THE IMPACT OF EUROPEAN RIGHTS ON NATIONAL LEGAL CULTURES

This book contributes to the debate about the impact of European Community law on the national constitutional orders and cultures of the respective Member States. The author examines the doctrine of sovereignty as a mechanism within which this impact may be best assessed and in particular how it underwrites the tension between European Union rights and the rights provided by the respective legal orders of the Member States, which, for the purposes of this book, have been taken to mean European rights.

In particular the book focuses on political, social and civil rights, drawing from TH Marshall's typology. In endorsing an appropriate analytical framework, the book challenges both existing law and secondary literature in order to argue that the terminology, the concepts and the tools which are used to assess the impact of EC law on the national constitutional orders are to be selected with great care. This is particularly apposite given the complexity of constitutional diversity, in terms of national constitutions and their reception of EC law. It is also important because of the variety of approaches involved in the constitutional adjustment provoked by the *acquis de l'Union* within the context of the increasing drive to constitutionalisation of the Union on the one hand and enlargement on the other.

Care must also be taken in ensuring that the analytical framework is in itself able to come to terms with the EU, an embryonic quasi-state, and the way in which it interacts with the legal systems and cultures of the EU Member States in the context of the move towards constitutionalisation and the effects of the emergence of an EU 'documentary' constitutionalism (foreshadowed in the European Convention established by the Laeken Declaration).

Volume 2 in the series, Modern Studies in European Law

Modern Studies in European Law

Volume 1: Soft Law in European Community Law
Linda Lenden

The Impact of European Rights on National Legal Cultures

MIRIAM AZIZ

·HART·
PUBLISHING

OXFORD AND PORTLAND OREGON
2004

Published in North America (US and Canada) by
Hart Publishing
c/o International Specialized Book Services
5804 NE Hassalo Street
Portland, Oregon
97213-3644
USA

Hart Publishing is a specialist legal publisher based in Oxford, England. To order further copies of this book or to request a list of other publications please write to:

Hart Publishing, Salters Boatyard, Folly Bridge,
Abingdon Rd, Oxford, OX1 4LB
Telephone: +44 (0)1865 245533 Fax: +44 (0) 1865 794882
email: mail@hartpub.co.uk
WEBSITE: http//:www.hartpub.co.uk

British Library Cataloguing in Publication Data
Data Available

ISBN 1-84113-309-4 (hardback)

Typeset by Olympus Infotech Pvt Ltd, India, in Sabon 10/12pt
Printed and bound in Great Britain by
TJ International Ltd, Padstow, Cornwall

This book is dedicated to
Professor J K Mason

Contents

Preface

The research undertaken which has led to the publication of this book was truly a pan-European effort during the ongoing process of continuing constitutional development and adjustment as part of two related developments: the move towards constitutionalisation of the European Union (EU) and the enlargement of the Union. I have tried in so far as is possible to incorporate the various 'constitutional moments'[1] which have arisen in this context including the European Convention which was established by the European Declaration in December 2002.[2] Generally speaking, the European Convention has proved to be an important constitutional moment, but one which will most likely provide a framework and catalyst for continuing constitutional development and adjustment rather than *the* final constitutional word. The successful conclusion of accession negotiations at the Copenhagen summit in December 2002 means that ten countries will join the European Union in the biggest wave of enlargement it has ever witnessed after which the Union will contain 25 members. The Accession Treaty, which is the legal basis for enlargement, was signed on April 16, 2003 under the Greek presidency in Athens. The Member States and the candidates are obligated to ratify the treaty in order to enable the accessions to proceed as planned on 1 May 2004.

To the best of my ability I have tried, where appropriate, to formulate my arguments so as to contribute to the development of an analytical framework within which the impact provoked by European rights on the respective constitutional cultures may be best understood within this overall context.

The research undertaken for this book began whilst I was a post-doctoral research fellow at the *Otto-Suhr Institut* based at the Department of Political and Social Sciences of the Free University of Berlin, Germany from 1997 to 1999. I would like to thank Professor Dr Ulrich K Preuβ, Tine Stein and Katja Stamm for their advice and their support. I would also like to thank the *Deutsche Akademische Austausch Dienst* (DAAD) and the *Studienstiftung des Abgeordnetenhauses von Berlin* for funding this research. I was also fortunate to be included in the Berlin contingent of a Framework 5 project directed by Richard Bellamy and Dario Castiglione, 'European Citizenship and the Social and Political Integration of the European Union' (EURCIT) funded by the European Commission. Many of

[1] The term has been coined by Bruce Ackerman in *We the People* (Cambridge MA, Harvard University Press, 1998) albeit in the context of constitutionalism in the United States.
[2] See the Laeken Declaration on the Future of the European Union available at <http://european-convention.eu.int/pdf/LKNEN.pdf>.

the ideas which appear in this book are the result of fruitful discussions with the participants in EURCIT as well as the participants at the conferences in Reading, Florence, Braga, Sardinia and Vienna. Indeed, Chapter Four on Social Rights is based on a paper I gave at the EURCIT conference in Sardinia entitled 'Social Rights and EU Citizenship' in June 2000. This research was financially supported by the European Union Social Science Information Research Facility (EUSSIRF) Library Grant and undertaken whilst on research leave at the library of the European University Institute (EUI), Florence in March 2000. I benefited greatly from two further periods of research leave, namely at the Department of Law at the University of Trento, Italy and the International Institute for the Sociology of Law (IISL) in Oñati, Spain. I would like to thank Professor Roberto Toniatti of the Department of Law at Trento University for his support and enthusiasm, both as a colleague and as a friend. I would also like to thank the staff of the IISL who made me feel extremely welcome during my stay in Oñati; in particular, I would like to thank William Felstiner, Manuel Calvo García and Malen Gordoa Mendizabal.

I was also fortunate in receiving invaluable feedback at a number of conferences. Many of my ideas on the doctrine of sovereignty would not have taken shape without the advice of Neil Walker who gave me an opportunity to present my ideas at a conference he organised at the Law Department of the European University Institute entitled 'Sovereignty in Transition' in September 2001. Many of the ideas in this book stem from my contribution, 'Sovereignty and the German Legal Order' which was later included in his edited collection for Hart Publishing as 'Sovereignty über Alles: (Re)Configuring the German Legal Order'. Indeed, Chapter Two draws from this contribution, which has also appeared as a Constitutionalism Web-Paper: 'Sovereignty Lost, Sovereignty Regained? Some Reflections on the Bundesverfassungsgerichts's Bananas Judgment', ConWEB No. 3/2003 <http://www.les1.man.ac.uk/conweb/>. Further thanks go to the participants at a conference held at the European Centre Natolin, Warsaw, Poland in January 2003 entitled *Enlargement and the European Constitutional Process* for feedback which was most helpful. I am also grateful for the constructive comments I received at the University of Zaragoza, Spain as a participant at the conference, *Los Derechos Fundamentales en la Unión Europea*, in November 2002.

Chapter Three on Political Rights is drawn from a paper I gave at the Law and Society Conference in Miami, entitled 'The Challenge of Immigration to EU Citizenship' in May 2000. Further inspiration for this chapter was gained by giving a presentation entitled, 'EU Citizenship and (An)Other' as part of the *Stranger* seminar series organised by James Kaye, Willfried Spohn, Bo Stråth and Anna Triandafyllidou at the Robert Schuman Centre for Advanced Studies at the European University Institute in November 2001.

Chapter Five draws from a paper, 'Language, Rights and Diversity: The Modesty of the Constitutional Moment', prepared for a Workshop on 'The Public Discourse of Law and Politics in Multilingual Societies' held at the International Institute for the Sociology of Law (IISL) in Oñati, Spain in June 2002. A later version was presented at the Trento Workshop on European Governance (TWEG) held in June 2002 at the University of Trento, Italy. I wish to thank the participants of both workshops for their feedback which was extremely instructive. Special thanks goes to Niamh Nic Shuibhne, Roberto Toniatti, Francesco Palermo and Marco Dani who helped me to see the limitations of constitutionalism in dealing with the thorny issue of linguistic diversity. I should also mention Philippe van Parijs, my co-author for a contribution to *European Law and Linguistic Diversity*, edited by Bruno de Witte and myself (Intersentia, 2004 forthcoming) entitled 'Linguistic Legislation for XXIst Century Europe' and which he kindly agreed to publish as a Working Paper for the Chaire Hoover d'éthique économique et sociale, Université catholique de Louvain. He was instrumental in enabling me to develop my ideas within an interdisciplinary framework and in encouraging me to address the theoretical nature of the debate, thereby unwittingly reminding me of ideas I first addressed in my doctoral thesis 'The Regulation of Medical Research Involving Human Subjects: A Comparative Study' at the University of Edinburgh (1997) on the issue of language and elites.

Helen Wallace, the director of the Robert Schuman Centre for Advanced Studies (RSCAS) at the European University Institute (EUI) continues to be a source of inspiration and together with Bruno de Witte encouraged me to convene the 'EUI Convention Working Group — Rencontres sur la Convention'. The Declaration of Laeken in December 2001 established a Convention as a framework for dialogue on the Constitution of the European Union. The RSCAS at the European University Institute organised a number of meetings related to this constitutional reform process early in 2002 and in 2003. In my role as academic co-ordinator, I was privileged to witness a microcosm of intellectual activity which the Convention generated as part of the EU's 'constitutional moment'. Participants to the meetings included academics from a variety of disciplines as well as members of the European Parliament and policy makers. Meetings which took place in 2002 included the European Constitutional Debate and Enlargement, the EU as an International Actor, the Institutional Matrix of EMU, the Constitution of Europe and the Role of the Regions, the European Social Model, Gender and the Convention and the Convention and the Third Pillar. Within this context, I also represented the EUI at a preparatory meeting (Academic Institutions and Think Tanks) for a plenary session of the Convention in June 2002 and was struck by the particular nature of civil society's mobilisation, which challenged my understanding of political rights and participation in the EU.

Further thanks goes to the following guides, philosophers and friends: Mike Artis, Fareda Banda, Zenon Bankowski, Ségolène Barbou de Places, Richard Bellamy, Galya Benarieh-Ruffer, George Berman, Agrado Betzold, Gráinne de Búrca, Dario Castiglione, Carlos Closa, Julio Baquero Cruz, Peter Cullen, Margarita de Leon, Neil Duxbury, Bardo Fassbender, Johannes Feest, Bob Hancké, Hanno Kube, Mary Lokken, Ingolf Pernice, Christian Joerges, Peter Kenneally, Horst Krenzler, Rita Krueger, Karl-Heinz and Marianne Ladeur, Neil MacCormick, Matthias Mahlmann, Begoña de la Marta, Yves Mény, Susan Millns, Machtheld Nijenhuis, Sylvie Pascucci, Miguel Poiares Maduro, Mark Pollack, Martin Rhodes, Wojciech Sadurski, Silvana Sciarra, Jo Shaw, Alex Warleigh, Jan Zielonka, Jacques Ziller and Peer Zumbansen. I must also thank *i Fiorentini* notably Renzo Angeloni, Brunella Casalini, Carlo Gaulino, Emilio Santoro, Deborah Spini, Betty, Anna and Simone.

I would also like to thank those lawyers with whom I was privileged to work as a legal practitioner such as David Anderson QC of Brick Court Chambers, London, Helmut Bergmann of Deringer/Freshfields, (Berlin), as it was then, Nicholas Forwood QC, now at the Court of First Instance, and Karl Pilny, then based at Coudert Schürman (Berlin). Further thanks go to my students at both the *Otto-Suhr Institut* in Berlin and the Faculty of Law at the University of Edinburgh who challenged my basic understanding of EU law enough for me to make numerous trips back to the drawing board. Indeed, their enthusiasm and curiosity regarding the socio-political implications of the European Integration project was both inspirational and infectious!

I would like to thank my family, who have continued to support my decision to write about the law instead of the life which goes on outside or indeed because of it. I confess that I have, at times, needed reminding that life does not exist because of the law but that law exists because of life. I am indebted to James Kaye, to Caterina and Maria Ferrari and to Germano, Franca, Carlo and Hugo Gentili, who have contributed to making the *Palagetto* my home throughout my time in Florence — although Dr Kaye would no doubt have something to say about the use of the word 'home'.[3] I must also thank Gillian Walker whose friendship has been a veritable lifeline, as has that of Neil and Lewis ('CL') Walker. Further thanks goes to Jim Hughes for his unwavering support and his unconditional friendship. Last but by no means least, I am grateful to Bruno de Witte, who helped me see that there is life in the law after all, though not necessarily as we lawyers know it nor indeed are always willing to admit.

This book is dedicated to Professor JK Mason, who supervised my PhD at the University of Edinburgh without whose faith and support, I would never have had the opportunity to develop ideas that I can call my own.

[3] J Kaye, *No One Such Place. 'Home' in Austrian and Swedish 'Landscapes'* (Doctoral Thesis) (Florence, European University Institute, 2003).

Indeed, his 'supervisory jurisdiction' extended beyond the call of duty on many occasions, both during the PhD and afterwards. This is a debt which I am unable to repay but for which I am and shall remain eternally grateful.

A final word of thanks to Hannah Hupfauer-Scotti for reminding me that the labyrinth of EU law and European rights is best entered with ample *Reiseführer* to which I hope that this book is a contribution.

Miriam Aziz
Florence, October 2003

This research was initially financially supported by the European University Institute through the award of a Jean Monnet Fellowship, by a Marie Curie Fellowship which was financed by the European Commission's Framework 5 programme and by CIDEL RTD Project under the 5th Framework Programme (Contract No HSPE-ct-2002-00144).

1

Introduction

THE MAIN PURPOSE of this book is to analyse systematically and comprehensively the process of constitutionalisation in the EU with regard to the theoretical and practical law and policy dimensions of European rights. It is a contribution to the development of an appropriate analytical framework governing the impact of European rights on the national legal cultures of the Member States in the European Union (EU),[1] focusing on the issue of implementation. I have elected to subsume the impact on the constitutional orders and legal systems and administrative practice in the Member States under the heading of 'culture' as opposed to limiting my analysis to the impact on legal systems.[2]

As part of this exercise, the doctrine of sovereignty has been selected as a mechanism within which the impact is assessed and in particular how it underwrites the tension provoked by fundamental rights and policies in the European Union. In endorsing an appropriate analytical framework, I challenge both existing law and secondary literature in order to argue that the terminology, the concepts and the tools with which the impact of European rights on the national constitutional orders may be best assessed must be selected with great care. This is particularly apposite given the constitutional diversity in the EU as well as the variety of conceptual, ideological and national approaches engendered by the process of constitutional adjustment within the context of the increasing drive to constitutionalisation of the Union on the one hand and enlargement on the other. Both have an impact on the EU's institutional architecture not to mention the values contained therein — latterly embodied in the Draft Treaty establishing a Constitution for Europe delivered to the European Council meeting in Thessaloniki on 20 June 2003 and later submitted to the President of the European Council in Rome on 18 July 2003.[3] They also engender an

[1] See generally J Ziller (ed), *The Europeanisation of Constitutional Law in the Light of the Constitutional Treaty for Europe* (Paris, L'Harmattan, 2003).
[2] I realise that the decision to refer to legal cultures as opposed to legal systems is somewhat contentious. See HP Glenn 'La tradition juridique nationale' (2003) 2 *Revue Internationale de Droit Comparé* 263 and also D Nelken and J Feest (ed), *Adapting Legal Cultures* (Oxford, Hart Publishing, 2001).
[3] CONV 820/03. This text was revised twice. (CONV 820/1/03 REV 1, CONV 820/1/03 REV 2). See also CONV 847/03, CONV 848/03.

impact on the legal and administrative elites who are responsible for the implementation of the *acquis communautaire* and in European rights arising therefrom. By 'elites', I hope to include all persons who are involved in rights implementation and have decided against limiting my findings to public authority officials;[4] I suggest that the term 'public authority officials' would be too narrow for the purposes of analysis. The privatisation of public services has led to elites being involved in the dispensation of 'public' services who are not, however, civil servants but who are employed by the private sector. This is linked more generally to the obfuscation of the public/private divide as well as the increasing role of governance both within and outwith the state's apparatus in the mediation of public services.

European rights are subjected to the interpretative device of the respective legal systems and administrative cultures of the Member States. It is often said that much may be lost in translation. It may also be the case, however, that much can be gained, given the rich tapestry of constitutional traditions in the EU which may have much to offer in clothing the skeleton of European rights. Much depends on how qualitative benchmarks, such as, for example, clarity, coherence, consistency and constitutional stability are assessed. Care must be taken in ensuring that the analytical framework is in itself able to come to terms with the EU, an embryonic quasi-state, and the way in which it interacts with the legal systems and cultures of the EU Member States in the context of the move towards constitutionalisation and the effects of the emergence of an EU 'documentary' constitutionalism (latterly portended in the European Convention established by the Laeken Declaration).

The European Convention was an important 'constitutional moment' in the sense that it will most likely provide a framework and catalyst for continuing constitutional development and adjustment rather than *the* final constitutional word. Rights are at the heart of the process of constitutional engineering in the EU, constitutionalism as a whole and the EU Constitution. They are integral to the basic constitutive question of governmental institutions and the fundamental relationship between the citizen and the polity. So too is the issue of implementation by EU Member States and the direct relationship between EU citizens and the public authorities[5] of the Member States in respecting European rights. It will be argued that the process of constitutional engineering and the implementation of European rights also has methodological implications for social scientists who are themselves engaged in a debate about the significance and the measurement of constitutional phenomena within the context of EU constitutionalism.

[4] Concerning the debate concerning the public/private divide, see generally D Oliver, *Common Values and the Public-Private Divide* (London, Butterworths, 1999).

[5] Whereas I refer to 'public authorities' throughout this book, my analysis can be extrapolated to apply to 'public' decision-making which occurs in the private sector.

EU CONSTITUTIONALISM

The notion of constitutionalism is used in a variety of ways in the European Union, given the diverse number and nature of legal cultures of the Member States. The process of the drafting of the EU Charter of Fundamental Rights provides a useful case in point.[6] The same may be said regarding the European Convention.[7] This has obvious implications at the level of the implementation of the Charter of Fundamental Rights, given the differing levels of both knowledge and understanding as to its remit by academics and practitioners alike as well as the motivation by national courts and public authorities to co-operate in their recognition and implementation. Indeed, the rule of law in the European Union is to some extent fragmented along national and regional lines,[8] given the different degrees of reception of the *acquis communautaire* as a whole and in terms of how the impact of European rights in particular is both perceived and interpreted by legal[9] and administrative elites in the Member States.[10] There is a need to distinguish between the formal process of implementation (the adoption of the *acquis*) and the legal norms and legal culture which will inform the implementation of the *acquis* in the day-to-day process.[11]

Detailed studies of the reception of the *acquis communautaire*, which extends to approximately 80,000 pages, have been conducted as regards national constitutional courts[12] on the implementation of directives[13] and

[6] [2000] OJ C 364/1. See J Schönlau, 'Drafting Europe's Value Foundation: Deliberation and Arm-twisting in Formulating the Preamble to the EU Charter of Fundamental Rights' in E Eriksen, JE Fossum and A Menéndez, *The Chartering of Europe* (Oslo, ARENA, 2001), 127; G de Búrca, 'The Drafting of the EU Charter of Fundamental Rights' (2001) 26 ELR 26; F Deloche-Gaudez, 'La Convention pour l'Élaboration de la Charte des Droits Fondamentaux: Une Méthode d'Avenir?' (2001) 15 *Études et Recherches* 1.

[7] J Shaw, 'Process, Responsibility and Inclusion in EU Constitutionalism' (2003) 9 ELR 45. See also J Ziller, *La nouvelle constitution européenne* (Paris, La Découverte, 2003).

[8] G Greco, 'Rapporti tra ordinamento comunitario e nazionale' in MP Chiti and G Greco, *Trattato di diritto amministrativo europeo* (Milan, Giuffrè, 1997), 566.

[9] L Azoulay, 'The Judge and the Community's Administrative Governance' in C Joerges and R Dehousse (eds) *Good Governance in Europe's Integrated Market* (Oxford, Oxford University Press, 2002), 109-137.

[10] S Kadelbach 'European Administrative Law and the Law of a Europeanized Administration' in C Joerges and R Dehousse (eds), *Good Governance in Europe's Integrated Market* (Oxford, Oxford University Press, 2002), 167; J Schwarze (ed), *Administrative Law under European Influence: On the Convergences of the Administrative Laws of the EU Member States* (London, Sweet & Maxwell; Baden-Baden, Nomos Volas, 1996).

[11] See, eg, the Commission White Paper on the Preparation of the associated countries of Central and Eastern Europe for integration into the internal market of the Union, COM (95) 163.

[12] A-M Slaughter, A Stone Sweet and JHH Weiler (eds), *The European Court and National Courts – Doctrine and Jurisprudence: Legal Change in its Social Context* (Oxford, Hart Publishing 1998). See also A Oppenheimer, *The Relationship between European Community Law and National Law. The Cases vol 1.* (Cambridge, Cambridge University Press, 1994); A Oppenheimer, *The Relationship between European Community Law and National Law. The Cases. Vol 2* (Cambridge, Cambridge University Press, 2003).

[13] S Prechal, *Directives in European Community Law* (Oxford, Clarendon Press, 1995).

in certain policy areas such as, for example, free movement,[14] EU environmental policy[15] and health.[16] However, little has been undertaken by way of systematic and targeted research as regards the day-to-day implementation of European rights across multi-levels other than preliminary research on the impact of the Charter of Fundamental Rights.[17] The legal response to EU constitutionalism is further amplified by the absence of a common analytical framework regarding the law of the European Union which has proved difficult to ascertain.[18] Legal education in the European Union as a whole has been unable to address this absence given that it has tended to focus on training lawyers to serve their own domestic legal orders,[19] despite claims of an undeniable presence of a unified European legal culture[20] not to mention the increase of transnational mobility of lawyers in private practice.

A key test of the EU constitutionalism is the issue of rights.[21] The implementation of the Charter of the Fundamental Rights of the European Union is likely to be one of the centrepieces of the current constitutionalising drive, as well as one of the key areas of contestation, particularly as there is no uniform model of a Bill of Rights in the existing Members States' Constitutions, nor in those of the new Member States.[22] Issues such as the horizontal applicability of constitutional rights, the justiciability of socio-economic rights, the nature and grounds of justified statutory limits upon constitutional rights are of central importance, as is the greater prominence in the European context of freedom of expression and the fight against discrimination, and the challenge of promoting diversity *within* all European states in relation to sensitive issues such as minority rights.

[14] M Jarvis, *The Application of EC Law by National Courts: The Free Movement of Goods* (Oxford, Clarendon Press, 1998).
[15] D Chalmers, 'Inhabitants in EC Environmental Law' in P Craig and G de Búrca, *The Evolution of EU Law* (Oxford, Oxford University Press, 1999), 653–92.
[16] TK Hervey, 'Community and National Competence in Health After Tobacco Advertising' (2001) 38 CML Rev 1421–46.
[17] P Eeckhout 'The EU Charter of Fundamental Rights and the Federal Question (2002) 39 CML Rev 945; J Dutheil, 'Droits de l'homme: La Charte des droits fondamentaux et au delà' (2002) 10/01 Jean Monnet Working Papers <http://www.jeanmonnetprogram.org.>
[18] R Dehousse, 'Comparing National Law and EC Law: The Problem of the Level of Analysis' (1994) 42 *American Journal of Comparative Law* 761.
[19] P Legrand, 'European Legal Systems Are Not Converging' (1993) 45 *International and Comparative Law Quarterly* 52.
[20] P Häberle, *Europäische Rechtskultur: Versuch einer Annährung in zwölf Schriften* (Baden-Baden, Nomos Verlag, 1994).
[21] W Osiatynski, 'Rights in New Constitutions of East Central Europe' (1994) 26 *Columbia Human Rights Law Review* 111; W Sadurski, 'Postcommunist Charters of Rights in Europe and the U.S. Bill of Rights' (2002) 65 *Law and Contemporary Problems* 223–50; A Williams, 'Enlargement of the Union and Human Rights Conditionality: A Policy of Distinction?' (2000) 25 ELR 601.
[22] Which during the period of pre-accession were referred to as the Central and East European Countries for Enlargement or 'CEECs'.

The purpose of this book is to explore these issues through the prism of the doctrine of sovereignty.

EUROPEAN RIGHTS AND SOVEREIGNTY

The juridical debate concerning sovereignty has tended to focus on the 'ultimate arbiter' or 'supremacy' debate in which the doctrine is framed in terms of being lost, pooled or divided.[23] Interestingly enough, it is constitutional lawyers who have tended to monopolise the debate, leaving their civil law colleagues to speak the language of sovereignty, rather like the lady who spoke prose, without being entirely aware of it. It is questionable whether a formulation of sovereignty based in terms of supremacy is the most appropriate method according to which the multi-faceted, multi-level and multi-dimensional challenge posed by European rights to concepts of people, territory and the state may be addressed. The decisions of the European Court of Justice and the constitutional courts of the Member States of the Union are of limited use, given that the main challenge — and indeed the more pressing challenge for many individuals — to state sovereignty posed by EU law is at the level of day-to-day practice in the 'constitutional regions'.[24]

It is easy to forget just how many spheres of the lives of individuals have been europeanised. Arguably this has led to the 'loss of control' over an area of national life, being achieved sometimes by default rather than by an informed decision.[25] One look at the incorporation of the *acquis communautaire* into the legal systems of the new Member States serves as a useful reminder of the extent to which domestic legal systems of the Member States have been europeanised. Thus, article 69 under Chapter III of Estonia's Europe Agreement lists customs law; company law; banking law; company accounts and taxation; intellectual property; financial services; rules on competition; protection of health and life of humans, animals and plants; protection of workers, including health and safety at work;

[23] See generally N MacCormick, *Questioning Sovereignty: Law, State and Nation in the European Commonwealth* (Oxford, Oxford University Press, 1999). See also the discussion by Christian Callies in the context of Art 1 TEU in C Callies and Ruffert (eds) *Kommentar zu EUV and EGV* (Neuwied, Luchterhand, 2002); P Zumbansen 'Making Day-to-Day Sense of European Governance' in P Zumbansen and R Miller (eds) *The Annual of German and European Law* (Oxford and New York, Berghahn Books, 2002).

[24] See N MacCormick, 'A Comment on the White Paper' in C Joerges, Y Mény and JHH Weiler (eds). *Mountain or Molehill? : A Critical Appraisal of the Commission White Paper on Governance*, Jean Monnet Working Paper 6/01 (Florence, Robert Schuman Centre for Advanced Studies at the European University Institute; New York, New York University School of Law, 2001).

[25] *Ex parte* Judge J in *R v Secretary of State for Home Dept, ex p Vitale and Do Amaral* The Times 18 April 1995.

consumer protection; indirect taxation; technical rules and standards; nuclear law and regulation; transport; telecommunications; environment; public procurement; statistics; and product liability as areas to which the approximation of laws shall extend. It is perhaps easier to list the areas of law that are outside the realms of EU competence, the contours of which are elastic.

EU competence has been reconfigured during the process of the evolution of the EU into a layered entity, hosting a host of legal sub-entities,[26] which has inter alia given rise to spheres of rights index linked to European integration in a differentiated sense.[27] The resolution of social, political and civil conflicts in a plethora of both fields and spheres of law is being swept along by an under current of europeanisation. Seen through the lens of the 'ultimate arbiter' debate, this statement appears somewhat abstract. It is, however, instructive to the extent that it reveals the lengths to which judges of the national constitutional courts of the Member States have attempted to resist the challenge posed by legal pluralism[28] and what I refer to in terms of 'multi-jurisdictionality'. Indeed, many judges have gone to considerable lengths in order to protect what they view as part of the 'national heritage' of rights. 'Rights protectionism' has been practised on the basis that the states which they serve protect human rights more vigorously than others or, alternatively, that they uphold certain rights and fundamental values which are not to be found in the constitutions of other states.[29] The decisions of the German Federal Constitutional Court concerning European integration, for instance, provide a useful case in point, both explicitly[30] and implicitly speaking.[31] The same may be said regarding constitutional courts of other EU Member States. Our concern here is, however, not about sovereignty per se. Rather, this book addresses the implications for state sovereignty of European rights and, in particular, the case studies provided by political

[26] Such as inter alia the Investment Bank, the European Central Bank, EUROPOL and EURODAC. See DM Curtin and IF Dekker, 'The European Union as a "Layered" International Organization: Institutional Unity in Disguise' in P Craig and G de Búrca (eds) *The Evolution of EU Law* (Oxford, Oxford University Press, 1998).

[27] See J Shaw, 'Constitutional Change in the EU: From Uniformity to Flexibility?' in G de Búrca and J Scott, *Constitutional Change in the EU: From Uniformity to Flexibility?* (Oxford, Hart Publishing, 2000), 337–58.

[28] I have addressed this in more detail elsewhere. See M Aziz, 'Sovereignty Lost, Sovereignty Regained? The European Integration Project and the Bundesverfassungsgericht' (2002) 9 *Columbia Journal of European Law* 109.

[29] As in the case of the protection of economic rights in the German Basic Law, for example.

[30] As in *Solange I* (BVerfGE 37, 271), *Solange II* (BVerfGE 73, 339) and in the Banana Decision (Decision of June 7, 2000–2 BvL 1/97).

[31] As in the *Maastricht* Case (BVerfGE 89, 155) or *Brunner v European Union Treaty* [1994] 1 CMLR 57. I have addressed this in more detail in M Aziz 'Sovereignty über Alles: (Re)Configuring the German Legal Order' in N Walker (ed) *Sovereignty in Transition* (Oxford, Hart Publishing, 2003).

and social rights at the level of implementation. I have elected against including civil rights as a case study on the basis that the impact of fundamental rights policies in the EU is less developed than in the case of political and social rights. Although many of the conclusions reached also have implications for civil rights in the EU.

This book extends the enquiry in such a way as to include *all* potential rights holders in the EU given that European rights seen through the prism of EU citizenship tell only part of the story, so to speak. Indeed, citizenship is inappropriate as the central vehicle of fundamental rights in the EU. Not only does it exclude vast categories of individuals who reside within the Union but also, it fails to come to terms with overlapping regulatory networks which govern rights at the national, supranational and international level, failing as it does, to come to terms with the state as a 'contested terrain' in the face of the destabilising effects of globalisation. Indeed, the citizenship discourse has tended to bury its head in the sands of legal monism, preferring instead to hide behind the skirts of its state fixation as opposed to standing up to legal pluralism in which law has arguably come of age.[32] The view of regulatory networks existing beyond the state as irretrievably fracturing the body politic or existing forms of political sovereignty informs much the debate's inherent denial.

The aim of widening the analytical framework is not normative. That is to say, whether all residents of the Union *ought* to benefit from rights is not the main concern of this book, although no doubt normative conclusions may be drawn from some of the arguments made which are constructed in such a way as to support the following thesis: an incremental challenge to the sovereignty of the Member States is being sustained in day-to-day legal practice in which inter alia political and social rights are being contested in national, supranational and international jurisdictions which sometimes overlap. Implementation of European rights incurs an ongoing reconfiguration of the Member States' legal cultures, thereby challenging their sovereignty and, by implication, their identity. I use the term 'inter alia' in order to clarify that whilst being aware of the many forms of rights, such as economic, environmental and cultural rights, I have elected to focus on those rights which are most relevant for the purposes of my argumentation, namely political and social rights. As will become apparent, however, it is not always possible to separate these categories.

In order to be able to assess and to evaluate this process of reconfiguration, I have elected to address each of the chapters on political and social rights by means of the following criteria. First, I argue that the

[32] See G Teubner, '"Global Bukowina": Legal Pluralism in the World Society' in G Teubner *Global Law without a State* (Aldershot, Dartmouth, 1997), 3.

impact of European rights on the legal cultures of EU Member States occurs across multi-levels of government and modes of governance. Secondly, European rights are dependent on elite compliance. Thirdly, there is inherent confusion regarding the conceptualisation of European rights which is divided along national and ideological lines. Lastly, the *sui generis* nature of European rights means that an appropriate analytical framework is needed which is able to come to terms with this confusion which has implications for future research agendas as well as for the substance, process and practice of EU constitutionalism as a whole.

POLITICAL RIGHTS

In Chapter Three, I argue that debates concerning political rights in the EU have focused on issues of identity and the notion of a European demos. However, the law cares little about identity or the absence of a European demos as regards issues of implementation. Political rights in the EU have substantially revised and reconfigured classical notions of representative democracy which have tended to be linked to citizenship. However, EU citizenship is inappropriate as the basis for political rights in the EU. First, the actors engaged in political participation in the EU include, de facto, EU citizens and non-EU citizens. Secondly, the forms of participation are more innovative than classical conceptions of representative democracy allow for. Indeed, in practice, political rights in the EU are framed more widely than the EU citizenship provisions contained in the treaties.[33] Political participation has also been achieved through recourse to the courts. Judicial activism of this nature has rendered the distinction between political rights *stricto sensu* and rights or interests with a political dimension ambiguous. Thirdly, the realisation of political rights is heavily dependent on national elites and, in particular, public authority officials and judges.[34] Their compliance and co-operation is essential. Member States have been exceedingly defensive, resisting those policy areas where EU-wide political rights challenge their sovereignty in ways that they deem unacceptable. The exclusions from public service employment under the free movement provisions provides a useful illustration of where the impact on state sovereignty provoked by European political rights is at its most dynamic, and indeed at its most acute, giving rise to implications which are more considerable than those provoked by the EU citizenship provisions in relation to political rights at a first glance. In sum: whilst policy makers have focused on achieving democratic legitimacy through citizenship provisions, appealing to the

[33] EC Treaty art 19.
[34] Though political participation through lobbying, for example, often involves elites such as those who work for Non-Governmental Organisations (NGOs).

notion of a demos of citizens, in so doing, they have tended to ignore the fact that the quest for legitimacy has been reconfigured by virtue of local and operational forms of administrative co-ordination.

Thus, for example, political rights have traditionally been linked to citizenship which has been taken to govern who legitimately belongs to the polity. According to definitions of sovereignty in the Kantian tradition, the polity is comprised of the authors of the normative framework in which they live. The mistrust with which third-country nationals are viewed has been generally articulated through citizenship's exclusionary tendencies, which have been well documented.[35] Policy choices are being made at a number of levels (namely at the national, supranational and international level) which serve to perpetuate what has been referred to as the 'wanted but not welcome' syndrome.[36] In effect, migrants are economically desirable but are culturally and politically unwelcome. What has generally been omitted from the analysis, however, is the assumptions upon which the categories of inclusion and exclusion work in such a way as to exclude categories of people who are resident in the Union as a whole, in other words those individuals who are 'accepted' Europeans but who do not feel at ease with a European identity. However, the implementation of political rights in the EU occurs in such a way that the broader dimension of culture and identity which is generally perceived to be so crucial is rendered largely irrelevant.

SOCIAL RIGHTS

Access to social justice has been challenged by the reconfiguration of solidarity, territoriality and nationality by supranational and international sources of authority which exist beyond the state.[37] Social rights are part and parcel of the welfare state. Welfare states are nation-states. Indeed, social rights have been customarily regarded as being within the exclusive competence of the nation-state, international obligations notwithstanding,[38] such as the general rights to social security,[39] primarily because it is national resources which are subjected to the added strain of having to internalise the risks of globalisation. The elastic criteria regarding those

[35] S Peers, 'Towards Equality: Actual and Potential Rights of Third-country Nationals in the European Union' (1997) ELR 341–51.
[36] See A Zolberg, 'Modes of Incorporation: Towards a Comparative Framework' in V Bader *Citizenship and Exclusion* (London, MacMillan, 1997), 140 at 141.
[37] See AP van der Mei, *Free Movement of Persons within the European Community. Cross-border Access to Public Benefits* (Oxford, Hart Publishing, 2002).
[38] Such as those provided by the International Covenant on Economic, Social and Cultural Rights.
[39] As provided by Art 22 UDHR, Art 9 ICESCR, ILO Convention No 102 concerning Minimum Standards of Security, Art 12 ES, referring to ILO Convention No 102.

individuals who may benefit from social rights and those who do not, illustrate the *malaise* with which states view rights holders who may or may not be transient, both nationals – and by extension EU citizens - and third-country nationals alike. The reference to nationals may seem curious. It is, however, motivated by the way in which nationals can distance themselves from their own brethren when matters of social equity are at stake. The view of the unemployed as social 'pariahs' given their dependence on state resources is a case in point. This is further amplified across regional lines through divides which arise as a consequence of fiscal federalism and regional autonomy.[40] A good example would be the financial equalisation exercise in Germany whereby revenue from income tax, corporation tax and turnover tax is shared jointly by the federation and the individual States or *Länder* of the Federal Republic of Germany.[41] This is an integral part of a federal system based on social justice, or what is referred to in the Basic Law as the *Sozialstaat*. Accordingly, the financial strength of the States is balanced in such a way as to give effect to federalist solidarity. Accordingly the financial strength of weaker States may be bolstered in a bid to maintain a degree of balance of inter alia living conditions of citizens. In practice, the more prosperous *Länder* such as Bavaria, have repeatedly attempted to isolate themselves from the less prosperous *Länder* through both political and judicial activism.[42] The politics of Umberto Bossi's *Lega Nord* in Italy have also been fuelled by similar concerns although its stance vis-à-vis the south of Italy has been dominated by separatist sentiments of an altogether more sinister nature. At the level of the European Union, the North/South divide has been particularly visible regarding the granting of subsidies to farmers as part of the Common Agricultural Policy (CAP). Here too, farmers from more prosperous regions and states have sought to distance themselves from their less fortunate counterparts. The same can be seen in the context of the adoption of the euro, where some Member States have repeatedly expressed concern and scepticism about the ability of less economically successful partners in sustaining growth so as to respect the criteria for and indeed stability of monetary union. These examples not only demonstrate the drive towards economic and political burden-sharing but also illustrate that the response

[40] See G Majone, 'Europe's "Democratic Deficit": The Question of Standards' (1998) 4 *European Law Journal* 5–28 at 14.

[41] As provided by the Financial Equalization Law ('FEL') or *Gesetz über den Finanzausgleich zwischen Bund und Ländern* or '*Finanzausgleichsgesetz*' Dated June 23, 1993 (BGBl I S 944, 977). See ss 1 (2) and (3), 2 (1) and (2), 4 to 10, 11 (1), (2), (3), (5), (7) and (8), 12 to 15 of the FEL.

[42] See the so-called 'Länderausgleich' judgment of BVerfG, 2 BvF 2/98, 3/98, 1/99, 2/99 vom 11.11.1999, Absatz-Nr. (1–347) of which I have written a brief case study. See M Aziz, 'The Federal Constitutional Court Decision Concerning the Financial Equalization between the States of the Federal Republic of Germany: the "Länderausgleich" judgment' (2000) 6 *European Public Law* (Survey).

to the challenge to sovereignty posed by social justice has arisen in relation to regions as well as vis-à-vis states.[43]

Social rights in the European Union have emerged in a variety of policy contexts, in particular in the area of social policy and labour. They have also arisen in the context of housing, education, discrimination and equal treatment for EU migrants, the co-ordination of social security entitlements and the impact of free movement and entitlements to health care in the realm of the internal market. I address the complex issue of social rights in the EU by concentrating on the application of rights to health care which have developed under the aegis of the free movement provisions. First, they illustrate the tension which arises as a consequence of the impact of European rights on the legal cultures of the Member States. Secondly, they illustrate how this impact gives rise to a challenge to state sovereignty which operates across the multi-levels of both government and modes of governance. The point of access for any EU citizen seeking medical treatment in an EU Member State other than their own is at the local or regional level. Moreover, it is dependent on elite compliance. Both the knowledge and the motivation of the elites, be they legal, medical, administrative or suchlike, are crucial elements of elite compliance, without which the right to cross-border health care remains relatively meaningless.

Thirdly, access to cross-border health care by EU citizens also illustrates the confusion between 'Rights' and 'Policies' and how this confusion serves the ends of certain parties. Thus, the extent of the conceptual gerrymandering is index linked to the attempts by the Union to be seen to be respecting the sovereignty of the Member States in relation to social policy. In other words, the vagueness of visions of a 'social area' or 'social space' serves instrumental ends. The ambiguity is partly explained by the diverse traditions regarding social rights in the Member States. Numerous levels of diversity must, however, be distinguished. Diversity exists as between Member States regarding social rights and the values upon which they are predicated and according to which they are articulated, constitutionally speaking. Diversity also exists, however, amongst the legal community within these Member States as to the concept of social rights. Indeed, it is difficult to assume the existence of a homogeneous approach to social rights amongst jurists, in which term I include judges and practitioners. The reasons may be partly explained by political affiliation. They may also be regionally marked. Moreover, there is further diversity across the academic disciplines as to definitions of social rights. It is also unlikely that one could

[43] See M Rossi, 'Anmerkung zu C–184/99 Grzelczyk' (2002) 7 *Juristen Zeitung* 249–353 who makes this point in relation to the decision of the ECJ in which social welfare provisions ordinarily restricted to nationals of an EU Member State were extended to an EU citizen.

assume the existence of a unified understanding of social rights amongst political actors. Variation further exists at the level of the EU citizen who will tend to view social rights in terms of his own constitutional order and the welfare policies enshrined therein. Here again, differential markers arise as a consequence of political affiliation and regional policies.

IMPLEMENTATION OF RIGHTS AND THE ROLE OF ELITES

In Chapter Five, I focus on the tension generated by European rights in terms of implementation rather than principle.[44] The first section addresses the deliberations of the European Convention in the context of its contribution to shaping the conditions for the implementation of rights rather than in the broad sense of the Convention as a community-mobilising and deliberative exercise. In particular, the deliberations concerning citizenship and loyal co-operation provide a useful case study of the resistance of some Member States to cede rights which, as they perceive it, are integral to their sovereignty and their identity. The second section focuses on language rights in the EU as part of the context of adjunctive or implementation rights which render effective various objectives bound up with the development of a rights regime. Both illustrate the generation of a just, engaged and active polity which requires not merely statements of rights (political, social and fundamental freedoms) but also a context of implementation which is itself at least partly legally grounded and supplied through, for example, a supportive generic conception of citizenship, an adequate reconciliation between national and supranational interest through a two-way loyalty clause and an effective language policy which reconciles respect for diversity with the need for effective communication. European rights are dependent on elite compliance. Both the knowledge and the motivation of legal and administrative elites are crucial elements of elite compliance, without which European rights remain rhetorical, an issue which the discussion concerning access to justice in the EU has tended to overlook.[45]

Rights are not worth the statute books they are written on if they are not realisable — if, in other words, there is no or little effect to the procedural

[44] Thus, I do not explicitly address civil rights in the minimalist sense envisaged by Marshall, ie minimum negative rights guaranteeing secure membership of a community and basic economic freedoms.

[45] Tending to concentrate on the relationship between Arts 230 and 234 EC Treaty. E Szyszczak, 'Making Europe More Relevant to its Citizens: Effective Judicial Process' (1996) 21 ELR 351; A Biondi, 'Effectiveness versus Efficiency: Recent Developments on Judicial Protection in EC Law' (2000) 6 *European Public Law* 311. See, however, D Chalmers, 'Judicial Preferences and the Community Legal Order' (1997) 60 MLR 164 at 167ff.

cause they seek to further and guarantee.[46] The testimony delivered by the 'living law'[47] of EU fundamental rights and policy as a whole paints a picture which is sometimes unrecognisable by EU policy makers who have paved the road between the citizen and the Union with the best of intentions. Logic, which may not be immediately identifiable, may be recognisable when exposed to the litmus test of the 'rough and tumble' of day-to-day implementation.

Rights provided mean very little if they are not accompanied by enabling measures which ensure that the access to justice is tailored in such a way that it bridges the gap between appearance and reality. The danger here is that legal provisions are cosmetic and by implication, rhetorical. Rhetoric can, as Schumpeter has shown, act as the medium according to which varying elites compete for the peoples' vote.[48] Obtaining the consent of the governed and securing democratic legitimacy through the use of ideology is an altogether different matter however. Manufacturing the electoral will[49] through inter alia legal provisions which act as public relations exercises does little to inspire the trust of rights holders. Legal provisions which promise, but which do not deliver, are even more dangerous given that they lull the addressees of rights holders into a false sense of security. Citizens who choose, for example, to rely on the free movement provisions in order to work in other EU Member States may find that the concrete, day-to-day recognition of their rights is in many cases impracticable. Not only is the individual faced with linguistic barriers but she is also at the mercy of rules of bureaucracy which may be significantly different to those which she is used to, particularly as many of these rules or 'ways of doing things' are integral to the legal and administrative culture of the state. Recognition is, however, central as it has implications concerning the realisability of rights, particularly because it becomes more difficult for a non-national to recognise when she is being discriminated against. That is to say, both when she is being treated differently to her national counterparts *and* when this

[46] This represents an issue which has been addressed particularly apt in relation to the implementation of directives in EC law. Indeed, the European Court of Justice recognised very early on that the procedures laid down in Arts 169 and 170 of the Treaty are inadequate in guaranteeing sufficient and direct legal protection of individuals. See Prechal, see n 13 above, at 145ff.

[47] The reference to the 'living law' draws from Oliver Wendell Holmes who firmly believed that jurisprudence ought to include the human element: 'The life of the law has not been logic: it has been experience.' See O Wendell Homes, 'Review of CC Langdell "Summary of the Law of Contracts"' (1880) 14 *American Law Review* 233 at 234.

[48] J Schumpeter, *Capitalism, Socialism and Democracy* (London, Allen & Unwin, 1942).

[49] A Downs, *An Economic Theory of Democracy* (London, Harper & Row, 1957). I am grateful to Paul Craig for drawing my attention to this issue as part of his contribution, 'The Nature of the Community: Integration Theory and Democratic Theory: Two Discourses Passing in the Night' to a Colloquium in Exeter in November 2000 on the Rule of Law.

differential treatment amounts to discrimination which cannot be objectively justified.[50]

The non-national is faced with a two-tier test. First, she must recognise differential treatment. Secondly, she must recognise that this treatment is discriminatory. As regards the latter, the non-national is not alone and may seek legal advice, if she is in the position to do so. Part of being in the position to do so — and indeed a pivotal part — is that she may only seek legal advice when she has satisfied the first part of the test. In other words, she will have had to recognise differential treatment in the first place, which is no mean feat given the unwritten rules of conduct and etiquette, not to mention the presence of codes which govern administrative practice and culture. Not all discriminatory measures are as easily identifiable as those which, for example, preclude individuals, as in the case of *Bickel and Franz*, from addressing a court in the same language as residents of a particular area.[51] Placing individuals on the same footing as a state's nationals by upholding their right to 'use a given language to communicate with the administrative and judicial authorities of a State'[52] is undeniably a step in the right direction. The importance of context must also, however, be acknowledged in which forms of discrimination can be far more subtle and nuanced, an issue which also affects nationals of a state. Judicial acknowledgement of indirect or covert discrimination can only go so far in identifying forms of discrimination.[53]

Nationals face the same dilemma regarding identifiability, albeit within parameters which are sometimes different and sometimes which are not. In short, there are spheres of discrimination within cultures of bureaucracy which, in many cases, also affect nationals of a Member State. National citizens may be discriminated against according to class, sex, profession and so on. The same applies to non-nationals. Thus, for example, an English lawyer working in Greece may receive better treatment at the hands of the administrative authorities than an English waiter. There is a great deal of overlap and cross-referencing between the spheres of differential and discriminatory treatment. (By electing to use the word differential, I hope to make it clear that not all differential treatment is discriminatory). However, non-nationals arguably stand even less of a chance in navigating

[50] See the anti-discrimination clause in Art 13 EC. See also Dir 2000/43 EC [2000] OJ L180/22 which implements the principle of equal treatment between persons irrespective of race or ethnic origin and the so-called frame-work employment Dir 2000/78 EC [2000] OJ L303/16 covering discrimination in the field of employment on the grounds listed in Art 13 (other than race, ethnic origin or sex, which are already addressed in other legislation. Thus: religion, belief, disability, age and sexual orientation). See generally M Bell, *Anti-discrimination Law and the EU* (Oxford, Oxford University Press, 2002).

[51] Case C–274/96 *Bickel and Franz* [1998] ECR I–7637.

[52] See *Bickel and Franz*, n 51 above, at paras 15–16.

[53] See Case C–33/88 *Allué v Coonan* [1989] ECR 1591. See also Case C–41/84 *Pinna v Caisse d'Allocations Familiales de la Savoie* [1986] ECR I.

the perilous straits of administrative cultures, particularly as in some cases, they may be discriminated against by virtue of being a foreigner, something which their national counterparts are not subjected to — although there here also discriminatory undertones may be present, as naturalised citizens would no doubt testify.

There is a price to pay for such treatment. In the case of social security provisions, for example, the shortfall for EU citizens working in a Member State other than their own can have lasting consequences which may, as in the case of pension rights, be difficult to reverse, leaving them in a precarious position if they choose to retire in a state other than the one in which they have made their pension contributions.[54] *Context is important.* Indeed, context is everything in a world where the recognition of rights of the individual is at the mercy of administrative authorities, whose discretion is not always subject to the supervisory jurisdiction of the courts. Significance found in what is often not said, or in the way in which something is said, takes on dimensions of a zero-sum game which the individual stands little chance of winning in the socio-legal context of implementation which is underpinned by power relations. Discrimination, however, may not only be the result of malevolent or insidious intent but may also be the consequence of ignorance on behalf of the gate keepers. Elites — that is, in this case, administrative personnel — may, at times, be as helpless in facing the challenge of navigating the straits of administrative law and procedure as the individual particularly given the presence of complex 'networked' or 'fused' administrative rules,[55] not to mention that supranational administrative law and procedure is embedded in a particular tradition[56] or context, which may be unrecognisable by some national administrative bureaucrats, whose loyalty is often called into question by the presence of a supranational order.[57] Capacity is often seen in terms of physical capacity like resources, personnel and structures. Capacity is also, however, about skill assets, training and trust. As I argue throughout this book, the recognition of rights is dependent on the motivation and willingness not only of states but also of their elites to co-operate and comply. In the absence of social mobilisation and social learning[58] in support of European rights, the

[54] As in the case of *Molenaar*. See Case C–160/96 [1998] ECR I–843. Although the plaintiff was successful in this case.

[55] See K-H Ladeur, 'Towards a Legal Theory of Supranationality: The Viability of the Network Concept' (1997) 3 *European Law Journal* 33 and also Kadelbach, n 10 above and K-H Ladeur (ed), *The Europeanisation of Administrative Law: Transforming National Decision-making Procedures* (Aldershot, Ashgate, 2002). Note that the word 'fusion' is a term which is used by Neil MacCormick in order to refer to the pooling between national and supranational normative systems. See N MacCormick, 'Beyond the Sovereign State' (1993) 50 MLR 1 at 16.

[56] Which is constituted by the 'pick and mix' of administrative borrowings from some of the administrative cultures of the Member States.

[57] See M P Chiti, *Diritto amminstrativo europeo* (Milano, A Giuffrè, 1999) at ch 7.

[58] See R Inglewood, *Culture Shift* (Princeton, Princeton University Press, 1990), 377.

danger is that constitutional provisions become merely cosmetic and, by implication, rhetorical.

THE IMPLICATIONS FOR THE DISCIPLINE OF EUROPEAN UNION LAW

The implications for the discipline of EU law in terms of analysis are considerable to the extent that it has neglected to address the issue of rights implementation. The 'analytical narrative' governing European rights has moved from focusing on citizenship in the early 1990s in order to address the citizenship provisions introduced by the Maastricht Treaty.[59] This was followed by a shift in emphasis from citizenship to constitutionalism[60] in the mid 1990s, inspired by the adoption of the Charter on Fundamental Rights proclaimed at Nice in December 2001.[61] More recently, at the end of the 1990s, attention has been transferred to issues of governance[62] — both multi-level and otherwise — a move catalysed by the publication of the Commission's White Paper.[63] Actors in academia, political actors as well as civil society have each had their part to play in both the *teoria* and *praxis* of European integration, in an array of networks which often overlap, sometimes drawing inspiration — or indeed, disenchantment — from one another. Each, in their own way, has articulated dissatisfaction with hierarchical understandings in attempting to deal with the complexity which the integration process generates and is generated by. The reconfiguration of legal science through the challenge posed by legal pluralism is a further case in point.

Generally speaking, law has traditionally been viewed as a normative order best understood in terms of a hierarchy.[64] In the German case, for

[59] See, eg, M La Torre (ed), *European Citizenship: An Institutional Challenge* (The Hague, Kluwer Law International, 1998).

[60] See L Dobson, 'Citizenship, Political Authority and Constitutionalism in the European Union: A Normative Theoretical Approach' (2002) 23 *Journal of European Integration* 335; S O'Leary, 'The Relationship between Community Citizenship and the Protection of Fundamental Rights in Community Law' (1995) 32 CML Rev 519.

[61] See generally G de Búrca, 'The drafting of the EU Charter of Fundamental Rights' (2001) 26 *European Law Journal* 126.

[62] Generally speaking, the literature on the socio-political dimension of governance agenda in both law and political science is vast. For an overview of the literature in political science see S Hix, 'The Study of the European Union II: The New Governance Agenda and Its Rivals' (1998) 5 *Journal of European Public Policy* 38 and also B Kohler-Koch, 'Catching up with the Change: The Transformation of Governance in the European Union' (1998) 3 *European Journal of Public Policy* 359. See further W Sandholz and A Stone Sweet (eds), *European Integration and Supranational Governance* (Oxford, Oxford University Press, 1998) and G Marks, L Hooghe and K Blank, 'European Integration from the 1980s: State-Centric *v* Multi-Level Governance' (1996) 34 *Journal of Common Market Studies* 341.

[63] Commission of the European Communities *European Governance: A White Paper* COM (2001) 428 final, Brussels 25 July 2001.

[64] Through, eg, the doctrine of precedent housed in the English legal system or the *Anwendungsvorrang* in German law. See H Kelsen *The Pure Theory of Law* (trans M Knight)

example, the prevailing hierarchy is constituted by the Basic Law, Federal Law and State Law. European Community (EC) law may also be understood according to a hierarchical model to the extent that, as the catechism provides, it prevails over national law[65] and consists of primary and secondary sources of law arranged according to a hierarchy of precedence. Whereas, however, EC law prevails over national law, it is also part and parcel of the legal systems of the Member States. EC law both informs and forms the national law through europeanisation which has led to a substantial degree of convergence between the legal systems of the Member States[66] — in both public[67] and private[68] law — not to mention mergers between those who serve them.[69] The hierarchical model does not provide an adequate response to the normative order upon which EC law resides.

The hierarchical model also fails to account for the generation of legal norms. It can be argued that the citizen formally creates the law but only through case law. However, the citizen provides the origin of the legal dispute and does not participate in the production of norms. To this extent, EC law is *Juristenrecht*,[70] which is to say, EC lawyers are making EC law. *Juristenrecht*, however, raises problems of democratic legitimacy if one accepts that judges and lawyers alike are supposed to be beneath the law and not, as the *praxis* of EC law testifies, before it. According to a judicial model, the citizen is never the originator of the norms. In political terms, however, the citizen is able to informally determine the content by way of Non-Governmental Organisations (NGOs) and lobbyists[71] who operate within and without the boundaries of comitology.[72] The normative order which constitutes EC law is not only the product of legal pluralism;[73] it is

(Berkeley and Los Angeles, University of California Press, 1967). This observation has also been made in the context of international law; see P Zumbansen, 'Die vergangene Zukunft des Völkerrechts' (2001) 35 *Kritische Justiz* 46.

[65] Case C–6/64 *Costa v ENEL* [1964] ECR 585. However, this principle has been derogated from and qualified by, eg, the *Maastricht* judgment of the German Constitutional Court. See 89 BVerfGE 155.
[66] Against, Legrand, n 19 above.
[67] See JWF Allison, 'Transplantation and Cross-Fertilisation' in J Beatson and T Tridimas, *New Directions in European Public Law* (Oxford, Hart Publishing, 1998), 169.
[68] B Markesinis, *The Gradual Convergence: Foreign Influences and English Law on the Eve of the 21st Century* (Oxford, Clarendon Press, 1994).
[69] See DM Trubeck, R Dezalay, R Buchanan and JR Davis, 'Global Restructuring and the Law: Studies of the Internationalization of Legal Fields and the Creation of Transnational Arenas' (1994) 44 *Case Western Reserve Law Review* 407.
[70] E Ehrlich, *Grundlegung des Soziologie des Rechts* (Berlin, Duncker & Humblot, 1989).
[71] J Greenwood, *Representing Interests in the European Union* (London, MacMillan Press, 1997). See also EB Haas, *The Uniting of Europe: Political, Economic and Social Forces, 1950–1957* (Stanford, Stanford University Press, 1968).
[72] See C Joerges and E Vos (eds), *EU Committees: Social Regulation, Law and Politics* 1999).
[73] N MacCormick, 'The Maastricht Urteil: Sovereignty Now' (1995) 1 *European Law Journal* 255.

also entrenched in multi-level governance[74] given that it is based on an increasingly interconnected international order. In other words, the agents in the law-making process behind EC law are to be found both within and outwith the nation-state,[75] a phenomenon which the hierarchical model of law fails to address in a significant manner.

Citizenship too has exposed the shortcomings of being viewed from within a vacuum. After Maastricht, much was written about the exclusionary tendencies of EU citizenship. Citizenship, by definition, categorically excludes a plethora of individuals, such as third country nationals, some of whom are long-term residents in the EU. At one level, policies which disenfranchise long-term residents are at odds which notions of justice and equality. There was also, however, a gradual recognition that citizenship means very little if it does not accommodate, and indeed is not underwritten by, constitutionalism in both a narrow and a wide sense. The narrow sense ascribed to here refers to a constitutional framework as provided by a constitution and a Bill of Rights. Constitutionalism in a wide sense refers to citizenship — in this case — being underscored by notions of constitutionalism which include concepts such as the rule of law, democracy, judicial review, equality and so on.

The battles waged, for instance, about the EU Charter of Fundamental Rights, both before and after Nice, provide a useful case in point.[76] Not only were they directed at form and substance but also, the decision to ensure that the Charter would not be binding illustrated how every choice, more often than not, involves loss. What was being given with one hand, in other words, was being taken with another. However, whereas this may be true at one level, it may not be the case at another. Thus, what is being taken away at one level, may be given at another. To some extent, the Commission's decision to publish its White Paper on Governance can also be viewed as a commitment to the articulation and recognition of rights and policies whilst honouring the competences of the Member States as well as the regions. Sceptics would no doubt argue that it is not so much a case of whether the glass is half empty or half full but whether there is a glass on the table to begin with. Leaving aside for one moment conspiracy theories in which the Commission has a starring role as an all-encompassing, dominant autocrat, technocrat and bureaucrat, it is clear that what the

[74] I Pernice, 'Multilevel Constitutionalism and the Treaty of Amsterdam: European Constitution-making Revisted?' (1999) 36 CML Rev 703.

[75] M Zürn, *Regieren jenseits des Nationalstaates: Globalisierung und Denationalisierung als Chance* (Frankfurt am Main, Suhrkamp, 1998); M Zürn and D Wolf, 'European Law and International Regimes: The Features of Law Beyond the Nation-State' (1999) 5 *European Law Journal* 272 and also D Grimm, 'Die Zukunft der Verfassung' in UK Preuß (ed), *Zum Begriff der Verfassung* (Frankfurt am Main, Fischer, 1994), 283.

[76] See G de Búrca, 'The drafting of the EU Charter of Fundamental Rights' (2001) 26 *European Law Journal* 126.

Commission did provide was a framework for Member States to adopt flexible forms of co-operation through the Open Method of Co-ordination and in other ways, in which rights and policies (as in the case of social policy) are both articulated and recognised in a way which is polycentric and more attuned to the de facto EU.[77]

The progression from citizenship to constitutionalism and then later to governance ought to be viewed in a non-linear fashion so that each concept is not overtaken by the events of the latter.[78] It is suggested that the three be viewed as mutually exclusive spheres, which sometimes overlap. Each, taken on its own is unable to bear the burden of rights recognition alone. Rather, an institutional and extra-institutional balance exists between the three. The task of lawyers is to endorse an analytical legal framework which is able to ensure that this balance is a fact and not a fiction,[79] an unenviable task given the sometimes overwhelming sense of complexity of the European integration process as the experience of the European Convention has shown.

The consequences, not only for the domestic legal cultures but also for the day-to-day lives of individuals are considerable. The multi-level nature of the 'network of interrelationships'[80] existing between the different instruments for the protection of European rights can mean greater protection within a system of mutually accommodating jurisdictions which draw strength from one another through symbiosis. By contrast, multi-jurisdictionality may also disaggregate rights protection so that it becomes fragmented across a number of borders both within and outwith the nation-state in which scattered networks of both institutional and extra-institutional actors operate.[81] Not only is the system opaque but it does not necessarily lend itself to the traditional 'checks and balances' formula of

[77] C Joerges, Y Mény and JHH Weiler (eds), *Mountain or Molehill?: A Critical Appraisal of the Commission White Paper on Governance* Jean Monnet Working Paper 6/01 (Florence, Robert Schuman Centre for Advanced Studies at the European University Institute; New York, New York University School of Law, 2001). See also E Szyszczak, 'Social Policy in the Post-Nice Era' in A Arnull and D Wincott (eds) *Accountability and Legitimacy in the European Union* (Oxford, Oxford University Press, 2002), 329.

[78] See generally C Joerges and R Dehousse (eds), *Good Governance in Europe's Integrated Market* (Oxford, Oxford University Press, 2002).

[79] Or to draw from Giscard d'Estaing's Déclaration de Rome on 18 July 2003 in his assessment of the success of the Convention, 'les équilibres nécessaires entre les peuples, entre les États, nouveaux et anciens, entre les institutions, entre rêve et réalité." See the Convention's Futurum website <http://europa.eu.int/futurum/index_en.htm>.

[80] C Tomuschat, 'The Interaction between Different Systems for the Protection of Human Rights' in R Bieber, K de Gucht, K Lenaerts and JHH Weiler, *Au nom des peuples européens – In the Name of the Peoples of Europe. Un catalogue des droits fondamentaux de l'Union européenne – A Catalogue of Fundamental Rights in the European Union* (Baden-Baden, Nomos Verlag, 1996), 29–43

[81] See generally C McCrudden, 'A Common Law of Human Rights?: Transnational Judicial Conversations on Constitutional Rights' (2000) 4 OJLS 499.

accountability — traditional in the sense of belonging to the tradition of state theory and practice.

The concept of the rule of law has become almost by definition linked to state building, leaving very little room for manoeuvre for conceptualisations which move beyond its borders[82] and which have to come to terms with addressees who are both transnational and supranational. After all, traditional conceptions of constitutionalism are predicated on the assumptions of homogeneity and uniformity of the people[83] which are, more often than not, at odds with the moveable feast of individual mobility across state borders. Those individuals who are mobile are heavily dependent on legal elites who are versed in the specialised knowledge needed in order to carve out a niche amongst a plethora of jurisdictions in order for their rights to be guaranteed.

European rights must be viewed within the context of the complex interplay of institutional reform provoked by the European Convention and the Inter-Governmental Conference (IGC) and enlargement. European integration studies have tended to regard the two processes as being distinct. A new enlargement creates tensions given the challenge of incorporating and assimilating legal systems and cultures of former socialist economies and societies into the EU, which the EC, as it was then, experienced in previous waves of enlargement (as, for example, in the case of Spain and Portugal[84] but never on such a vast scale. The question of the *viability* of the modes of implementation of European rights through law and governance is of a particular relevance for the transformation of the societies, legal systems and administrative practices, economies and polities of the new Member States. Moreover, issues of implementation arise in ways from which lessons may be learned by all of the EU Member States which are faced with the double challenge of europeanisation and transition. This topic is particularly relevant as regards contemporaneous developments in the EU such as the European Convention, the subsequent Intergovernmental Conference and further treaty revisions.

This book will seek to demonstrate the complexities which arise in endorsing an appropriate legal framework for addressing and accommodating the diversity generated by the national legal cultures of the Member States

[82] See also generally D Dyzenhaus (ed), *Recrafting the Rule of Law* (Oxford, Hart Publishing, 1999).

[83] J Tully, *Strange Multiplicity: Constitutionalism in an Age of Diversity* (Cambridge, Cambridge University Press, 1995).

[84] G Ruiz and R Ruiz, 'La libertà di impresa nella costituzione economica spagnola: con particolare riguardo al principio di libera concurrenza' in L Mezzetti *Costituzione economica e libertà di concurrenza* (Torino, G. Giappichelli, 1994), 37–71; See also the contribution by MM Leitão Marques, 'Iniziativa economica e concurrenza nell'ordinamento giuridico portoghese' in the same volume at 75.

as regards implementation of European rights. Case studies will be conducted in individual policy fields, namely in the field of political and social rights, the purpose of which is to assess the extent to which the emerging constitutional framework in the EU is a viable method for addressing the needs of individuals, both EU citizens and non-citizens alike.

2

European Rights and Sovereignty

INTRODUCTION

WHICH OF THE following words could be used to most usefully describe the development of fundamental rights and policies in the European Union? Is it (A) *éclat*; (B), *eclectic*; or (C) *eclipse*? Whereas one might be tempted to select (B), the answer is of course (D), that is to say, *all of the above*. The reason, as this chapter will show, is not because (A) and (C) are conveniently placed at either side of *eclectic* in the *Concise Oxford Dictionary*.[1] Rather, it is because they have evolved in some instances through a brilliant display or effect (*éclat*) in which the European Court of Justice (ECJ) has had a visible hand. Moreover, they have derived ideas and style from a broad and diverse range of sources which include inter alia 'the constitutional traditions common to the Member States'[2] (*eclectic*). They have also, as in the case of an eclipse, obscured the light from one celestial body (in this case, the legal orders of the Member States) by the passage of another (EU law), thereby, as some would argue, depriving the former of significance, power and prominence.

The impact of European rights on the national legal cultures has been part and parcel of the debate concerning the challenge posed by EU law on the legal systems of the Member States as a whole. The juridical debate concerning the relationship between EU law and national law has become so polarised, in some cases, that it might be more appropriate to replace the word *eclipse* with *eclipsing binary* which is used to refer to a binary star whose 'brightness varies periodically as the two components pass one in front of the other'.[3] One is tempted to add — *if only it were that simple*! Consider, for example, the primacy clause inserted in the Draft Constitutional Treaty, Article 10 (1) of which states that the Constitution, and the law adopted by the Union institutions in exercising competences conferred on it, shall have primacy over the law of the Member States.[4] Whereas the provision may in

[1] J Pearsall (ed) *The Concise Oxford Dictionary* (Oxford, Oxford University Press, 2001), 453.
[2] Art 6 (2) TEU. See also AG Roemer's opinion in *Stauder* in which he refers to the 'comparative evaluation of national constitutional concepts and fundamental rights'. See Case C–29/69 *Stauder v City of Ulm* [1969] ECR 419.
[3] See n 1 above.
[4] CONV 820/03.

effect do little more than codify the principle of supremacy as developed by the European Court of Justice,[5] it is unlikely that it is able to resolve the controversial debates surrounding the supremacy debate.[6]

The phenomenon of legal pluralism and multi-jurisdictionality which has led to the (re)configuration of jurisdictional boundaries does little to reduce the complexity with which rights holders in the European Union are faced, not to mention those who are responsible for their implementation. Generally speaking, human rights have been framed in a number of national, supranational and international legal spheres, some of which have significantly challenged states' legal orders in terms of both legal and political authority.[7] No more so has the challenge been so acute than at the interface between states' national constitutional traditions and other sources of fundamental rights provided by inter alia the European Convention on Human Rights and Fundamental Freedoms (ECHR), the International Covenant of Civil and Political Rights and the European Social Charter.[8] This problem exists as regards EU law as a whole and in particular in relation to the overlap between the Charter of Fundamental Rights and other provisions of EU law.[9] It is also likely to arise in the context of the Charter and other sections of the Draft Constitutional Treaty.[10] This somewhat qualifies references to the word *eclipse* in relation to the impact of European rights on national legal cultures of the Member States given that the word is generally taken to refer to where one entity obscures the other. For those who view EU law solely in terms of international law[11] or cosmopolitan law[12] this may be unproblematic. For others, the tension between the two is more contentious given that, contrary to international law,

[5] Case C–6/64 *Costa v ENEL* [1964] ECR 585.

[6] See M Dougan, 'The Convention's Draft Constitutional Treaty: A "Tidying-up Exercise" That Needs Some Tidying-up of its Own' (2003) <http://www.fedtrust.co.uk>. See also P Craig, 'What Constitution does Europe Need? The House that Giscard Built: Constitutional Rooms with a View' (2003) <http://www.fedtrust.co.uk>.

[7] See C McCrudden, 'A Common Law of Human Rights?: Transnational Judicial Conversations on Constitutional Rights' (2000) 4 OJLS 499. See also N Walker, 'Human Rights in a Postnational Order: Reconciling Political and Constitutional Pluralism' in T Campbell, KD Ewing and A Tomkins (eds) *Sceptical Essays on Human Rights* (Oxford, Oxford University Press, 2001), 119.

[8] See J Shaw, 'What's in a Convention? Process and Substance in the Project of European Constitution-building' (2003) *Political Science Series* 89.

[9] Art 52 (2) of the Charter recognises this overlap and requires that rights recognised by the Charter which are based on EU law are exercised in accordance with the conditions of the EU treaties. This provision has also been included in the Draft Constitutional Treaty in Art II–52 (2).

[10] See E Vranes, 'The Final Clauses of the Charter of Fundamental Rights: Stumbling Blocks for the First and Second Convention' (2003) European Integration OnLine Papers <http://eiop.or.at.eiop/texte/2003-007a.htm>.

[11] M Pechstein and M Koenig, *Die Europäische Union: Die Verträge von Maastricht und Amsterdam* (Tübingen, Mohr, 1998). See also F Sorrentino, *Profili costituzionali dell'integrazione comunitaria* (Torino, Giappichelli, 1996) and F Capotorti (ed), *Il primato del diritto comunitario e i guidici italiani* (Milan, Franco Angeli Editore, 1978).

[12] P Eleftheriadis, 'Cosmopolitan Law' (2003) 9 *European Law Journal* 241.

EC law creates rights upon which individuals can directly rely,[13] which has implications for the legal cultures of the Member States and the division of competences.[14]

The expansion of EU competence as a whole generated a process whereby the architecture of the Union was restructured into layers of legal entities,[15] of which the EC was only one.[16] This gave rise to spheres of direct effect of rights and interests of individuals where some were framed in a thick sense, namely under the first pillar of the EC, and others in a thin sense, namely under the other two pillars, the Common Foreign and Security Policy (CFSP) and Cooperation on Justice and Home Affairs (CJHA). In the case of the latter, rights are not exposed to the supervisory jurisdiction of the European Court of Justice and are also, as in the case of EUROPOL, outside the remit of parliamentary control.[17] Elements of differentiated integration give rise to differential spheres of rights which forms part of the many faces, and many personalities of a polity which is both non-static and flexible.[18] This will be further amplified by the amendments to the institutional and constitutional architecture introduced by the Draft Constitutional Treaty which inter alia envisage the abolition of the Pillar Structure and the introduction of a single Treaty.[19] This new Treaty will be divided into fours parts. Part I sets out the Union's constitutional structure which is divided into nine Titles. Part II contains the Charter of Fundamental Rights, Part III outlines the policies and functioning of the Union and Part IV contains general and final provisions.[20] Rights will be scattered across the four parts of the Treaty.

[13] Case C–26/62 *Van Gend en Loos v Nederlandse Administratie der Belastingen* [1963] ECR 1.

[14] See generally V Constantinesco and J P Jacqué, 'L'Application du droit international et communautaire au regard de la Constitution' in P Koernig and W Rüfner (eds) *Le contrôle de la constitutionalité en France et en République féderale d'Allemagne* (Paris, Heymann, 1985), 174; J Wouters, 'National Constitutions and the European Union' (2000) 27 *Legal Issues of European Integration* 25.

[15] Such as inter alia the Investment Bank, the European Central Bank, EUROPOL and EURODAC.

[16] Referred to by some as constituting a type of Russian Doll. See DM Curtin and IF Dekker, 'The European Union as a "Layered" International Organisation: Institutional Unity in Disguise' in P Craig and G de Búrca (eds) *The Evolution of EU Law* (Oxford, Oxford University Press, 1998). This is, however, disputed by those who subscribe to the 'fusion thesis' according to which the EU is regarded as an international legal entity with a single legal system. See A von Bogdandy and M Nettesheim, 'Die Europäische Union: Eine einheitlicher Verband mit eigener Rechtsordnung' (1996) *Europarecht* 3.

[17] Although see the *Airport Transit Case* in which a joint action was held to have legally binding effects in the context of CJHA. See Case C–170/96 *Commission v Council (Air Transport Visas)* [1998] ECR I–2763.

[18] See generally, J Shaw, 'Constitutional Change in the EU: From Uniformity to Flexibility?' in G de Búrca and J Scott (eds) *Constitutional Change in the EU: From Uniformity to Flexibility?* (Oxford, Hart Publishing, 2000), 337.

[19] See Art IV–2 in conjunction with Art IV–3 on legal continuity in the transition from the existing Treaties to the new Constitution.

[20] There are also additional Protocols which are annexed to the Treaty. See Art IV–6 of the Draft Constitutional Treaty.

Whereas EU law does contain elements of international law, it cannot be exclusively understood in these terms, particularly given that Community law has priority over national legal provisions,[21] damages can be obtained for the non-implementation of EC law[22] and where there is a conflict between national law and Community law, the latter prevails,[23] judicial 'conscientious objectors' notwithstanding. The stand made by the conscientious objectors is instructive for the intents and purposes of this chapter given that those national constitutional courts which have elected to object to the supremacy rule, have done so inter alia on the basis of fundamental rights and the protection of values enshrined in their respective legal orders through the prism of competence.[24]

Indeed, the issue of fundamental rights has further consolidated the role of national constitutional court judges as ombudsmen patrolling the borders of their constitutional cultures.[25] In some cases, as in the Italian case *Frontini*,[26] this has been achieved on the basis of outright rejection of the supremacy rule. In other cases, the rejection has been more subtle and nuanced. Thus, for example, the Spanish *Tribunal Constitucional* has tended to disregard European Community law as raising constitutional issues. It has, however, inferred, most notably in its declaration concerning the Maastricht Treaty,[27] that there are limits of the impact of EC law on fundamental rights contained in the Spanish Constitution.[28]

Moreover, the dexterity with which courts have framed their objection to the supremacy rule has been such that it is not always clear when derogations are being made. Restatements of community law being conceptually distinct from national law as made in *Granital*[29] illustrate that for some judges, whether the road is less travelled or not is immaterial given that there are in fact two roads. One road runs through the 'country they know best'.[30]

[21] Case C–6/64 *Costa v ENEL* [1964] ECR 585.

[22] Case C–6/90 and Case C–9/90 *Francovich and others v Italy* [1992] IRLR 84.

[23] *Factortame Ltd v Secretary of State for Transport* (No.2) [1991] AC 603. See also cases C–46/93 and C–48/93, *Brasserie du Pêcheur SA v Germany, R v Secretary of State for Transport, ex p Factortame Ltd* [1996] ECR I–1029.

[24] Regarding the discussion concerning the promotion of constitutional values by the European legal order see D Blanchard, *La Constitutionalisation de l'Union Européenne* (Rennes, Apogée, 2001), 65ff.

[25] JHH Weiler, 'Epilogue: "Comitology" as Revolution' in C Joerges and E Vos (eds) *EU Committees: Social Regulation, Law and Politics* (Oxford, Hart Publishing, 1999), 339 at 343.

[26] *Frontini v Ministero delle Finanze* [1974] 2 CMLR 372.

[27] DTC 108/1992.

[28] See generally R Alonso Garcia, *Derecho comunitario y derechos nacionales: autonomia, integración e interacción* (Buenos Aires, Abeledo-Perrot, 1999) and GC Rodríguez Iglesias, D Liñán Nogueras and V Abellán Honrubia (eds) *El derecho comunitario europeo y su aplicación* (Madrid, Civitas, 1993).

[29] *SpA Granital v Amminstrazione delle Finanze*, an unofficial translation of which has been published by G Gaja (1984) 21 CML Rev 756.

[30] The formulation used by Commissioners at College meetings of the Commission when making an intervention that refers to their home country. See M Egeberg, 'Transcending

The other road also runs through their country, but is separate. It is national judges, so the reasoning goes, who retain the 'ultimate' choice as to which road to take, as well as determining both the level and extent of their awareness of the existence of what many view as the 'Other', that is to say, European Union law.

As this chapter will show, however, the politics of resistance or dissent[31] is not always as identifiable as those achieved under the aegis of the 'two legal orders' doctrine. As regards the development of European rights, it is not only a case of asking 'whose rights are they anyway?', but also, 'who is right?' and 'who decides who is right?' The debate concerning the ultimate authority, or *Kompetenz-Kompetenz* does not necessarily lend itself to the reductive components of multiple-choice questions (or *MCQs*). As all those who have suffered at the hands of *MCQs* know best, where there is an 'all of the above' box, there is generally a request or, indeed a summons, to '*Discuss*'.

WHO FRAMED EU FUNDAMENTAL RIGHTS AND POLICIES?

The European Court of Justice has been a driving force[32] of the European integration process.[33] It has, however, not acted alone but has been assisted by lawyers and national judges who have contributed to the development of the legal integration process according to their means and their respective ends. This has, to some extent, created a type of 'spill over',[34] the dynamics of which have fed back into the greater political environment.[35] Governments are not, as has been suggested, the only actors who are unable to control this behaviour. National constitutional courts find themselves faced with the same predicament in spite of their attempts to 'claw back' the remit of their jurisdiction. The best they can hope to achieve, as I will go on to argue, is to provide a theoretical blueprint for

Intergovernmentalism. Identity and Role Perceptions of National Officials in EU Decision-making' (1999) 6 *European Journal of Public Policy* 456.

[31] See M Aziz, 'Constitutional Tolerance and EU Enlargement: The Politics of Dissent?' in P Zumbansen and R Miller (eds) *The Annual of German and European Law* (New York, Berghahn, 2002).

[32] See generally M Poiares Maduro, *We, the Court* (Oxford, Hart Publishing, 1998).

[33] See E Stein, 'Lawyers, Judges and the Making of a Transnational Constitution' (1981) 75 *American Journal of International Law* 1; A–M Burley and W Mattli, 'Europe before the Court: A Political Theory of Legal Integration' (1993) 47 *International Organisation* 41. See also A Stone Sweet, *Governing with Judges* (Oxford, Oxford University Press, 2000).

[34] First identified by Haas although he did not have the law and the courts in mind. See EB Haas, *The Uniting of Europe: Political, Economic and Social Forces, 1950–1957* (Stanford, Stanford University Press, 1968).

[35] See A Stone Sweet and TL Brunell, 'Constructing a Abovenational Constitution: Dispute Resolution and Governance in the European Community' (1998) 92 *American Political Science Review* 63 at 64.

national judges who operate across the judicial spectrum so as to advise them how to contain the impact of European rights on their domestic legal cultures. Regarding the development of EU fundamental rights and policies as a whole, the European Court of Justice has in some cases rushed in where policy makers feared to tread.[36] It has also, however, had to come to terms with the process of differentiated integration as mediated through legal and extra-legal frameworks in which its supervisory jurisdiction has been contained.[37]

Originally, the Court spoke about what the ECSC and the EEC Treaties, adopted in the 1950s, passed in silence. Rights were later incorporated, first on an informal basis[38] and then formally incorporated through Treaty amendment later,[39] culminating in the *éclat* caused by the adoption of the Charter on Fundamental Rights proclaimed at Nice in December 2001,[40] a non-binding instrument which nevertheless commits the Member States to the rights contained therein when they implement Union law,[41] whilst 'having regard' to the principle of subsidiarity.[42] As regards the ECJ, the

[36] Starting with *Stauder*. See Case C–29/69 *Stauder v City of Ulm* [1969] ECR 419. See also Case C–11/70 *Internationale Handelsgesellschaft* [1970] ECR 1125. For a general appraisal of the European Court of Justice's rights jurisprudence see P Alston and JHH Weiler, 'An "Ever Closer Union" in Need of a Human Rights Policy: The European Union and Human Rights' in P Alston, M Bustelo and J Heenan (eds) *The EU and Human Rights* (Oxford, Oxford University Press, 1999), 3 and also JHH Weiler and SCF Fries, 'A Human Rights Policy for the European Community and Union: The Question of Competences' in P Alston, M Bustelo and J Heenan (eds) *The EU and Human Rights* (Oxford, Oxford University Press, 1999), 147.

[37] See, however, Case T–135/96 *UEAPME v Council* [1998] ECR II–2335 in which the Court of Instance interpreted laws adopted under the Social Policy Agreement as Community law. See also Case C–170/96 *Commission v Council (Air Transport Visas)* [1998] ECR I–2763 in which the European Court of Justice extended its jurisdiction to CJHA. See also the cases concerning transparency and access to documents such as, for example, Case T–194/94 *Carvel v EU Council* [1995] ECR–II 2765 (access to third pillar documents); Case T–174/95 *Tidningen Journalisten v Council* [1998] ECR II–2289 (access to third pillar documents); Case T 14/98 *Hautela v Council* [1999] ECR II–2489 (access to second pillar documents) and also Case T–188/97 *Rothmans International v Commission* [1999] ECR I–19 July 1999 (access to comitology committees).

[38] See the Joint Declaration by the European Parliament, the Council and the Commission on fundamental rights of 5 April 1977, [1977] OJ C103/1.

[39] See Art 6 TEU and also Art 46 TEU which grants the European Court of Justice jurisdiction.

[40] [2000] OJ C 364/1. See N Walker, 'Protection of Fundamental Rights in the European Union: The Charter of Fundamental Rights' in P Cullen and P A Zervakis (eds) *The Post-Nice Process: Towards a European Constitution* (Baden-Baden, Nomos Verlag, 2001), 119, K Lenaerts and E De Smijter, 'A "Bill of Rights" for the European Union' (2001) 38 CML Rev 273 and also R Toniatti (ed), *Diritto, diritti, giurisdizione: La carta dei diritti fondamentali dell'Unione Europea* (Padova, CEDAM, 2002).

[41] See G de Búrca, 'The Drafting of the EU Charter of Fundamental Rights' (2001) 26 *European Law Review* 126. Although the status of the Charter is due to be re-evaluated at that next Intergovernmental Conference. See declaration 23 adopted by the Nice Intergovernmental Conference at [2001] OJ C 80/85.

[42] Thus, the explanatory note to Art 51 of the Charter provides that:

> Paragraph 2 confirms that the Charter may not have the effect of extending the competences and tasks which the Treaties confer on the Community and the Union. Explicit reference is made here to the logical consequences of the principle of subsidiarity and to

Charter has been referred to in a number of opinions of Advocates General as one of the sources from which it derives its *eclectic* rights jurisprudence, a logical step for a court which regards the Charter as confirming and consolidating its judicial activism of the past.[43]

For those who regard the 'creative jurisprudence'[44] of the ECJ as illegitimate,[45] its development of fundamental rights and policies exemplifies recidivist behaviour of the very worst kind. However, where would human rights be without the interpretative skills of judges? As Dworkin has written concerning the relationship between judges and democracy:

> Democracy does not insist on judges having the last word, but it does not insist that they must not have it.[46]

The fundamental question is whether the influence judges of the ECJ have exerted over the European integration process is disproportionate, bearing in mind, however, that a degree of differentiation has prevailed. The different degrees of judicial activism[47] have in effect given rise to different degrees of *taking rights seriously.*

The Market Mentality of the European Court of Justice

Fundamental rights were not developed as ends in themselves but in order to meet the needs and demands of market integration as well as a vehicle to

> the fact that the Union only has those powers which have been conferred upon it. The fundamental rights as guaranteed in the Union do not have any effect other than in the context of the powers determined by the Treaty.

See CHARTE 4473/00, 11 October 2000. For an erudite discussion of the principle of subsidiarity see A Estella, *The EU Principle of Subsidiarity and its Critique* (Oxford, Oxford University Press, 2002).

[43] See, eg, Advocate General Tizzano's opinion at paras 26–28 in Case C–173/99 *The Queen v Secretary of State for Trade and Industry, ex p Broadcasting, Entertainment, Cinematographic and Theatre Union (BECTU)* [2001] ECR I–4881 in which the Charter was referred to as a 'substantive reference point'. See also Advocate General Jacob's opinion of 14 June 2001 in Case C–377/98 *Netherlands v European Parliament and Council* at paras 197 and 210. Note that the Court of First Instance did explicitly refer to the Charter in Case T–54/00 *max.mobil Telekommunikation Service v Commission*, judgment of 30 January 2002 at paras 47–48. See generally: P Eeckhout, 'The EU Charter of Fundamental Rights and the Federal Question' (2002) 39 CML Rev 945; R Alonso Garcia, 'The General Provisions of the Charter of Fundamental Rights' (2002) 8 *European Law Journal* 492.

[44] See T Tridimas, *The General Principles of EC Law* (Oxford, Oxford University Press, 1999), 205.

[45] See TC Hartley, *Constitutional Problems of the European Union* (Oxford, Hart Publishing, 1999).

[46] R Dworkin, *Freedom's Law: The Moral Reading of the American Constitution* (Cambridge MA, Harvard University Press, 1996), 7.

[47] See Poiares Maduro, n 32 above, at 89.

extend the scope and impact of European law as a whole.[48] However, whereas the 'market mentality'[49] of the ECJ is a noticeable part of its rights jurisprudence, it does not account for, neither does it inform all of, its decisions. Notwithstanding, the predilection of the ECJ for recognising those rights which are significant for market building is a thesis which merits consideration given its propensity to view the individual as a 'factor of production' or *homo economicus*.[50] Indeed, comparisons with Karl Polanyi's concept of the 'market mentality' are not entirely inappropriate.[51] The ECJ has also, however, developed human rights *beyond* their economic significance for market integration. Thus, in *P v S* and in *Grant*,[52] which concerned discrimination against transsexuals and homosexuals and lesbians in employment, the dignity of the individual and the value of equality were at the forefront of the Court's reasoning and not the economic aims upon which sex discrimination under EC law is based. It is not my intention to discuss the ECJ's human rights jurisprudence as a whole.[53] Neither is it my aim to join the rank of sceptics who view its decisions solely through the lens of market integration. However, the 'market mentality' of the ECJ is relevant to the extent that it exposes the degree to which it has differentiated between different categories of rights, vesting some with more authority than others, sometimes by design, and sometimes by default.

The economic emphasis on rights derived from general principles of EC law, namely, the protection of fundamental rights, the right to privacy, the principle of proportionality, legitimate expectations, legal certainty and equality,[54] together with the highly developed legal and administrative structures enacted for their implementation highlights *degrees or spheres* of, to draw from the title of Ronald Dworkin's book,[55] *taking rights seriously*. Competition law and policy is a useful example of rights 'with teeth' given the jurisdictional hold over its implementation and administration by the Commission which presides over legal and administrative structures which leave little room for doubt that rights contained therein are anything but rhetorical.[56] Indeed, this is an area of EU fundamental rights and policies

[48] J Coppel and A O'Neill, 'The European Court of Justice: Taking Rights Seriously?' (1992) 29 CML Rev 669.
[49] See below.
[50] M Everson, 'The Legacy of the Market Citizen' in J Shaw and G Moore (eds) *New Legal Dynamics of the European Union* (Oxford, Clarendon Press, 1995), 73.
[51] K Polanyi, *The Great Transformation* (Boston, Beacon Press, 1944), 76.
[52] See Case C–13/91 *P v S and Cornwall County Council Case* [1996] ECR 2143 and also Case C–249/96 *Grant v South-West Trains Ltd* [1998] ECR I–621.
[53] See B de Witte, 'The Past and Future Role of the European Court of Justice in the Protection of Human Rights' in P Alston, M Bustelo and J Heenan (eds) *The EU and Human Rights* (Oxford, Oxford University Press, 1999), 859.
[54] See Tridimas, n 44 above.
[55] R Dworkin, *Taking Rights Seriously* (Cambridge, Cambridge University Press, 1978).
[56] See, eg, Council Regulation 17/62 and also Council Regulation 4064/89, OJ 1989 L 395/1 rectified by OJ 1990 L 257/13 amended in 1997, OJ 1997 L180/1 which govern merger control.

which the policy makers were less silent about given their role in relation to market integration. For some, the European Court of Justice 'broke the silence of the Treaty' as regards fundamental rights and policies in *Stauder*.[57] For competition lawyers, however, the Treaty spoke the prose of rights from the outset, without most constitutional lawyers being aware of it.

Constitutionalising Competition Law

Traditionally seen as an instrument of private law, most public law lawyers are unaware that both the vocabulary and grammar of competition law is the language of rights as underwritten by constitutionalism.[58] This version of events — and it is a version as this view is debatable — is one in which the founding Treaties of the European Economic Community, as it was then, feature as a charter of economic rights. The original Treaty of Rome (1957) is viewed as a covenant to ensure against the outbreak of war by fostering a Franco-German alliance. In other words, it was designed in such a way as to ensure that their economies would be so intertwined that hostilities between them in the future would be unthinkable with the second political objective being to increase their political and economic weight in international affairs.[59] Thus, the Treaties created a powerful central authority with extensive powers in order to ensure that a highly planned and regulated market among the member countries was maintained, which has encouraged some scholars to regard the Treaties as an economic constitution.[60]

Given the increase in EU competence and its gradual transformation into a body which promotes and protects human rights, this view of the Treaties is debatable. Notwithstanding, the implications of regarding the Treaties in terms of an economic constitution are mainly twofold. First, it illustrates the nexus of market building with certain categories of rights. Secondly, it also highlights the cultural dimension of EU fundamental rights and policies, without expressly appearing to do so. As I noted in the Introduction,

See Council Regulation 659/1999, OJ 1999 L 83/1 (control of State aids) and also Council Regulation 384/96, OJ 1996 L 56/1 (anti-dumping).

[57] See de Witte, n 53 above, at 867.
[58] See generally J Baquero Cruz, *Between Competition and Free Movement: The Economic Constitutional Law of the European Community* (Oxford, Hart Publishing, 2002).
[59] See K Nicolaïdis and R Vernon, 'Competition Policy and Trade Policy in the European Union' in EM Graham and J D Richardson (eds) *Global Competition Policy* (Washington DC, Institute for International Economics, 1997), 273 who argue that such was the thinking behind the implementation of the European Recovery Program that, together with the financial support of the United States and the institutional support of the Organisation for European Economic Cooperation, the countries of western Europe sought to breach the gap in productivity and technological achievement between European industry and US industry.
[60] C Joerges, 'European Economic Law, the Nation State and the Maastricht Treaty' in R Dehousse (ed) *The European Union Treaty* (München, CH Beck, 1994), 29.

constitutions incorporate rights which reflect certain values.[61] The perennial link between values and culture means that they constitute statements of identity.[62] In other words, the constitutional identity of a multinational society is its basic constitutional structure.[63] The link between the two has implications for identity though not in a way in which it is customarily recognised nor perceived. The range of the rights debate as regards identity politics does not, at first glance, appear to be relevant to the concept of rights as vehicles for market integration. What do the constitutional recognition and accommodation of identities of inter alia individuals, women, gays, lesbians, linguistic diversity, ethnic, religious and cultural minorities have in common with a market mentality approach to fundamental rights? The literature of identity politics is vast.[64] However, little mention is made of the role of economic rights in promoting and perpetuating a particular, if not dominant identity. The literature in which the Treaties have a starring role as an economic constitution is also sizeable,[65] but here also, scant attention is paid to the fact that the identity politics contained therein form an integral part of the established political culture, both in institutional and in ideological terms. Left up to the devices accorded to it by the Member States, the ECJ has been able to develop economic rights in such a way that it has redrawn the maps which detail how cohesion and unity may be achieved, thereby side stepping the customary tools used to accomplish state building such as, for instance, education, conscription and a common language. Where the Court has been challenged as having addressed the issue of culture in a too interventionist manner, it has side stepped the accusation by pointing to the severability from the main case at hand. For instance, not all language issues, as the Court has been at pains to point out, are linked to cultural heritage.[66] Thus in *Parliament v Council*[67] the Parliament sought to have a Council decision on the multi-annual programme

[61] See, eg, the exposition of this thesis by Advocate General Léger as part of his opinion of 10 July 2001 in Case C–353/99 P *Council v Hautala* at paras 51ff in which he states that the principle of access to documents is included in the Charter (see Art 42) by virtue of representing a value which is unanimously shared by the Member States.
[62] This is discussed further in ch 5.
[63] See James Tully's introduction to J Tully and AG Gagnon (eds) *Multinational Democracies* (Cambridge, Cambridge University Press, 2001). He draws from the Canadian context in order to substantiate this argument which has also been made in relation to the German constitution. See EW Böckenförde, (1974) NJW 1529.
[64] See generally S Benhabib (ed) *Democracy and Difference* (Princeton, Princeton University Press, 1996); B Parekh, *Rethinking Multiculturalism: Cultural Diversity and Political Theory* (Cambridge, Cambridge University Press, 2000); W Kymlicka, *Multicultural Citizenship* (Oxford, Oxford University Press, 1995) and also J Tully, *Strange Multiplicity: Constitutionalism in an Age of Diversity* (Cambridge, Cambridge University Press, 1995).
[65] See K Füßer, 'Grundrecht auf wirtschaftliche Freizügigkeit und Art. 8 a EGV als Auffangbeschränkungsverbot des Gemeinschaftsrechts' (1999) *Die öffentliche Verwaltung* 96. See also Poiares Maduro, n 32.
[66] This is addressed in further detail in ch 5, the section on Language Rights Policies at p 153.
[67] Case C–42/97 *European Parliament v Council of the European Union* [1999] ECR I–869.

to promote the linguistic diversity of the Community in the information society[68] annulled on the grounds that it should have specified Article 151 as part of its legal basis. In its decision, the Court drew a distinction between the 'essential and indissociable' and the 'incidental' components of the measure. If, as the Court argued, the industrial component was the main or predominant component, then the appropriate legal basis was Article 157 of the EC Treaty. In essence, the Court held that the cultural aspects of the contested measure were incidental and that the marginalisation which the legislature sought to ward off was in the commercial sphere of the information society and not the sphere of cultural heritage. What the Court omitted to address, however, was that there are many cases in which the spheres overlap.[69] The *Sunday Trading* decisions are a further case in point, where the decision to allow shops to open on a Sunday has obvious cultural dimensions, an overlap which the Court was less willing to acknowledge.[70]

Through competition law and policy, the Commission is able to influence the content of cultural politics in an indirect manner through the medium of procedure. Its competence concerning culture is not extensive. It is, however, able to exert considerable influence by its transmission through, for example, competition policy and the drive towards harmonisation through standardisation, the latter being seen as representing the consumer's best interests. Thus, for example, in *the Council Resolution on the development of technology and standards in the field of advanced television services,*[71] the emphasis is placed on the need for Europe have a

> coherent global approach to the development of technology and standards for new digital television systems which is to be achieved by ensuring that all new television transmission and encryption systems to be used in the Community be standardised.

In the *Council Resolution on a framework for Community policy on digital video broadcasting,*[72] it is stated that its aim is inter alia, fair and open competition, consumer protection and what it refers to rather cryptically as 'other significant public interest'.[73] The process of standardisation of digital television is to be 'encouraged' by issuing briefs to European standardisation bodies,[74] a measure which extends its jurisdiction albeit in an administrative manner. The logic of what has been referred to as

[68] Aimed particularly at the needs of small and medium-sized companies facing different language markets within the EC. See [1996] OJ L306/40.
[69] See N Nic Shuibhne, *EC Law and Minority Language Policy* (The Hague, Kluwer Law International, 2002), 145.
[70] See M Jarvis, *The Application of EC Law by National Courts: The Free Movement of Goods* (Oxford, Clarendon Press, 1998), 180ff.
[71] OJ C 209 of 03/08/1993, Document 393Y0803(01).
[72] OJ C 181 of 02/07/1994, Document 394Y0702(02).
[73] See OJ C 181 of 02/07/1994, Document 394Y0702(02) at para 3.2. (ii).
[74] See OJ C 181 of 02/07/1994, Document 394Y0702(02) at para 5.2.

'jurisdictionalized administration' is achieved by extending discretionary powers of the administration whilst at the same time increasing the respect for procedural guarantees. Not only does this ensure that the grounds of review are limited[75] but also, it masks the extent of the Commission's influence. There is a fine line between standardising the method of transmitting culture and standardising its substantive elements.

Secondly, the nature of Europeanness or the leading culture or *Leitkultur*[76] which is promoted through competition law reflects a particular version of economic liberalism which has implications for the implementation of European rights, as Chapter Four on Social Rights will demonstrate. This version is distinct from the United States, as the Court of Justice is fond of pointing out. Indeed, the ECJ has consistently rejected the American Chicago model of 'pure or perfect competition' in favour of a social justice model based on 'workable competition'[77] thereby exposing the nexus of values inherent in competition law and policy. In the case of the German Act Against the Restrictions of Competition (ARC) or *Gesetz gegen Wettbewerbsbeschränkungen* ('GWB'), which regulates restrictive practices,[78] a clear statement of values is made through the medium of a constitutionalist approach. This is particularly apparent when one regards the way in which it was last amended in 1998. The passing of the Act was heralded as the 'constitution' of the free market or the 'magna carta' of the nation's economy by the then Federal Minister of Economy, Günter Rexrodt of the FDP.[79] The context of Rexrodt's remarks is more apparent when taken in conjunction with the historical significance of the link between economic and political stability,[80] a fact of which Ludwig Erhardt the 'father of the ARC' was only too aware.[81] The sixth amended version of the ARC not only consolidated the developments in competition policy since its original enactment in 1958[82] but

[75] cf L Azoulay, 'The Judge and the Community's Administrative Governance' in C Joerges and R Dehousse (eds), *Good Governance in Europe's Integrated Market* (Oxford, Oxford University Press, 2002), 109 at 113.

[76] To use the term used in the German debate regarding identity politics. See the discussion in ch 2, the section One Legal Order or Two at p 51.

[77] Briefly stated, the adherents to the Chicago school believe in minimal intervention and that the market has the inherent ability to correct itself. Moreover, a maximalist approach hinders the efforts of industry to compete in a global market. Thus, policy tends to prefer regulation of a small category of corporate behaviour. See H Fleischer, 'Gezielte Kampfpreisunterbindungen im Recht der Vereinigten Staaten: der Supreme Court zwischen Chicago School and Post-Chicago Economics' (195) 10 *Wirtschaft urd Wettbewerb* 798.

[78] See generally V Emmerich, *Kartellrecht* (München, CH Beck, 1994) at 30ff.

[79] *Der Tagesspiegel*, 10 May 1998 at 22 and also the *Frankfurter Allgemeine Zeitung*, 7 May 1998 at 19.

[80] See K-U Kühn, 'Germany' in EM Graham and JD Richardson (eds) *Global Competition Policy* (Washington DC, Institute for International Economics, 1997), 117.

[81] See *40 Jahre Bundeskartellamt 1958–1998* (Berlin, Bundeskartellamt, 1998).

[82] *Gesetz v 27.7.1957*, BGBl I S 1081, which entered into force on 1 January 1958.

it also substantively harmonised German competition law with EC competition law provisions.[83]

The Act was a central element of the decartelisation policy imposed by the US after the second world war. An effective competition regime was regarded as constituting an essential pillar, limiting private power as the Basic Law limited state power. The ARC was couched in constitutional terms from the outset thereby not only explicitly acknowledging the power interests at stake[84] but also recognising a particular orientation, or to paraphrase from the original German source: that an economic constitution of this nature forms the economic policy of a political democracy.[85] Indeed, it vests the political democracy with part of its identity through the medium of sovereignty in no uncertain terms. In effect, the europeanisation of competition law of the respective Member States has exported certain values which have led to a reconfiguration of their constitutional orders as well as the values contained therein.[86] This has been particularly the case as regards countries which, like Portugal and Spain, had to satisfy the requirements of membership by embracing the value of a market economy whilst eschewing their socialist past.[87]

To some extent, this makes a mockery of the judicial sovereignty debate which has raged across the constitutional courts of the Member States who have focused their attention on those fundamental rights and values upon which EU law has had less impact than in those fields of law more directly linked to market integration. Arguments concerning the threat to their respective legal orders by EC competition law, for instance, by constitutional judges have been notable for their absence.

The jurisprudence of the ECJ as regards *justice as fairness* linked to market building is prolific. The principle of fairness as articulated in competition

[83] See a speech by the President of the Federal Cartel Office (FCO), Dieter Wolf, 'Die Erwartungen des Bundeskartellamts an die 6. GWB Novelle — Mehr Konvergenz mit europäischen Recht?' or 'The Expectations of the FCO arising out of the Sixth amendment of the ARC — More Convergence with European Law? at the XVII. International Forum of EC Competition Law, 15–16 May 1997, Brussels. See <http://www.bundeskartellamt.de/sechste.htm> for a full transcript of the speech.

[84] E Braun, *EC Competition Rules in National Courts (III): Germany* (Baden-Baden, Nomos Verlag, 1996).

[85] 'Eine derart geordnete Wirtschaftsverfassung bildet das wirtschaftspolitische Gegenstück zur politischen Demokratie. Während deren Inhalt als das politische Mitbestimmungsrecht jedes Staatsbürger anzusehen ist, stellt die Wettbewerbsordnung die wirtschaftlichen Grundrechte der Freiheit der Arbeit und der Verbrauchswahl sicher.' BT–Drucks II/1158 at IV. Die Wettbewerbsordnung.

[86] See generally L Mezzetti (ed) *Costituzione economica e libertà di Concurrenza* (Torino, G Giappichelli Editore, 1994).

[87] See G Ruiz and R Ruiz, 'La libertà di impresa nella costituzione economica spagnola: Con particolare riguardo al principio di libera concurrenza' in L Mezzetti (ed) *Costituzione economica e libertà di concurrenza* (Torino, G. Giappichelli, 1994), 37 and also the contribution of MM Leitão Marques, 'Iniziativa economica e concurrenza nell'ordinamento giuridico portoghese in the same volume at p 7.

law through third-party access to a private asset, for instance provides a useful case in point.[88] Although the ECJ has not made explicit mention of the essential facilities doctrine, as such, it has upheld the doctrine in principle.[89] Thus, for example, in the *Magill* case[90] the Court of First Instance held that *Magill* must be allowed to use the copyrighted weekly TV programme listings of each of the BBC, the RTE and the ITP (the Broadcasters) in order to produce a comprehensive weekly TV listings of the Broadcasters.[91] The doctrine of essential facilities has lent itself as a vehicle to suit the ends of European integration based on a particular conception of fairness. This selective interpretation is also further evidenced by the legal and administrative structures within which competition law is ensconced, over which the Commission continues to preside. Indeed, the concept of natural justice which exists in matters of competition is somewhat unique. This is particularly the case as regards the rules of procedure. Thus, for example, the rule which provides that it is the Commission which decides to which documents companies have access in order to prepare their defence so that they may examine the defence before trial would seem to undermine most notions of natural justice.[92] This is not, however, to say that notions of natural justice are absent. Thus, for example, in *Hoechst*,[93] the ECJ held that whilst the right to defence should be protected, undertakings could not benefit from the same protection afforded to natural persons as provided by Article 8 (1) of the European Convention on Human Rights which protects the inviolability of the home. In this case, the Commission had imposed a penalty of periodic payments on an undertaking it suspected of engaging in

[88] '... the essential facilities doctrine imposes a liability when one firm, which controls an essential facility, denies a second firm reasonable access to a product or service that the second firm must obtain in order to compete with the first.' *(Alaska Airlines v United States et al.* 948 F 2d 536 (9th Cir 1991). Decision of 29 October 1991.)

[89] Thereby emulating the position in the United State to the extent that the Supreme Court has supported the doctrine by implication only. See P Areeda, 'Essential Facilities: An Epithet in Need of Limiting Principles' (1990) 58 *Antitrust Law Journal* 841. It is arguable that the ECJ has not had to make explicit reference to the doctrine given that the Commission has referred to it in less ambiguous terms. See Commission Decision EC/94/19 (*Sea Containers / Stena Sealink*). OJ 1994 L15/8. M Furse, 'The "Essential Facilities" Doctrine in Community Law' (1995) 8 ECLR 469.

[90] Commission Decision: *Magill TV Guide / ITP, BBC and RTE* OJ 1989 L78/43. Case T–69/89 *RTE v Commission* [1991] ECR II–485 (C–2241/91P); Case T–70/89 *BBC v Commission* [1991] ECR II–535; Case T–76/89 *ITP v Commission* [1991] ECR II–575 (C–242/91).

[91] See R Subiotto, 'The Right to Deal with Whom One Pleases under EEC Competition Law: A Small Contribution to a Necessary Debate' (1992) 6 ECLR 234; R Greaves, 'Magill est arrivé ... RTE and ITP v Commission of the European Communities' (1995) 4 ECLR 244.

[92] See R Wesseling, *The Modernisation of EC Antitrust Law* (Oxford, Hart Publishing, 2000) at 165–66.

[93] Case C–46/87 and 227/88 *Hoechst AG v Commission* [1989] ECR 2859, [1991] 4 CMLR 410.

anti-competitive practices which had refused to permit the Commission to carry out its investigation.[94]

In *Hoechst*, the ECJ acknowledged that fundamental rights are an integral part of the general principles of EC law as are the constitutional traditions common to the Member States taken in conjunction with international treaties such as the European Convention for the Protection of Human Rights and Fundamental Freedoms to which most if not all are signatories.[95] However, it openly stated that rights contained therein, such as the right of defence, must not impair preliminary inquiry procedures including investigations which 'may be decisive in providing evidence of the unlawful nature of conduct engaged in or by undertakings for which they may be liable.'[96] The limited extent to which the jurisprudence of the European Court of Human Rights is to be followed was also reaffirmed in *Mannesmannröhren-Werke AG v Commission*.[97] In this case, which involved the interpretation of Regulation 17, the Court of First Instance held that the decisions of the ECHR are as such not part of Community law.[98] Needless to say, the interpretation was more restrictive than that adopted by the ECHR, thereby illustrating the extent of the 'special significance' attributed to the European Convention it referred to in *Emesa Sugar*.[99] Regarding the interpretation human rights in the context of Commission competition policy, the reaction amongst the academic community[100] has been more vociferous than that of the constitutional court judges of the Member States, a curious omission, given the obsession of the latter for the protection of fundamental rights, which they have stated and restated on numerous occasions.[101]

It may be the case that these constitutional ombudsmen arguably painted themselves into a corner by choosing to articulate their concerns in terms of the competence issue. Thus, the explicit competence of the EU over matters of competition law undeniably constrained these judges from voicing their concerns in this policy sphere. As the EU's human rights profile expanded, many national judges seemed content to withdraw their voices of concern as in the *Solange II* decision of the German Federal Constitutional Court.[102]

[94] Powers it enjoys as part of Art 14 of Regulation No 17.
[95] See *Hoechst*, n 93 above, at para 13.
[96] See *Hoechst*, n 93 above, at para 15.
[97] Case T–112/98, [2000] ECR II–729.
[98] *Ibid* at para 59.
[99] See Case C–17/98 *Emesa Sugar (Free Zone) NV v Aruba*, Order of the Court of 4 February 2000, para 8 citing Case C–260/89 *ERT* [1991] ECR I–2925, para 41.
[100] A Clapham, 'A Human Rights Policy for the European Community' (1990) 10 *Yearbook of European Law* 309 at 331. See also P Beaumont, 'Human Rights: Some Recent Developments and Their Impact on Convergence and Divergence of Law in Europe' in P Beaumont, C Lyons and N Walker (eds) *Convergence and Divergence in European Public Law* (Oxford, Hart Publishing, 2002), 131.
[101] See below.
[102] See below.

Some judges have allowed themselves to stray beyond the limits of their judicial mandate by participating in public debates concerning sovereignty which illustrates how debates being conducted in various spheres can, at times, overlap.[103] As a result, the boundaries are not always clear thereby creating, in some cases, a certain amount of 'spillover' which in turn influences the content of the respective debates. The legitimacy of allowing judges to express dissent in other spheres, particularly if they are adjudicating on certain contentious cases, in the press, is perhaps questionable.[104] What is apparent is how the debates concerning sovereignty in the various networks feed in to one another in substantiating not only *Visions of Europe*[105] but also *Versions of Europe*. It is not so much a case of seeing different worlds but rather, it is that the same world is viewed differently.[106]

ENDOGENOUS JUDICIAL REASONING: ONE EUROPE AND/OR SEVERAL?

Part of the legacy of the law's role in state formation is that lawyers tend to think of law in terms of the nation-state.[107] Indeed, the nation-state lies at the apex of legal reasoning.[108] Few legal disciplines, other than the law of the European Union, encourage the legal profession to think beyond the

[103] Which some social theorists have elected to term a 'sphere of publics'. See C Calhoun, *Critical Social Theory* (Oxford, Blackwell, 1995), 242. See also J Habermas, *Between Facts and Norms* (Cambridge, Polity Press, 1997) 373–374 who conceptualises this in terms of overlapping international, national, regional, local and subcultural networks.
[104] See an interview with the former German constitutional judge in the German magazine *Focus* from 13 February 1999 at p 11 which was given whilst he was still a judge at the Constitutional court.
[105] See generally A Moravcsik, 'Review Essay on Larry Siedentop, *Democracy in America*: Despotism in Brussels? Misreading the European Union' (2001) 80 *Foreign Affairs* 114 who does not, however, expressly address the sovereignty debate.
[106] Indeed, more modest claims which shy away from claiming to represent reality are all too often rarely made. See, however, E Philippart and M Sie Dhian Ho, 'From Uniformity to Flexibility: The Management of Diversity and its Impact on the EU System of Governance' in G de Búrca and J Scott (eds) *Flexibility and Models of Governance for the EU* (Oxford, Hart Publishing, 2000), 299 at 308 who write in relation to models of governance for the EU that:

> These models do not pretend to represent 'reality', but in a stylised way each of them says something about what are, will and/or should be EU policies, methods of integration, institutional architecture and legitimacy.

[107] See generally D Nelken and J Feest (eds), *Adapting Legal Cultures* (Oxford, Hart Publishing, 2001).
[108] One is reminded of the social anthropologist Mary Douglas who describes a professional collective as one which 'leads perception and trains it and produces a stock of knowledge'. This includes drawing up and maintaining criteria as regards what constitutes a reasonable question and a true or false answer. In short, it provides the context and sets the limits for any evaluative judgment about what is objective. See M Douglas, *How Institutions Think* (London, Routledge, 1987), 12ff.

limits of their national legal training, a notable exception being the discipline of public international law and comparative law not to mention the recent development of supranational legal bodies such as the arbitration authority established by the World Trade Organisation.[109] Turning our attention to comparative lawyers[110] there is no doubt that comparative law fosters the pursuit of ideas. The *ratio* of this discipline, however, remains the domestic legal system which is first and foremost the point of departure of this form of legal analysis which encourages a compartmentalised view of law along the lines of the state.[111]

By contrast, jurists in the 17th and 18th centuries made use of the same legal grammar as part of the *ius commune*.[112] The common language was Latin, and the common heritage was Roman law[113] which arguably constituted a unified, European culture.[114] Justinian's *Corpus Iuris Civilis* and the first European university at Bologna, the *universitas magistrorum et scholarium*, were pivotal in the gestation of law as a discipline[115] which was based on Roman and canon law. Thus, law or legal reasoning

[109] The role of the state is, however, not obsolete as the rules regarding standing provide: States and not individuals have standing as parties to the proceedings. Individuals are still dependent on institutions of the state for the implementation of their rights.

[110] '... by the international exchanges which it requires, comparative law procures the gradual approximation of viewpoints, the abandonment of deadly complacency, and the relaxation of fixed dogma. It affords us a glimpse into the form and formation of legal institutions which develop in parallel, possibly in accordance with laws yet to be determined, and permits us to catch sight, through the differences in detail, of the grand similarities and so to deepen our belief in the existence of a unitary sense of justice.' K Zweigert and H Kötz, *An Introduction to Comparative Law* (Amsterdam, North-Holland, 1977), 3.

[111] See generally R David, *Les grands systèmes de droit contemporains* (Paris, Dalloz, 1988); A Harding and E Örücü (eds), *Comparative Law in the 21st Century* (The Hague, Kluwer Law International, 2002); B Markesinis, *Foreign Law and Comparative Methodology* (Oxford, Hart Publishing, 1998); D Nelken, *Comparing Legal Cultures* (Aldershot, Dartmouth, 1997).

[112] See R Zimmermann, 'Savigny's Legacy: Legal History, Comparative Law and the Emergence of a European Legal Science' (1996) 112 LQR 576.

[113] E Hondius, 'Towards a European Civil Code' in A Hartkampf, M Hesslink, E Hondius, C Joustra and E du Perron (eds) *Towards a European Civil Code* (The Hague, Kluwer Law International, 1998), 8.

[114] See R Zimmermann, 'Civil Code and Civil Law: The Europeanisation of Private Law within the European Community and the Re-emergence of a European Legal Science' (1994) 1 *Columbia Journal of European and Transnational Law* 82.

[115] See U Wesel, *Juristische Weltkunde: eine Einführung in das Recht* (Frankfurt am Main, Suhrkamp, 1984), 64–65. It was during the 11th century, that Irnerius, a teacher of rhetoric who neglected his studies in grammar in favour of teaching Roman law, managed to obtain a copy of a transcribed version of Justinian's *Digest* (transcribed in the so-called writing F) which had been copied directly from the *Digest* in the sixth century. The *Digest* had disappeared from Italian legal practice only to re-emerge in Constantinople in the Byzantine empire, where it prevailed over the legal system until the fall of the empire in the 15th century. Prior to the rediscovery of the *Digest*, its principles had only existed as basic law in Italy and other areas of the former Western Roman Empire. After the 11th century, however, the *Digest* was the foundation of legal education at Bologna and other Italian universities.

was rooted in the notion that it was an application of legal principles instead of being territorially based within a context constituted by customary law, a project which we would now term as being a quest for universals.[116]

During the 19th century, for example, German legal scholars were schooled in Roman law and canon law as opposed to local customary law, regardless of where they originated from in Germany primarily due to the influence of the church and Roman law.[117] Lawyers who had completed their legal training in one country could occupy a chair in another. The German case is partly explained because there was no single Germanic law or people at this time. Indeed, the German state as a single entity, namely, the German Reich, was only founded as late as 1871. Thus, in 1495 when the *Reichskammergericht* was established, judges had to swear that they would uphold the common law of the *Reich* thereby acknowledging its primacy over the individual laws of the German territories. The reason for this is not exclusively to do with geography but also refers to the evolution of law as a science, namely, the implementation of rational, supra-regional, and neutral laws. The German jurists who had studied in Italy excelled in the formal rigour of legal reasoning which was not dependent on a local context[118] but on methodical, disciplined scientific reasoning.[119] To conclude: a common European legal culture which centred around a common legal science once existed.[120] Legal reasoning according to principles was, however, reversed at the turn of the 19th century for it was at this time that the nation-state as defined by territorial, essential, a priori elements prevailed. The instrumentalisation of law for the purpose of state formation are still very much part of the heritage of legal science. It is a heritage which must, however, not only be challenged, but must also be qualified in the face of the increasing inter-dependency of states in the light of globalisation. A challenge could arguably draw on a number of sources. Thus, for instance, it could draw from Kant's concept of the *Weltbürger*[121] in order to assess to what extent it gives rise to a possible corollary of a *Weltjurist*.

[116] Albeit universals which are predominantly in the Western tradition.
[117] See N Foster, *German Law and Legal System* (London, Blackstone, 1993), 14–15. Indeed, in 1200, one thousand law students were registered at the University of Bologna, half of whom were not of Italian nationality. Many of these scholars came from Germany. See U Wesel, *Geschichte des Rechts: Von den Frühformen bis zum Vertrag von Maastricht* (München, CH Beck, 1997), 312 and 360.
[118] *Ibid.*
[119] It is arguable that the laws were not as neutral as they appeared to be as the legal reasoning inherent to Roman law was underpinned by economic objectives.
[120] See R Zimmermann, 'Roman Law and European Legal Unity' in A Hartkampf, M Hesslink, E Hondius, C Joustra and E du Perron (eds) *Towards a European Civil Code* 2nd rev ed (The Hugue, Kluwer, Law International, 1998), 27.
[121] I Kant, *Die Metaphysik der Sitten, Rechtslehre* (Frankfurt am Main, Suhrkamp, 1977) at § 62 or see I Kant, *Political Writings* (Cambridge, Cambridge University Press, 1991) 172–73.

According to Kant, the rationality behind an international community is based on a principle of right as opposed to a philanthropic principle.[122] Thus, this is not an ethical principle but a legal principle. Moreover, Kant maintains that, if sovereign states could agree in certain legal principles embodied in an international binding agreement, a new and just legal order for all mankind could develop.[123] This position is not dissimilar to the arguments taken up as part of the debate concerning cosmopolitan citizenship which is based on a rejection of the Westphalian system of governance[124] which recognises the sovereignty of states as being absolute.[125] This was qualified by inter alia the Universal Declaration on Human Rights which accords inalienable rights to people irrespective of membership of a state. Thus, cosmopolitan citizenship recognises transnational or post-national agents.[126] As regards legal theory, one is again reminded of Eugen Ehrlich's emphasis on the independence of law from the nation-state, that is to say, law exists independently from the framework of the nation-state[127] which can be contrasted to Kelsen, for instance, who believed that law may only be realised within the hierarchical structures of the state.[128] The discussion of the *ius commune* serves a particular purpose and is *not* being used as an example or as evidence of a future trend. Rather, it is designed to illustrate the link between law and the nation-state which, as regards the juridical debates concerning European integration, is regarded as being intrinsic. In effect, this restricts the debate in such a way that alternative conceptions of law have no standing such as a pluralist position, for example, in which agreement can be reached regarding the similarity of key concepts such as fundamental rights, which go beyond national perceptions of these concepts.[129] Juridical debates are structured in such a way so that such considerations are noticeably absent which is partly explained by the loyalty to the nation-state or *Rechtspatriotismus* which legal education fosters by providing access to knowledge and the opportunity to be educated

[122] *Ibid.*

[123] See I Kant, *Zum ewigen Frieden: Ein philosophischer Entwurf* (Königsberg, Nicholovius, 1795) and also U Vosgerau, 'Der Begriff des Rechts bei Kant' (1999) 30 *Archiv der Rechtstheorie* 277.

[124] Arising from the Treaty of Osnabrück (1648). See A Linklater, *The Transformation of Political Community: Ethical Foundations of the Post-Westphalian Era* (Cambridge, Polity Press, 1998).

[125] Thus, according to the *ius territoriale* principle, no state could interfere in the affairs of another state.

[126] See D Archibughi and D Held (eds), *Cosmopolitan Democracy: An Agenda for a New Word Order* (Cambridge, Polity Press, 1995) and also D Archibughi, D Held and M Kohler (eds), *Reimagining Political Communities* (London, Polity Press, 1998).

[127] See E Ehrlich, *Grundlegung des Soziologie des Rechts* (Berlin, Duncker & Humblot, 1989).

[128] See H Kelsen, *A Pure Theory of Law* (Berkeley and Los Angeles, University of California Press, 1967).

[129] Taking into account the fact that this may be a similar starting point and that different national values may continue to influence their interpretation.

within the constraints of the state, which arguably explains why lawyers primarily identify with institutions of the nation-state.[130]

For national constitutional judges, the straight and narrow path is sign-posted by their respective constitutions which are to be protected in the face of European integration. The German case is particularly instructive as the distinctiveness of the state is perceived as being based on a *Staatsvolk*[131] as well as culture, which is defined in terms of language, religion, art and history.[132] Indeed, constitutional judges have been pivotal in ensuring that the state remains open to the persuasion of the European ideal (referred to as *Europaoffenheit*), whilst, at the same time, ensuring that the state does not 'dissolve', a phenomenon which is referred to as *Enstaatlichung*.[133] Appeals for tolerance vis-à-vis constitutional courts have been made in relation to the European integration project[134] whilst at the same time, it is precisely language and culture which are instrumentalised in order to demarcate boundaries and to erect borders. Here we see a 'spill over' from German debates regarding integration as a whole conducted in the media and amongst politicians where the presence of a 'leading culture' or *Leitkultur* is instrumentalised as exclusionary criteria[135] as part of an overriding fear of 'cultural subversion'.[136] Quite apart from cultural influences, and the different historical processes which led to the drafting of the respective constitutions, the assumption which prevails is that the conceptions contained therein are so distinct or 'essential' that they merit vigorous protection, a position which is supported by certain strands of German state theory.[137] The German constitutional judges have not been alone in adopting the stance that to allow for 'outside' influences would further

[130] This is the general notion espoused by two sociologists, Ramirez and Boli who write about mass education (they do not confine their findings to any particular branch of education) as the primary source of formal socialisation of the individual. See FO Ramirez and J Boli, 'The Political Construction of Mass Schooling: European Origins and Worldwide Institutionalisation' (1987) *Sociology of Education* 2.

[131] That is to say, people who are related by birth and origin.

[132] See P Kirchhof, 'Europäische Einigung und der Verfassungsstaat der Bundesrepublik Deutschland' in J Isensee (ed) *Europa als politische Idee und als rechtliche Form* (Berlin, Duncker & Humblot, 1993), 79.

[133] *Ibid.* See also P Kirchhof, 'Deutsches Verfassungsrecht und Europäisches Gemeinschaftsrecht' (1991) *Special Edition of Europarecht* 12.

[134] See P Kirchhof, 'Editorial' (1999) 12 *Europäische Zeitschrift für Wirtschaft* 353. See also JHH Weiler, *The Constitution of Europe: 'Do the New Clothes Have an Emperor?'* (Cambridge, Cambridge University Press, 1999).

[135] See *Frankfurter Allgemeine Zeitung* 30 October 2000 at p 1.

[136] For an interesting analysis of the concept of 'cultural subversion' see A Sen, *Development as Freedom* (Oxford, Oxford University Press, 1999) at ch 10, 'Culture and Human Rights', pp 227–48.

[137] Thus, Hegel writes of the special historical role of people in history which is a consequence of the dialectical development of Spirit. There are the *Völkergeister* which denote the special differentiated modes of the existence of people, that is to say, there is such a thing as the 'Germanness' of Germans, the 'Englishness of the English' and so on which play their role on the stage of world history. See Hegel, *Grundlinien der Philosophie des Rechts* (Frankfurt am Main, Suhrkamp, 1970) at § 344ff.

contribute to the 'withering away' of the state's sovereignty. Similar concerns have been articulated by judges of other national constitutional courts.[138]

This is not a rejection of the universality of human rights but is premised on the position that some states protect human rights more vigorously than others.[139] Moreover, so the argument continues, some states have protected certain rights which are, as in the case of the protection of economic rights in the German Basic Law, for example, not to be found in the constitutions of other states, an argument also made in the context of biotechnology, albeit not by members of the judiciary.[140] Generally speaking, German courts and jurists are convinced that the German legal system establishes a level of protection which far outdoes supranational and international legal orders.[141]

The reasoning outlined above as regards the German approach to the 'straight and narrow' path to be adopted in the face of the process of European integration also constitutes one *Version of Events*, of which the there are several amongst German jurists. It is not so much a case of *One Europe or Several?*[142] but rather *One Europe AND Several.* Indeed, it would be erroneous to assume the presence of consensus regarding the version of events outlined above, let alone the way in which it is recounted, conceptually speaking. As I have written elsewhere, whilst German jurists bicker about the terms of reference for the sovereignty debate,[143] politicians

[138] See A-M Slaughter, A Stone Sweet and JHH Weiler (eds) *The European Court and National Courts: Doctrine and Jurisprudence. Legal Change in its Social Context* (Oxford, Hart Publishing, 1998) and also F Mayer, *Kompetenzüberschreitung und Letztentscheidung* (München, CH Beck, 2000).

[139] Reasoning which was employed by Ireland in the adoption of Protocol 17 of the TEU in which the Irish Government successfully protected the Irish constitutional prohibition on abortion and on information and referral services from the impact of Community law. See generally DR Phelan, 'Right to Life of the Unborn v Promotion of Trade in Services: The European Court of Justice and the Normative Shaping of the European Union' (1992) 55 MLR 670.

[140] Indeed, it is interesting to see how concerns regarding biotechnology in Germany are articulated in terms of rights which correspond to certain values which are enshrined in the German constitution in extra-legal spheres. In essence, the arguments made are based on a view of the German Basic law which provides a level of protection which is far superior to that accorded in other countries, such as in the United Kingdom, the regulation of which is more permissive. Note that these concerns have been made both within and without the context of the European Union. These fears have, to some extent, been addressed in *Netherlands v European Parliament and Council*, opinion of 14 June 2001, at paras 185–215 which concerned the Biotechnology Directive (OJ 1998, L 213/13) in which the right to human dignity was referred to by Advocate General Jacobs as being part of Community law by virtue of Art 1 of the EU Charter of Fundamental Rights.

[141] The consequences of such a stance has been examined in the case of international law. See B Simma, 'The Role of German Courts in the Enforcement of International Human Rights' in B Conforti and F Francioni (eds) *Enforcing International Human Rights in Domestic Courts* (Oxford, Oxford University Press, 1997), 107.

[142] This is unashamedly borrowed from the title of a ECRC Programme which was directed by Professor Helen Wallace entitled *One Europe or Several?*. See <http://www.one-europe.ac.uk>.

[143] See M Aziz, 'Sovereignty Lost, Sovereignty Regained? The European Integration Project and the Bundesverfassungsgericht' (2002) 9 *Columbia Journal of European Law* 109.

have seized the initiative in formulating a vision of Europe which clearly moves beyond classical conceptions of constitutionalism which are umbilically linked to the state[144] arguably placing constitutional judges in the role as the caretakers — and, as some might see it, as undertakers, of the concept of sovereignty which is no longer appropriate as a method according to which the impact of European legal integration on national legal cultures can be best understood.

For their part, politicians have been able to allow others to voice the politics of dissent, whether through constitutional court decisions and public reaction thereto, referendums and other debates which have been conducted in civil society across the Union. The impact of the judicial voices of dissent has been contained by the fact that they have had little to say concerning where sovereignty has been challenged the most, namely in matters of market building. This has not been the case of the new Member States, where the constitutional court in Hungary, for example, has already taken a firm stance in this matter, stating that competition law is under the exclusive jurisdiction of state sovereignty which it interprets as signifying that the state may dispose of its sovereign rights in its international relations.[145] This leads to the following question: has the jurisprudence of the constitutional courts of the Member States as regards fundamental human rights and policies been *much ado about nothing*?

Sovereignty and the Constitutional Ombudsmen: Who Is Right?

The judicial 'dialogue' amongst the national constitutional courts and the ECJ has been well documented.[146] This is not the case as regards the lower legal instances.[147] The word dialogue draws from the formulation of what

[144] See Joschka Fischer's speech at the Humboldt University in Berlin on 12 May 2000 and Jacques Chirac's speech before the German *Bundestag* on 27 June 2000 in which both argue in favour of the drawing up of a European Constitution. See *Frankfurter Allgemeine Zeitung* of 15 May 2000 at p 15 and also of 28 June 2000 at p 1. See <http://www.auswaertiges-amt.de/6_archiv/2/r/r000512b> and also C Joerges, Y Mény and JHH Weiler (eds) *What Kind of Constitution for What Kind of Polity? Responses to Joschka Fischer* Florence, Robert Schuman Centre for Advanced Studies at the European University Institute; Cambridge MA, Harvard Law School, 2000).

[145] See J Volkai, 'The Application of the Europe Agreement and European Law in Hungary: The Judgment of an Activist Constitutional Court on Activist Notions' (1999) <http://www.jeanmonnetprogram.org> who cites Judgment 4 of 22 January 1997 (the so-called 'Preliminary Issues Judgment') and Judgment 30 of 25 June 1998 which dealt with the merits of the submission (the so-called Europe Agreement Judgment).

[146] See generally Slaughter *et al*, n 138 above; Mayer, n 138 and also Wouters, n. 14 above.

[147] See, however, F Ramos, 'Judicial Cooperation in the European Courts: Testing Three Models of Judicial Behavior' (2002) 2 *Global Jurist Frontiers* 1 and also KJ Alter, *Establishing the Supremacy of European Law: The Making of an International Rule of Law in Europe* (Oxford, Oxford University Press, 2001).

the German Constitutional Court endorsed as a 'cooperation relationship'.[148] Both are referred to here in inverted commas given that it is questionable as to whether some of the decisions can be regarded in terms of dialogue or whether they resemble edicts more commonly found in monologues by soliloquists who speak not so much when alone, but rather, regardless of the listeners. The listeners, however, may not always be interested in what the courts have to say. The jurisdictional tug of war which has prevailed between the ECJ and the constitutional courts of the Member States serves to illustrate the lengths to which jurists will go to have the last word as regards the locus of the ultimate authority. Whilst the ECJ has acknowledged that it is bound to 'draw inspiration from constitutional traditions common to the Member States',[149] it has reserved itself the competence to decide which traditions to 'pick and choose' from.[150] Notwithstanding, some national constitutional courts state that the competence is all theirs and that accordingly it is they who decide on the applicability of Community law with reference to their domestic legal order as opposed to treating it as having authority within its own right. The issue of competence is not, however, as static as is assumed to be the case.[151] Indeed at times, it resembles a 'moving target' as is illustrated, *pars pro toto* by the decision concerning the Tobacco Directive in which the Court of Justice sought to reassure the angst concerning powers of the Community which extend beyond its competence in annulling the directive.[152] Thus, according to the Court, article 100a(1) EC (now article 95(1)) did not vest the Community legislature with a general power to regulate the internal market as not only was it contrary to the express wording of the directive but also it was incompatible with article 3b (now article 5 EC) which provides that powers of the Community are limited to those specifically conferred on it.[153] The preoccupation with the issue of competence by politicians during the course of the proceedings of the Laeken Convention illustrates that judges are not alone in being concerned with the demarcation of EU and national competences.[154]

[148] A concept it endorsed in the Maastricht Judgment. See below.
[149] See Case C–4/73 *J Nold KG v Commission* [1974] ECR 491. See also Case C–55/88 *Wachauf v Germany* [1989] ECR 2609. The TEU now provides that the constitutional traditions common to the Member States form part of the general principles of Community law (Art 6 (2) TEU).
[150] See Opinion 2/94 on Accession by the Community to the ECHR [1996] ECR I–1759.
[151] See G de Búrca and B de Witte, 'The Delimitation of Powers between the EU and its Member States' in A Arnull and D Wincott (eds) *Accountability and Legitimacy in the European Union* (Oxford, Oxford University Press, 2002),
[152] Case C–376/98 *Germany v European Parliament and Council* [2000] ECR I–8419.
[153] *Ibid* at para 83.
[154] Indeed, the issue is one of the four subjects which constitute the Convention's mandate. See Laeken Declaration on the Future of the European Union available at <http://european-convention.eu.int/pdf/LKNEN.pdf>.

The Draft Constitutional Treaty's provisions on competence are contained in Title III of Part I. Article 9(1) provides that Union competences are based on conferral and that their exercise is governed by the principles of subsidiarity and proportionality.[155] Article 9(2) further provides that the Union must act within the limits of the competences conferred on it by the Member State and that competences not conferred on the Union remain with the Member States. Article I-III outlines categories of competence which include inter alia categories of exclusive competence,[156] shared competences,[157] co-ordination of economic and employment policies[158] and areas of supporting, co-ordinating or complementary action.[159] The debates concerning competences have, however, illustrated the difficulty of categorisation which is in itself revealing of the tensions which are likely to arise during the ratification process and even further, if ever the Union is faced with a 'living constitution'.[160]

For their part, the constitutional courts have focused their attention on sovereignty by addressing the issue of fundamental rights, sometimes directly, at other times, in a more indirect manner.[161] Indeed, what is interesting about the German case is how the judges of the Federal Constitutional Court (FCC) have instrumentalised their institutional constraints in such a way as to appear as apolitical participants in the political debate on European integration. As I have suggested elsewhere, whereas most of their decisions regarding the European integration project are not explicitly about sovereignty, the court has managed to frame the judgments in such a way as to issue judgments which have considerable implications for the concept.[162] The purpose of this next section is to examine the FCC's jurisprudence in order to consider the implications for EU fundamental rights and policies. References will be made to the decisions of other national constitutional courts, which have, as this section will show, adopted similar approaches. The main focus, however, is Germany given that its jurisprudence as regards the process of European integration has been prolific, at times, viewing the impact of EU law on their legal order as a mixed metaphor, one which may leave their national legal order shaken but not by no means stirred. If European legal integration can be viewed as a cocktail, the main question upon which the constitutional decisions have hinged is whether it ought to be served with *one legal order or two*.

155 CON 820/03.
156 Art I–12.
157 Art I–13.
158 Art I–14.
159 Art I–16.
160 See the remarks of Professor Siegfried Broß, a judge in the German Federal Constitutional Court made in relation to the Draft Constitutional Treaty. *Die Welt* of 6 August 2003.
161 See DJ Liñán Nogueras and J Roldán Barbero, 'The Judicial Application of Community Law in Spain' (1993) 30 CML Rev 1135.
162 M Aziz, 'Sovereignty über Alles: (Re)Configuring the German Legal Order' in N Walker (ed) *Sovereignty in Transition* (Oxford, Hart Publishing, 2003).

The *Bundesverfassungsgericht* and the Politics of Dissent

The nation-state is a vital premise of the legal reasoning which informs the reception of EU law into the jurisdictions of the Member States of which consensus has, generally speaking, bifurcated into two schools of thought. Accordingly, either a state's membership of the EU is understood as a categorical acceptance of the supremacy doctrine, whereby EC law is placed at the pinnacle of the normative hierarchy.[163] Alternatively, the state's judiciary retains the right to set the supremacy doctrine aside in certain cases, rendering the qualification of state sovereignty conditional and avoiding a situation which might lead to an *eclipse*.[164]

These two schools of thought are particularly prevalent in the German juridical debate concerning European integration.[165] It is one in which the legal academic community[166] continues to exert a considerable degree of influence on the jurisprudence of the *Bundesverfassungsgericht*,[167] in contrast to other Member States of the EU. The ultimate arbiter debate in Germany is underpinned by a tension between these two versions of events, predominantly spoken in statist terms and concepts,[168] a phenomenon which has also been identified in other EU Member States.[169]

[163] Although it is important to add a reminder that no explicit notion of hierarchy is to be found in written European law but has been referred to by the European Court of Justice as an unwritten principle of EC law. See Case C–38/70 *Tradax/Einfuhr-u. Vorratsstelle* [1971] ECR 145; Case C–34/78 *Yoshida/Kamer van Koophandel* [1979] ECR 115; Case C–145/79 *Roquette v France* [1980] ECR 2917, 2940. See generally R Bieber and I Salomé, 'Hierarchy of Norms in European Law' (1996) 33 CML Rev 907.

[164] See, eg, Art 91 (3) of the Polish Constitution which provides that foreign law prevails only over statutes. Judges only have jurisdiction through Polish law and are precluded from having independent means of reviewing foreign law.

[165] They have also led to a split in the judiciary in France, with one branch accepting the doctrine of supremacy and the other refusing it. See generally JHH Weiler, 'The Community System: The Dual Character of Supranationalism' (1981) 1 *Yearbook of European Law* 267.

[166] Which Kokott refers to as *La Doctrine* which, in her opinion, is composed of professors of public, European and international law including former and future justices. The fact that Kokott does not include academics from the lower ranks of academia says much about the hierarchical structure within which German academia is entrenched. See J Kokott, 'Report on Germany' in Slaughter *et al,* at n 138 above at p 79.

[167] Indeed, the extent of the influence exercised by German legal academia on judicial decisions may be regarded as surprising by common law lawyers. It is often the case in Germany that judges are also academics. Historically, universities played an important role in the development and the systemisation of German law. Academic opinion, outlined in periodicals and commentaries (*Kommentare*) is regarded as persuasive authority. This is in direct contrast to the position in common law jurisdictions. See Lord Goff's *dicta* in *Spiliarda Maritime v Consulex Ltd* [1987] 1 AC 460 at 488. The position in Scotland can be distinguished on the grounds that it is more common to cite opinions of academics, which may influence the outcome of litigation.

[168] See K-H Ladeur, 'Towards a Legal Theory of Supranationality: The Viability of the Network Concept' (1997) 3 *European Law Journal* 33 at 34.

[169] See, eg, the case of Spain. Whereas the *Tribunal Constitucional* has not gone as far as the German Federal Constitutional Court, scholars in Spain have proposed similar limits based on fundamental rights in attempting to 'defend' the Spanish constitution. See A Mangas Martín, *Derecho comunitario europeo y derecho español* (Madrid, Tecnos, 1987).

Thus, what I have referred to as the 'etatist' view provides that EC law prevails over national law; there are, however, exceptions. The 'post-etatist' view, however, categorically accepts the order of precedence of EC law.[170] Academic opinion in Germany amongst jurists falls into precisely these two positions.[171] Both positions represent competing schools of thought in a debate which is highly vitriolic, defensive, confrontational, rhetorical and ideological. Nowhere have the debates been so heated as in the case of fundamental rights.

In its *Solange I* decision,[172] the court held that as long as ('*solange*') the EC has not proved itself to provide adequate protection of basic rights, the Federal Constitutional Court remained the ultimate arbiter concerning issues of human rights and would assess the level of protection afforded to human rights in *specific*[173] cases. In *Solange II*,[174] the EC was held to protect human rights in line with the protection of fundamental rights enshrined in the German Basic Law thereby enabling the FCC to relax its jurisdictional hold over questions of basic rights. Accordingly, as long as the general level of protection was secured by the ECJ, the FCC would not review the level in specific cases. The fundamental rights issue was not directly relevant for the *Maastricht* judgment.[175] It is arguable that the FCC reaffirmed the position it adopted in *Solange II*,[176] that is to say that the FCC would only look at general cases in the event of a decrease in the general level of human rights protection. It was this interpretation of the *Maastricht* decision which was of particular significance regarding the FCC's *Banana* decision[177] where a group of third-country banana importers[178] challenged the constitutionality of the conditions of trade for third countries imposed by virtue of an EU Regulation before a Frankfurt Administrative Court.[179] The FCC held that fundamental rights in the European Communities, as the ECJ's decisions indicate, are sufficiently protected.[180] That is to say that the level of protection

[170] Also referred to in terms of 'pro-nation State' versus 'pro-integration' positions. See A von Bogdandy, 'The Science of European Law' (2000) 6 *European Law Journal* 213.
[171] For the FCC being the ultimate arbiter, see R Scholz, *Neue Juristische Wochenschrift* (1993) 1690 and against G Hirsch, *Neue Juristische Wochenschrift* (1996) 2457. See also an article by the latter, a former judge at the ECJ, G Hirsch in the *Frankfurter Allgemeine Zeitung* on 9 October 1996 at p 15.
[172] BVerfGE 37, 271.
[173] Author's own emphasis.
[174] BVerfGE 73, 339.
[175] BVerfGE 89, 155 or *Brunner v European Union Treaty* [1994] 1 CMLR 57. It is important to point out that the *Maastricht* decision was based on arguments concerning democratic legitimacy and competence. The human rights nexus of the case is obiter dicta only.
[176] Indeed, there are several interpretations of the case. See, eg, P Kirchhof, 'The Balance of Powers between National and European Institutions' (1999) 5 *European Law Journal* 225.
[177] Decision of 7 June 2000 – 2 BvL 1/97.
[178] Referred to as the Atlanta Group.
[179] In Germany, prior to the enactment of the regulation, the majority of the bananas on the market emanated from third countries.
[180] The FCC was thereby reaffirmed its *Solange II* decision. See BVerfGE 73, 378–81.

is commensurate with the protection guaranteed by the provisions of the German Basic Law. The Court further held that as long as this continues to be the case, it will not exercise its jurisdiction concerning the applicability of secondary EC law. In other words, the FCC shall not review secondary EC law[181] unless the ECJ fails to protect fundamental rights to the degree envisaged in *Solange II*.

Fundamental rights and values are pivotal to the FCC's decision, particularly when one bears in mind the constitutional basis provided by the amendment to the Basic Law (Art 23 (1) Sentence 1),[182] which was enacted prior to both the *Maastricht* decision and the ratification of the Maastricht Treaty, an amendment which provides constitutional limits to European integration. Thus, the EC Treaties and any secondary legislation arising therefrom should be read in the light of other provisions of the Basic Law, such as the provisions falling under the so-called 'eternity clause'[183] which contains a reference to human dignity and the value of human life[184] as well as to the federal, democratic and social principles upon which the Federal Republic of Germany is founded.[185] The eternity clause provides that these principles may not be set aside by the legislature.[186]

In order for a challenge to succeed before the FCC, a court must prove that European law, which includes the decisions of the ECJ taken after the *Solange II* decision, has sunk below the necessary level of basic rights protection. This necessitates reconciling basic rights protection at the national level with the European level according to the method envisaged by the FCC in *Solange II*. The FCC held that not only had the administrative court

[181] Or 'Solange dies so ist, wird das BVerfG seine Gerichtsbarkeit über die Anwendbarkeit von abgeleitetem Gemeinschaftsrecht nicht mehr ausüben. Vorlagen von Normen des sekondären Gemeinschaftsrechts an das BVerfG sind deshalb unzulässig.' Here the court cross referred to its Solange II decision. See BVerfGE 73, 339.

[182] As amended on 21 December 1992. Art 23 (1) of the Basic Law provides that:

> (1) To realize a unified Europe, Germany participates in the development of the European Union which is bound to democratic, rule of law, social, and federal principles as well as the principle of subsidiarity and provides a protection of fundamental rights essentially equivalent to that of this Constitution. The federation can, for this purpose and with the consent of the Senate, delegate sovereign powers. Art 79 (2) & (3) is applicable for the foundation of the European Union as well as for changes in its contractual bases and comparable regulations by which the content of this Constitution is changed or amended or by which such changes or amendments are authorized.

[183] Art 79 (III) of the Basic Law.

[184] Art 1 of the Basic Law.

[185] See Art 20 of the Basic Law.

[186] In the event of conflict, the competing constitutional principles must be balanced in accordance with the principle of maximum effectiveness or 'practical concordance'. See K Hesse, *Grundzuge des Verfassungsrechts der Bundesrepublik Deutschland* (Heidelberg, Müller, 1995) at 28 and 72. For a succinct yet informative outline of the applicability of Art 23 of the Basic Law, see C Schmidt, 'From Pont d'Avignon to Ponte Vecchio: The Resolution of Constitutional Conflicts between the European Union and the Member States through Principles of Public International Law' (1998) 18 *Yearbook of European Law* 415 at 418–19.

(VG) failed to undertake such an assessment but also the ECJ's case law illustrated that basic rights are sufficiently protected at the level of the EU.[187]

The questions addressed in the *Maastricht* decision do, to some extent, overlap with those raised in the *Banana* case. The judgments are, however, by no means interchangeable. *Maastricht* concerned the issue of competence of the German state, under its constitution to ratify the Maastricht Treaty. By contrast, the *Banana* case was based on the issue of fundamental rights. Whereas these issues are substantively different, they both raise the question of the ultimate arbiter and by implication, the doctrine of sovereignty. It is of interest to note that the ease with which the FCC dealt with the human rights issue in a case which was essentially based on competence — albeit obiter dicta — was noticeably absent in the *Banana* case.[188] That is to say, that it elected not to address the issue of competence by way of obiter dicta in a case based on fundamental rights, a move which would have been in line with the tactics it adopted in its *Maastricht* decision. What begins to emerge is a picture of the court's power of definition or 'frame of reference',[189] that is to say, that it has repeatedly reserved the right to interpret the issues which it deems most salient in a case. Thus, whilst appearing to address fundamental rights protection, it has in effect developed its 'sovereignty jurisprudence' so to speak, based on a vision of itself as the ultimate guardians of the unity of the German state. The 'euro' decision is a further case in point[190] of a tactic which would be surmised thus: *sovereignty by any other name*. Indeed, the jurisprudence of national constitutional courts as regards sovereignty must be regarded within the context of the historical and socio-political importance with which the concept has been vested in its role in state formation.[191] In the case of Germany, the importance vested in sovereignty as being quintessential to state formation is perhaps somewhat distorted given that after 1949, West Germany was conceded sovereign powers by the Allies whilst not being recognised as a sovereign state, strictly speaking. Indeed, the power base from which both the West and East German constitutions were framed

[187] Such as the right to property, the right to economic activity, the freedom of association, the right to equality and the prohibition against arbitrary conduct, the freedom of faith, the protection of the family and the principle of proportionality.

[188] See also BVerfG NJW 2000, 3124 and BVerfG *EuZW* 2001, 255.

[189] Also referred to as the concept of 'field constitution' in which the frames of reference correspond to a particular normative field. See M Koskenniemi, 'The Effect of Rights on Political Culture' in P Alston, M Bustelo and J Heenan (eds) *The EU and Human Rights* (Oxford, Oxford University Press, 1999), 99 at p 106 and fn 22 in particular in which he cites the dissenting opinion of Fitzmaurice at para 23 of *Golder v United Kingdom,* ECHR Series A No 18 (1975).

[190] *Ibid.*

[191] M Stolleis, *Geschichte des öffentlichen Rechts in Deutschland* (München, CH Beck, 1992).

was, lest one need reminding, military occupation.[192] The tactics to regain as much sovereignty as possible had to be subtle. The German general strategy in 1948–49 to regain full national sovereignty within parameters framed by military occupation by the Allies provides a useful illustration of how tactics were adopted to preserve as much national unity of the country as possible.[193]

One Legal Order or Two?

The German debate concerning the need for a European constitution is a good illustration of the extent to which theories of the state both form and inform the discussion concerning the European integration project.[194] Broadly speaking, the etatist school of thought provides that the European Union is unable to have a constitution in view of it not being a state.[195] The state is thereby viewed as being both the object and the prerequisite of a constitution.[196] Moreover, a constitution must be reflected upon by the state bearers of authority, the people (*Staatsvolk*). The *pouvoir constituant* is viewed as being absent in relation to the EU in view of the lack of a European *Staatsvolk*.[197] The so-called post-etatistic school, provides that a prerequisite for a constitution is the existence of a political community.[198] Thus, the state is shaped by the constitution, which is defined as the basic legal order of a political system.

The schools of thought also have different interpretations of the concept of sovereignty. According to the first view, legal sovereignty is linked to the nation-state. The EU is viewed as 'supranational' or even intergovernmental[199] and only legitimate to the extent that it provides a mechanism for furthering the interests of the nation-state, including those associated with fundamental rights.[200] The second view provides that rights

[192] See B Fait, 'In einer Atmosphäre von Freiheit: Die Rolle der Amerikaner bei der Verfassunggebung in den Ländern der US Zone 1946' (1985) 33 *Vierteljahrshefte für Zeitgeschichte* 420. See also the commentary for the East German constitution; S Mampel, *Die sozialistiche Verfassung der DDR* (Frankfurt am Main, Metzner, 1982), particularly at pp 56–57.
[193] See E Spevack, *Allied Control and German Freedom: American Political and Ideological Influences on the Framing of the West German Basic Law* (Münster, Hamburg, 2001), 322–23.
[194] See the symposium reproduced in (2001) 2 *German Law Journal* (Issue of September 1) available at <http://www.germanlawjournal.com>; see also J Murkens, 'The Integrative Function of a European Constitution:Discussion of Christian Dorau's Book: *Die Verfassungsfrage der Europäischen Union*' (2002) 3 *German Law Journal*.
[195] See D Grimm, 'Does Europe need a Constitution?' (1995) 1 *European Law Journal* 282.
[196] See C Dorau and P Jacobi, 'The Debate over a "European Constitution": Is it Solely a German Concern?' (2000) 6 *European Public Law* 413.
[197] See A Augustin, *Das Volk der Europäischen Union* (Berlin, Duncker & Humblot, 2000).
[198] See P Häberle, 'Die Europäische Verfassungsstaatlichkeit' in P Häberle *Europäische Verfassungslehre in Einzelstudien* (Baden-Baden, Nomos, 1999), 65ff.
[199] See, eg, Pechstein and Koenig, n 11 above, at 275.
[200] See below.

are not tied to culture or territory; thus, it is perfectly possible to have a legal system which is transnational or 'trans'-state-like which is focused on the interpretation and elaboration of these fundamental principles.

The former, however, view the latter as undermining the concept of unity in which, as they see it, sovereignty is predicated. Unity must, therefore, be preserved by ensuring that the state is impermeable, that is to say, that it must be protected from outside influences, which is easily achieved by adopting a view of EU law as constituting a separate legal order. Locating sovereignty in the state was one of the most cogent tools of state formation during the earlier 19th century which explains why it has been coveted by German lawyers. Sovereignty, as they view it, represents the essential characteristic to state formation in the tricky relationship they have had reconciling territory with identity, particularly given the presence of two German states prior to reunification.[201] The importance with which the concept of unity has been vested by adopting the two legal orders approach is also recognisable in other decisions of the national constitutional courts which have hinged not only on whether EC or national law prevails but also, and more importantly, *who decides* as such. It is of little surprise that the answer arrived at by the national constitutional courts is one in which they have central roles.

Thus, for example, in *Frontini*, derogation was effected by the Italian constitutional court through a strict separation of competences.[202] The court held that the EC, as it was then, had competence exclusively in matters concerning market integration thereby considering EC law as a distinct or 'autonomous' legal order,[203] a position it had already adopted in 1965.[204] This reasoning was further developed in *Granital* in which the Court restated its 'distinct legal order' thesis by further stating that it reserved the rights not only to adjudicate on the question of EC law and fundamental Italian constitutional rights but also on the basic question of the division of competence, a position it reaffirmed in 1989 in *Fragd*.[205] It is of interest to note that in *Granital*, the Court reached its decision by adopting a test more commonly found in private international law. Thus, where local judges were faced with two conflicting norms, the EC law norm was the applicable law if it related to the competences held by the EC. The national law was simply disapplied and was not thereby deemed to be void.

[201] Although some would no doubt dispute the reference to the former German Democratic Republic as a 'German' state. See below and also generally A Grunenberg, 'Zwei Deutschlands–zwei Identitäten?' in G-J Glaeβner (ed) *Die DDR in der Ära Honecker* (Opladen, Westdeutscher Verlag, 1988), 94–107.

[202] See, generally, M Cartabia and JHH Weiler, *L'Italia in Europa* (Bologna, Il Mulino, 2000); see also G Strozzi, 'Alcuni interrogativi a proposito della limitazione di competenza dell'Unione Europea' (1994) *Rivista di Diritto Internazionale* 136.

[203] Sentenza 27 dicembre 1973 n 183, Giurisprudenza Costituzionale, p 2401.

[204] Sentenza 27 dicembre 1965 n 98, Giurisprudenza Costituzionale, p 1322.

[205] See *Spa Fragd v Amministrazione delle Finanze*, Dec 232 of 21 April 1989 (1989) 72 RDI.

In *Fragd*, the Court held that those measures which contravened fundamental principles of the Italian Constitution concerning human rights protection would not be upheld.[206] Moreover, the decision as to whether this was the case was to be made by reference to internal constitutional law, a position which split the French judiciary along similar lines. Thus, for the *Cour de Cassation*, the supremacy of Community law was a direct consequence of international acts which, if properly ratified, exerted their power from *within* their national legal order.[207] Not so, according to the *Conseil d'Etat* which held that decisions on the constitutionality of legislation were matters for the French Constitutional Council,[208] a position it later qualified on the basis of the pragmatics of giving effect to international commitments.[209]

Similar tactics were deployed by the French *Conseil Constitutionelle* by recourse to the 'essential conditions' doctrine or *conditions essentielles de l'exercice de la souveraineté nationale*.[210] Thus in 1997,[211] it held that European asylum law would necessitate an amendment of the French Constitution.[212] In particular, the court held that Title IV of the Amsterdam Treaty violated the principle of national sovereignty.[213] In contrast to the position in Germany,[214] the French constitution does not contain an enabling provision concerning the European Union. It primarily contains a declaratory regulation as regards the co-operation of France in the Union.[215] This does not, however, provide for a transfer of competence. The point of departure for an assessment of the constitutional ramifications of the ratification of the Treaty is provided by article 3 which provides for the monopoly of public authority on behalf of representatives of the French nation.[216]

[206] See, however, the decision 135/2002 in which the Court directly refers to the EU Charter of Fundamental Rights.
[207] See *Administration des Douanes v Société 'Café Jacques Vabres' et SARL Weigel et Cie* [1975] 2 CMLR 336.
[208] See *Syndicat Général de Fabricants de Semoules de France* [1970] CMLR 395.
[209] See *Nicolo* [1990] 1 CMLR 173.
[210] See generally A Ondoua, *Étude des rapports entre le droit communautaire et la Constitution en France: l'ordre juridique constitutionnel comme guide au renforcement de l'intégration européenne* (Paris, L'Harmattan, 2001); J Cloos, *Le Traité de Maastricht: genèse, analyse, commentaires* (Paris, Bruylant, 1993).
[211] Decision Nr. 97–394 DC, Journal officiel de la République Française from 3 janvier 1998, p 165ff (AJDA 1998, 186ff).
[212] See S Millns, 'The Treaty of Amsterdam and Constitutional Revision in France' (1999) 5 *European Public Law* 61; A Bonnie, 'The Constitutionality of Transfers of Sovereignty: the French Approach' (1999) 4 *European Public Law* 517.
[213] Which the court failed to define in detail. See however its 'Maastricht I' decision from 9 April 1992 — Nr 92–308 DC, Rec 55. According to Art 54 of the French Constitution, the Treaty can only be ratified once the constitution has been amended.
[214] See Art 23 of the Basic Law.
[215] See Art 88–1.
[216] Indeed, the court mainly concentrated on this provision in its judgment as opposed to Art 88–1 of the French Constitution.

Generally speaking, the French Republic may participate in international organisations which have their own legal personality and which contain the transfer of competence with concomitant decision-making powers. However, the authorisation for integration (as provided by subsection 15 of the 1946 Preamble) does not cover an intrusion into the 'essential conditions' for the exercise of national sovereignty. In its *Maastricht I* decision, the Court had listed the basic rights which belonged exclusively to national sovereignty.[217] Strictly speaking, the *Conseil Constitutionelle*'s 1997 decision was not based on an assessment of basic rights but was limited to an examination of sovereignty. However, the two are linked. Emulating its German counterpart, the *Conseil Constitutionelle*, tactically side stepped the rights issue by directly addressing sovereignty, in so doing, electing to frame its deliberations in terms of procedure.

In particular, the Court held that the *conditions essentielles* formula provided that Title III of the Amsterdam Treaty,[218] which concerns the duty of third-country nationals to obtain a visa and measures implementing a uniform visa for the EU, was contrary to the French Constitution.[219] As regards asylum and immigration,[220] the court maintained that during the five-year transitional period where unanimity prevailed, the essential conditions for the exercise of national sovereignty was not adversely affected,[221] reasoning it originally adopted in its *Maastricht I* decision.[222] The court was less satisfied, however, with the position after the five-year period had elapsed. In particular, it held that the essential conditions formula was violated by the fact that not only do Member States lose their right of initiative[223] but also by the introduction of the co-decision procedure and its concomitant introduction of qualified majority voting. Thus, whilst the decision-making process was regulated by unanimity, the essential conditions formula was not affected.[224] In other words, through the exercise of their supervisory jurisdiction, the Court ensured that fundamental values contained in the French Constitution were not undermined by European commitments.

It is difficult to predict to what extent the juridical debate concerning sovereignty seen through the prism of fundamental rights will be taken up in the new Member States.[225] From the outset, it is important to differentiate between the position of sovereignty in the constitutions of the new

[217] Above n 211, para 17 and 18.
[218] Art 73j Nr 2 b) i), iii).
[219] See n 211 above, at para 9. See also the Maastricht I decision, n 213 above.
[220] Arts 73k, 73j Nr 1,3.
[221] See n above 213 at point 23.
[222] See Maastricht I, n 213 above, at paras 46–50.
[223] See para 24.
[224] See n above 213 at para 23.
[225] I have addressed this is further detail elsewhere. See Aziz, n 31. Indeed, the following section draws from this article.

Member States.[226] Within the communist systems in Eastern Europe, communism operated differently, was received differently by elites and populations, while relations between these countries and the Soviet Union were also different. Countries like Hungary after 1956, Czechoslovakia after 1968, Poland from 1945, the German Democratic Republic (GDR), Romania and Bulgaria were all different in the way in which the communist system(s) operated, the way they were perceived by elites and populations and the way these communist states interacted with the Soviet Union. They were all sovereign states but subject to limited sovereignty by virtue of the Brezhnev doctrine.[227]

Sovereignty and the Legacy of Communism in the New Member States

Briefly stated, the Brezhnev doctrine was embedded in Article 30 of the 1977 Soviet Constitution (the so-called 'Brezhnev Constitution'), which committed the Soviet Union to 'friendship, cooperation and comradely mutual assistance' in accordance with the principle of 'socialist internationalism' and also to participate in 'economic integration'.[228] Accordingly, important principles of equality, territorial integrity, independence, non-interference in domestic affairs were subject to particular interpretation in the interests of 'fraternal assistance' towards other Eastern bloc countries. In other words, support for Soviet interventionism was justified on the grounds of the need to protect the socialist community of states. This self-imposed limitation on state sovereignty in the socialist bloc was a device to cloak Soviet interventionism to sustain its hegemony in Eastern Europe, and in particular its military occupation of the German Democratic Republic.[229] The Soviet Union,

[226] See A Albi, 'Postmodern versus Retrospective Sovereignty: Two Different Discourses in the EU and the Candidate Countries' in N Walker (ed) *Sovereignty in Transition* (Oxford, Hart Publishing, 2003).

[227] For a discussion of the Brezhnev doctrine and its demise under Gorbachev see C Gati, *The Bloc that Failed Soviet-East European Relations in Transition* (Oxford, Oxford University Press, 1990), 71–79. For an exposition of the doctrine in Brezhnev's own words see the extract from his 'Speech to the Fifth Congress of the Polish United Workers' Party (12 November 1968), *Current Digest of the Soviet Press* 20 (46), 1968 at pp 3–5.

[228] I must apologise from the outset that I have elected to concentrate on the new Member States which were formerly referred to as Central and Eastern European Candidate Countries in view of their communist legacies.

[229] The Soviet military interventions in Hungary in 1956, Czechoslovakia in 1968, Afghanistan in 1979, and the pressures on Poland in 1980, were seen as legitimate measures to defend the socialist bloc. Those socialist states which did not accede to the hegemony of the Soviet Union, such as Yugoslavia (which broke with Moscow under Tito in 1948) and Albania, were isolated on the grounds that they had pursued the road of 'nationalism' — the ultimate form of deviation from the socialist cause. Note that a 'special relationship' which was maintained until the end as the discussions between Gorbachev and Honecker illustrate. See D Küchenmeister (ed) *Honecker-Gorbatschow: Vieraugengespräche* (Berlin, Dietz, 1993), 95. See also H Schulze, *Staat und Nation in der Europäischen Geschichte* (München, CH Beck, 1994), 323.

as its interventions in Hungary and Czechoslovakia illustrate, was unable to accept a 'national' form of communism. To do so would have called into question its hegemony over the socialist bloc and even its leadership of the Warsaw Pact.[230] Consequently, in the aftermath of the crushing of the Hungarian revolution of 1956, the Soviet Union imposed a doctrine of limited sovereignty on the socialist bloc of states, which was referred to as 'proletarian internationalism'.[231] Thereafter, any development of national forms of communism which was perceived to threaten Soviet hegemony was met with the 'fraternal assistance'[232] of military intervention, as the Warsaw pact invasion of Czechoslovakia in 1968 demonstrated. This so-called *pax sovietica* was also secured by a process of integration in the socialist bloc whereby ruling elites (the communist party *nomenklatura*), economies, militaries, and national interests were locked into Soviet-controlled supranational organisations such as Comecon and the Warsaw Pact. The special relationship or the 'fraternal assistance' between the countries of the Soviet bloc and the Soviet Communist party was never explicitly addressed. In the case of the German Democratic Republic, for instance, it was placed on a legal footing in a 1964 Treaty[233] which provided that in the event of any attack by an another country or force.[234] Indeed, the Treaty goes further in providing that if any state which was a signatory to the Warsaw Pact had come under attack, the others were obligated to give immediate support[235] to each other through economic aid and the exchange of economic and technical know-how.[236]

Some countries had room for manoeuvre under the shadow of the Brezhnev doctrine which others did not. The three Baltic States (Latvia, Lithuania and Estonia) were units in the Soviet Federation after their annexation. The reality was that there were important differences regarding how the Soviet Union treated them and the other members of the

[230] *Ibid.*
[231] As proclaimed in Moscow in October 1957 in the declaration of the communist parties in power to commemorate the 40th anniversary of the October 1917 Russian Revolution. The full text of 'the twelve' is reproduced in D Jacobs (ed) *The Communist Manifesto and Related Documents* (New York, Harper Torchbooks, 1962), 176.
[232] Referred to as 'comradely cooperation' in the Czechoslovak Constitution (Art 14 (2) at 145, 'friendship and cooperation' in the Polish Constitution (Art 6 (2)) and 'friendship, cooperation, and mutual assistance' in the Bulgarian Constitution (Art 3 (1)) above n 231.
[233] Vertrag über Freundschaft, gegenseitigen Beistand und Zusammenarbeit zwischen der Deutschen Demokratischen Republik und der Union der Sozialistischen Sowjetunion vom 12 Juni 1964 (GBl I S 132).
[234] *Ibid.*
[235] See Art 5 of the Vertrag über Freundschaft, gegenseitigen Beistand und Zusammenarbeit zwischen der Deutschen Demokratischen Republik und der Union der Sozialistischen Sowjetunion vom 12 Juni 1964 (GBl I S 132).
[236] The relationship between the GDR and the USSR was viewed in the West as one of forced dependency or a *Zwangsverhältnis*. The relationship was not regulated by transparent legal norms or the courts, but by non-transparent formal and informal agreements of communist party leaderships.

Soviet bloc in terms of their sovereignty. Poland, for example, had privatised agriculture (other Communist countries had socialised collective farming),[237] and the Catholic Church in Poland operated in a less constrained way than Orthodox or Protestant churches elsewhere. Indeed, the legacy of the Catholic Church's political leverage during communism is still felt today as the discussions concerning abortion and the EU's Charter of Fundamental Rights and latterly the European Convention in Poland testify.[238] From the early 1960s, Hungary was allowed to introduce the socialist market, which introduced limited decentralised reforms in the economy and privatisation. The country whose sovereignty was most limited was the GDR, which was under military occupation,[239] thereby illustrating the extent to which the Soviet Union both adopted and implemented a differentiated approach.[240]

It would be as erroneous to view the new Member States in a non-differentiated manner under the mantle of communism, and what came next, the period of transition which arose as a consequence of post-communism after 1989.[241] Indeed, the transition period was also differentiated, as illustrated by, for instance, the diverse and respective experiences of the roundtable talks between regimes and opposition groups that took place in 1988 and 1990.[242]

[237] See D Stark, 'Path Dependence and Privatisation Strategies in East Central Europe' (1992) 6 *East European Politics and Societies* 17 for an excellent typology of Central and Eastern European privatisation strategies.

[238] See W Sadurski, 'Charter and Enlargement' (2002) 8 *European Law Journal* 340. See also R Trzaskowski, 'National Report Poland' in C Franck and D Pyszna (eds) *Positions of 10 Central and Eastern European Countries on EU Institutional Reforms: Analytical Survey in the Framework of the CEEC-DEBATE project* (Louvain-la-Neuve, Université catholique de Louvain, 2003), 70. At the end of January 2003, Poland tabled a request to the EU to include a declaration safeguarding Polish laws on the 'protection of human life'. Whereas the request was made rather late in the days of the drafting stage of the Accession Treaty it may be granted the possibility to have a unilateral declaration on this issue attached to the Treaty, similar to the position of Ireland. Notwithstanding, the Polish church has expressed doubts over the clause. According to archbishop *Tadeusz Goclowski* the declaration approved and put forward by the Polish government did not fully meet expectations as bishops had asked clearly for human life to be protected from conception to natural death and a definition of marriage as a legal union of a man and woman. The original proposal for the text put forward by the Polish government which was submitted for consideration reads as follows:

> The government of the Republic of Poland understands that none of the provisions of the Treaty on European Union, or in the Treaties establishing the European Communities, or in the Treaties or Acts modifying or supplementing those Treaties, shall disturb the right of the Republic of Poland to regulate on issues of moral importance and concerning the protection of human life. (Reported in <http://www.eu-observer.com> in January 2003.)

[239] See Aziz, n 162 above.

[240] See generally G Ajani, *Diritto del'Europa Orientale* (Torino, UTET, 1996).

[241] See J Elster, C Offe and UK Preuß (eds) *Institutional Design in Post-communist Societies: Rebuilding the Ship at Sea* (Cambridge, Cambridge University Press, 1997).

[242] J Elster (eds) *The Roundtable Talks and the Breakdown of Communism* (Chicago, University Press, 1996).

In the case of the GDR, for example, the very existence of the state was at the heart of the deliberations.[243] This was in direct contrast to the position of the other countries involved in roundtable talks. The Baltic states, for their part, claimed independence and, in terms of sovereignty, aspired to a return to the status quo which existed prior to 1946. In the case of Poland, the agenda of the initial talks did not include a revision of the Constitution or the introduction of political democracy.[244]

Constitutionalism as a whole in the case of the new Member States was pivotal as part of the break with the legacy of communism.[245] Much significance was attached to state sovereignty as a symbol of independence and its role in upholding and protecting the integrity and identity of a state.[246] This goes some way towards explaining the preoccupation by some of the new Member States of the impact of European rights on their respective legal cultures. Indeed, much of the response of the new Member States to the Draft Constitutional Treaty has been framed in terms of the impact of rights and furthermore, on the need for clarification concerning the hierarchy of legal provisions adopted by EU institutions.[247] It is impossible to say as yet to what extent these concerns are shared by judges in the new Member States.[248]

The constitutional courts in the old Member States have tended to adopt hierarchical understandings of the application of EC law in which more often than not, EC law is regarded as constituting a separate legal order. In effect, this places the constitutional courts in the role of being the 'ultimate' guardians of the European Treaties,[249] a tactic which is underpinned by understandings of EC law as constituting an international legal order based on intergovernmentalism. The threat to their legal orders is thereby contained,

[243] See UK Preuß, '*The Roundtable Talks in the German Democratic Republic*' in J Elster (ed) *The Roundtable Talks and the Breakdown of Communism* (Chicago, University Press, 1996), 99.

[244] Instead, the idea was to obtain official recognition of Solidarity in exchange for Western Aid and Solidarity's support of the economic reforms that the government deemed necessary.

[245] R Elgie and J Zielonka, 'Constitutions and Constitution-building' in J Zielonka (ed) *Democratic Consolidation in Easten Europe, Vol I: Institutional Engineering* (Oxford, Oxford University Press, 2001), 33. See also W Sadurski, 'Conclusions: On the Relevance of Institutions and the Centrality of Constitutions in Post-communist Transitions' in J Zielonka (eds) *Democratic Consolidation in Eastern Europe. Vol I: Institutional Engineering* (Oxford, Oxford University Press, 2001), 455.

[246] See Albi, n 226 above.

[247] See C Franck and D Pyszna-Nigge, *Positions of 10 Central and Eastern European Countries of EU Institutional Reforms: Analytical Survey in the Framework of the CEEC-DEBATE project* (Louvain-la-Neuve, Université catholique de Louvain, 2003).

[248] Although an informal consensus amongst Polish lawyers at a conference held at the European Centre, Natolin in Warsaw on 31 January–1 February, 2003, *Enlargement and the European Constitutional Process* was that the majority of Polish constitutional lawyers regarded EC law in terms of international law.

[249] See T Schilling, 'The Autonomy of the Community Legal Order: An Analysis of Possible Foundations' (1996) 17 *Harvard International Law Journal* 389.

unlike the position which recognises that EC law is the product of a synthesis of principles of national and supranational legal systems which operate at a number of levels. One wonders to what extent the machinations of the constitutional courts resemble shutting the door after the trusted steed of sovereignty has already bolted. This argument has been made above in relation to competition law and policy. However, it may also be transposed to apply to the national legal orders as a whole, particularly given the wide range of competences which the EU possesses. Indeed, the elasticity of EU competence has ensured that more fields of national law have been 'europeanised' than the Treaties permit, strictly speaking, which has led to a disaggregation to the challenge to state sovereignty. By adopting a strict hierarchical understanding of the application of law, these courts in effect constrain their own outlook to the extent that they fail to furnish themselves with the appropriate analytical tools in which to appropriately view the challenge to state sovereignty. The challenge is multi-faceted, multi-level and multi-dimensional, a fact which the protagonists of the 'ultimate arbiter' debate are perhaps aware given that their decisions could be construed as providing guiding principles for lower courts, whose dissent may not always as identifiable as that of their colleagues in the constitutional colleagues.

THE JUDICIARY AS SOVEREIGNTY'S CARE(UNDER)TAKER?

Implementation of the *acquis communautaire*, also referred to as the *acquis de l'Union*, has a considerable impact on regions, both in terms of budgetary implications and the implications for courts and administrative bodies. The prospective burden which local and regional administrative authorities will be facing post-accession, for example, has already been recognised regarding the implementation and enforcement if EU Environmental Policy in the new Member States.[250] Some financial assistance has been provided in order to facilitate the process from pre-accession instruments.[251] In the case of EU Environmental Policy, the budgetary impact of compliance has been estimated as constituting approximately 80–110 billion euros.[252]

[250] See Press Release DN:IP/03/81 published on 21 January 2003, European Commission on Track to Ensuring an Enlarged Europe is a Greener Europe. See also reports in <http://www.euobserver.com> on the anti-competitive impact of the implementation of EU Environmental policy in the new Member States on 26 September 2003.

[251] Namely, PHARE which supports priority measures related to the adoption of the *acquis communautaire*, the instrument for Structural Policies for Pre-Accession (ISPA)-Finances infrastructure in the environment and transport sector and SAPARD Finances measures to support agriculture and rural development.

[252] This includes the implementation of the Urban Wastewater Treatment Directive (over 25 billion euros), the Landfill Directive (10–12 million euros). See Press Release, *ibid*.

Generally speaking, administrative institutions such as local administrative courts are pivotal in the process of constitutional adjustment and implementation as they act as the gatekeepers to European rights. The recognition of European rights which arise as a consequence the law of the European Union is dependent on knowledge as well as the willingness of these judges to apply it, both of which are essential as a means of ensuring meaningful access to Union's constitutional order. The experience gained in both the old and the new Member States regarding EC law is sobering, with reports of both knowledge and access being poor which has culminated in an appeal for judges and for legal practitioners to acquaint themselves with the EC Treaties.[253] Article 234 EC, whereby preliminary references may be made to the European Court of Justice regarding questions which regard the interpretation of the EC Treaties, is pivotal as it is the procedural mechanism according to which individuals may gain access to the ECJ's supervisory jurisdiction concerning the recognition of their rights albeit framed within the first Pillar.[254] However, even the best case scenario gives cause for concern by which the following is meant: judges may be all too aware of the remit of the Treaties. They may also be willing to apply or 'draw inspiration from them'. There is, however, a fundamental distinction between knowledge and understanding. Thus, if judges of the lower courts adopt the theoretical basis outlined by their constitutional court brethren, who argue that recognition of Community law is mediated through the authority of their own national legal order as opposed to being by virtue of its inherent nature, much of the substance of the rights of individuals may be lost as a consequence of national judicial translation. This not only means that they may, as some have pointed out, be unlikely to recognise that Community law might prevail over their own national legal orders[255] but also, even where they do recognise this, the substance of this recognition may leave much to be desired.

Theories of cognitive mobilisation appear to address this head on.[256] They do, however, by assuming that support is interchangeable with information or level of awareness. Accordingly, cognitive mobilisation, namely, whereby a citizen is integrated into modern organisations and extensive communication networks through social learning, is supposed to act in such a way that it guarantees support of elites. Thus, the higher the awareness,

[253] Sacha Prechal, National Courts in European Constitution, Paper given at a conference at the European University Institute, The Emerging Constitution of the European Union on April 19 and 20, 2002 which deals with the position in the Netherlands. See also F Emmert, 'Administrative and Court Reform in Central and Eastern Europe' (2003) 9 *European Law Journal* 288.

[254] See generally M Adenas (ed) *Art 177 References to the European Court: Policy and Practice* (London, Butterworths, 1994).

[255] B de Witte, 'Community Law and National Constitutional Values' (1991) 2 *Legal Issues of European Integration* 1 at 4.

[256] See R Inglewood, *Culture Shift* (Princeton, Princeton University Press, 1990), 377.

the more supportive a citizen becomes of the dominant values, expectations and institutions of a political community. It is questionable whether this can be taken at face value, particularly given that this theory confuses knowledge with understanding in attempting to determine levels of support.

Access to European rights by rights holders is mediated inter alia through national judges, who retain a filter of considerable importance by virtue of the preliminary reference procedure. According to article 234 EC, any court or tribunal

> *may*, if it considers that a decision on the question is necessary to enable it to give judgment, request the Court of Justice to give a ruling thereon.[257]

The word *shall* only applies to courts against whose decisions there is no judicial remedy. The aim of article 234 EC is inter alia the uniform application of EC law which may be jeopardised where conditions under which national courts must refer preliminary questions are too lax.[258] Whilst case studies of the use of the preliminary reference procedure go some way towards tracking the issue of access to justice as framed by the EC Treaties,[259] they are unable to monitor those forms of dissent which are more subtle and nuanced. There is a need for further differentiation as the more sensitive the area in which rights are embedded, the more unwilling a court is to relinquish its jurisdictional hold, a factor which has, to some extent, been acknowledged by the innovative application of article 234 EC in relation to matters pertaining to asylum. Thus, whereas the ECJ has jurisdiction over matters falling within Title IV (Visas, Asylum, Immigration and Other Policies Related to Free Movement of Persons),[260] it may only receive a preliminary reference once each legal instance has been exhausted.[261] Moreover, the ECJ does not, as is ordinarily the case, have the capacity to evaluate previous decisions reached by national courts.[262] The key to understanding nuance is often not what is said, but how. As regards legal reasoning, the trace elements of nuance are generally to be found in questions of procedure as opposed to substance. The two are, of course, linked, and at times, inextricably so.

[257] Author's own emphasis.
[258] See A Arnull, 'Modernising Community Courts' (2000) 3 *Cambridge Yearbook of European Legal Studies* 37 at 62.
[259] See, eg, *Data Set on Preliminary References in EC Law* (1961–98), Robert Schuman Centre, European University Institute, 1999 available at <http://www.iue.it/RSC/RSC_TOOLS/>. The Court of Justice also published Annual Reports on Monitoring the Application of Community Law. See that of 2000, for example: COM (2001) 309 final.
[260] See Art 68 EC.
[261] *Ibid.*
[262] See Art 68 (3) EC.

Whereas some national courts have been willing to accept procedural principles enshrined in EC law, they have been less willing to do so regarding matters of substance. Thus, for example, a court in England was prepared to enforce the duty of a national administrative authority to respect the EC law principle of legitimate expectations of individuals in relation to procedural matters. It is clear that it would have been less enthusiastic had the matter concerned a substantive decision of the administration.[263] The same may be said as regards the principle of proportionality which has been applied in relation to administrative decisions[264] and to Acts of Parliament.[265] It has, however, been held not to apply where it is deemed that no community measure is at stake.[266] Two observations must be made. First, the distinction between community measures and national measures is not always as clear cut as many may assume. In other words, it is not always so clear when a state's legal order has been europeanised let alone identify the extent to which the process has influenced and transformed this order. Secondly, much depends on who applies the distinction and, as the section above makes clear, on what theoretical basis.

A useful case in point is provided by the so-called 'Community interest' test in matters relating to competition law, which has been endorsed instead of one based on the effect on inter-state trade in Member States.[267] However, restatements such as 'Where there is Community interest, only Community antitrust law applies. If there is no Community interest, Member State laws may apply'[268] fails to come to terms with the advanced state of convergence between the legal orders of the EU Member States, rendering it difficult — if not sometimes impossible — to delineate 'community interests' from 'national interests' as neatly as is envisaged. Moreover, there is a difference between a national court which evaluates the presence of a Community interest with reference to its own domestic legal order and one which views the interest being defined by virtue of the Community legal order's inherent authority per se. The gradual realisation which has been expressed in the political science literature on elites in the Central and Eastern Europe is that the implementation of the *acquis communautaire* is dependent

[263] See *Council for Civil Service Unions v Minister for the Civil Service* [1985] AC 374 as interpreted by Geddes. See A Geddes, *Protection of Individual Rights under EC Law* (London, Butterworths, 1995), 108.

[264] See, eg, *R v Minister of Agriculture, Fisheries and Food, ex p Bell Lines Ltd* [1984] 2 CMLR 502.

[265] See, eg, *B & Q v Shrewsbury and Atcham Borough Council* [1990] 3 CMLR 535 which concerned the Shops Act 1950 and also *R v Secretary of State for Employment, ex p Equal Opportunities Commission* [1992] 1 All ER 545 which concerned the Employment Protection (Consolidation) Act 1978.

[266] *R v Secretary of State for the Home Department, ex p Brind* [1991] 1 AC 696.

[267] As originally proposed by AG Trabucchi in the Belgian Wallpaper case (C73/74 *Papier Peints de Belgique v Commission* [1975] ECR 1491).

[268] See R Wesseling, *The Modernisation of EC Antitrust Law* (Oxford, Hart Publishing, 2000), 152.

on the co-operation of elites to accept the consequences of EU membership for the national institutions which they serve.[269] This may be transposed to apply to legal elites to the extent that their role is crucial in the process of consolidation of the European legal order in the new Member States. Not only must the knowledge of EC law be imparted and disseminated, but the legal and administrative elites must be persuaded to apply them and moreover recognise that it is in their own interest to do so.[270] Tracking the changes of the adaptive capacity of the legal systems of the new Member States may, however, be an easier task than conducting the same exercise in the old Member States. The courts in the former are under considerable pressure to be seen to be honouring the spirit of the *acquis communautaire*, given the magnifying glass of conditionality which they have been subjected to during the period of pre-accession. Indeed, it would perhaps be easier to ascertain how legal elites in the new Member States regard the impact of EU law to their legal orders and its concomitant challenge to their loyalty than it would be to monitor the capacity of legal elites across the judicial spectrum in the Member States to honour EU law as a legal order in its own right. On the other hand, courts of the Member States may have more room for manoeuvre in articulating their resistance or dissent given that the hurdles for continuing EU membership are lower than those for the new Member States. A case of *'do as we tell you to do but not what we do'*?[271] It is doubtful whether a court in any of the new Member States could afford to ignore decisions of the European Court of Justice as has been the case in some of the old Member States. Be that as it may, however, the distinction between formal implementation and substantive implementation is an important one. The recognition of rights is dependent on elites, who, as in the case of many of the new Member States

[269] J Hughes, G Sasse and C Gordon, 'Saying "Maybe" to the 'Return to Europe': Elites and the Political Space for Euroscepticism in Central and Eastern Europe' (2002) 3 *European Union Politics* 3. See also W Mischler and R Rose, 'Learning and Re-learning Regime Support: The Dynamics of Post-communist Regimes' (2002) 41 *European Journal of Political Research* 5.

[270] I draw from the analogy of arguments advanced in the context of democratic consolidation in Central and Eastern Europe. See, eg, L Anderson (ed) *Transitions to Democracy* (New York, Columbia University Press, 1999) outlined inter alia in IL Markovitz, 'Constitutions, The Federalist Papers, and the Transition to Democracy' at 45.

[271] See the Prologue of JHH Weiler and SCF Fries, 'A Human Rights Policy for the European Community and Union: The Question of Competences' in P Alston, M Bustelo and J Heenan (eds) *The EU and Human Rights* (Oxford, Oxford University Press, 1999), 147. See also G de Búrca, 'Convergence and Divergence in European Public Law: The Case of Human Rights' in P Beaumont, C Lyons and N Walker (eds) *Convergence and Divergence in European Public Law* (Oxford, Hart Publishing, 2002), 131 at 140ff. Note that the issue of double standards existing as a consequence of the disparity between the internal and external dimension of the EU's human rights policy was to some extent recognised by the 'Leading by Example: A Human Rights Agenda for the EU for the year 2000 (Florence: EUI, 1998)' report by the *Comité des Sages* in contrast to the first EU Annual Report on Human Rights adopted in 1999 which concentrated on the EU's external relations. See First Annual Report reproduced at <http://www.europa.eu.int/comm/external_relations/human_rights/doc/report_99_en.pdf>.

have had to re-learn political support in relation to a new regime in the age of transition post-1989 and currently, as regards the EU in the accession process.[272] Both elites and citizens in these new democracies have spent most of their lives under an undemocratic regime.[273] A corollary to willingness to implement the *acquis communautaire* by the legal elites is the reception and recognition of the norms by citizens. In addressing this question, one must bear in mind that legal elites have a low standing in the new Member States due to the fact that law was traditionally politicised and was subject to the administration of political power. Capacity is often seen in terms of physical capacity like resources, personnel and structures. Capacity is also, however, about skill assets, training and trust.

The latter is particularly important, for if citizens do not trust those who are responsible for rights implementation, this erodes the rule of law. The French response to decisions of the European Court of Justice in which equal treatment in social security to associated third-country nationals from Morocco and Algeria was upheld illustrates this. In effect, the French authorities simply ignored the implications of the *Kziber* decision,[274] even after an Algerian national successfully appealed for a supplemental income benefit from the French *Cour de Cassation*.[275] The French administrative authorities continued to regard these cases as being individual cases which had no implications for administrative practice, a position it maintained even after a French court received a preliminary ruling on the case of an Algerian national in 1995.[276] Thus, French authorities ordered offices distributing supplemental income benefits to provide benefits only to those individuals who initiated proceedings in French courts[277] giving rise to a conundrum for administrative personnel faced with diverging commands. What has been referred to as the *dédoublement fonctionnel* as a part of the conflict of loyalty posed by two administrative orders gives rise to selective interpretation and selective application of EU law, which is not open to the scrutiny of the ECJ given that administrative authorities are unable to refer questions to the ECJ.[278] The response of national courts to the ECJ's decision in *Grzelczyk* in which a French student studying in Belgium was held

[272] See S Bartole, 'Organising the Judiciary in Central and Eastern Europe' (1998) 7 *Eastern European Constitutional Law Review* 62. See also L Sólyom and G Brunner (ed) *Constitutional Judiciary in a New Democracy: The Hungarian Constitutional Court* (Ann Arbor, Michigan, University Press, 2000).
[273] See Michler and Rose, n 269 above.
[274] Case C–18/90 [1991].
[275] Which ruled with *Kziber* in mind but omitted to acknowledge this as being the case. For an insightful discussion of these cases see L Conant, *Justice Contained: Law and Politics in the EU* (Ithaca, Cornell University Press, 2002).
[276] See Case C–103/94 *Krid*.
[277] See 'Condition d'attribution du Fonds National de Solidarité', No 347 1994, and No 365 1996; Lettre-circulaire No 169–95, 1995.
[278] See S Kadelbach, 'European Administrative Law and the Law of a Europeanized Administration' in C Joerges and R Dehousse (eds) *Good Governance in Europe's Integrated*

to be able to qualify for social benefits customarily reserved for Belgian nationals remains to be seen.[279] Indeed, the decision points to a reconfiguration of classical conceptions of citizenship which have been traditionally framed within the 'sacred' triumvirate of people, territory and the state. In effect, the sovereignty of the Member States, which appeared to remain untouched by the citizenship provision enshrined in the Maastricht Treaty, appears to have been challenged in terms which may not find favour amongst national judges, which as the following chapters will show is a *Leitmotiv* of considerable significance as regards the recognition and implementation of European rights.

CONCLUSION

Recognition and implementation of European rights is somewhat constrained by the fact that they are located in spheres of law and modes of governance which are scattered across a plethora sites of authority both internally speaking, that is to say within the EU's pillar structure and externally speaking, namely in the courts and spheres of bureaucracy of the Member States. It is questionable whether elites and judges in particular are aware of the extent to which EU fundamental rights and policies have europeanised their respective constitutional cultures. Raising awareness, however, must be seen in terms of a process. In other words, it is unlikely to be resolved by, for example, enacting a primacy provision, as contained in the Draft Constitutional Treaty. Indeed, such a provision is unlikely to resolve the ultimate arbiter issue and the *ompetenz/Kompetenz* debate. The provision may in effect be merely symbolic. However, its significance may only be discernible within the wider context of the simplification exercise regarding the constitutional architecture of the EU as a whole including inter alia the abolition of the Pillar structure, the attempt to delineate competences and the incorporation of the Charter and accession to the ECHR when taken in conjunction with innovation of the primacy issue. Until now, the issue of primacy concerned the law of the European Community. The Draft Constitutional Treaty refers to primacy of the law of the European Union.

European rights illustrate the diversity of 'jural relations'[280] both in terms of substance and as to source of authority. Coming to terms with this

Market (Oxford, Oxford University Press, 2002), 167 at 176–177 and also MP Chiti, *Diritto amminstrativo europeo* (Milano, A. Giuffrè, 1999).

[279] Case C–184/00 *Grzelczyk* discussed by M Rossi, 'Anmerkung zu C–184/99 Grzelczyk' (2002) 7 *Juristen Zeitung* 249.

[280] See WN Hohfeld, *Fundamental Legal Conceptions as Applied in Judicial Reasoning* (New Haven, Yale University Press, 1978).

diversity is a challenge, both for elites and for rights holders alike. Regarding the former, the co-operation of elites is crucial given their role as gatekeepers to access to justice.[281] Much depends on how they view the impact of European rights on the legal culture which they serve and whether they are able to appreciate the extent to which their loyalty has been europeanised. Court decisions alone are unable to expose judges' motivations. They are, however, indicative of certain trends whereby judges have sought to contain the impact of europeanisation. However, most of the literature on judicial activism in relation to fundamental rights has tended to focus on constitutional courts with scant attention being paid to courts across the levels of the judicial and indeed the bureaucratic spectrum. For the system to work, national judges and other related elites have to be persuaded not only to work within the new system of rules which are generated by European rights but also there will have to an incentive and indeed a motivation for them to do so. Much depends on how the issue is framed. As Amartya Sen has pointed out, albeit in the context of economic adjustment, few tears are shed for superseded methods of production. Thus, the elimination of old methods of production are regarded as being justifiable in favour of methods which are more efficient.[282] The same cannot be said, according to Sen, in the case of culture where lost traditions may give rise to deep sense of loss and anguish[283] and where individuals are more likely to seek solace in bygone days, in some cases, presumably electing to maintain that they are a feature of the present and not the past. The process of constitutional adjustment may be said to involve both. The challenge for legal scholarship is to endorse an appropriate analytical framework within which the impact of European rights on national legal cultures can be best understood. This challenge also has practical implications given that it is only once the impact is understood correctly that a framework for tracking and monitoring their implementation can be developed. The purpose of the subsequent chapters is to evaluate the impact of certain categories of European rights in order to evaluate the types of benchmarks which ought to inform the process of implementation of European rights, both in theory and in practice.

[281] This point has been generally made by Weiler and Lockhart who refer to as the 'agency situation' who have not, however, applied this to multi-level governance. See JHH Weiler and N Lockhart, '"Taking Rights Seriously": The European Court of Justice and its Fundamental Rights Jurisprudence' (1995) 32 CML Rev 73.

[282] Here Sen draws from Darwinism by referring to improvement in terms of being 'fitter' and 'better'. See n 283 below.

[283] A Sen, *Development as Freedom* (Oxford, Oxford University Press, 1999), p 241.

3

Political Rights

INTRODUCTION

THE ROLE OF rights as vehicles for expressing the *volonté générale* has been central to classical understandings of democratic legitimacy.[1] Political rights have customarily been extended to citizens of a state as a medium by which they may participate in the articulation and formation of the general will. Political rights seen through the looking glass of classical understandings of representative democratic theory are systemically unable to cope with a process of will formation which exists both within and outwith state borders. I would suggest as a first point that the language of recognition of political rights is one which is framed in the lingua franca of classical state theory. In the European Union, it is not so much a case that the language of political rights is being framed 'beyond hierarchy' but that, in practice, it is being spoken in such a way that it has substantially revised and reconfigured notions of representative democracy by a supranational 'community'.[2] This argument has been developed in debates concerning the democratisation of the EU generally.[3] It has also

[1] The notion of the *volonté générale* owes much to Rousseau who, in his *Du contrat sociale*, ensured its inclusion in the history of ideas. It must be stressed, however, that Rousseau did not invent the notion, an issue which he acknowledges in relation to the inspiration gained from the ideas of inter alia Port-Royal, Locke, Malebranche, Leibnitz and Descartes. See J-J Rousseau, 'Les Confessions' in B Gagnebin and M Raymond (eds) *Oeuvres complètes de Jean-Jacques Rousseau* (Paris, Pléiade, 1959), 237. See also A Postigliola, 'De Malebranche à Rousseau: Les Apories de la volonté générale et la revanche du "raisonneur violent"' (1980) 39 *Annales de la Société Jean-Jacques Rousseau* 134.

[2] See M Wilkinson, 'Civil Society and the Re-imagination of European Constitutionalism' (2003) 9 *European Law Journal* 451.

[3] See generally A S Milward, *The European Rescue of the Nation-State* (London, Routledge, 1992); See also C Joerges and J Neyer, 'From Intergovernmental Bargaining to Deliberative Political Processes: The Constitutionalisation of Comitology' (2001) 3 *European Law Journal* 273. A Héritier, 'Elements of Democratic Legitimation in Europe: An Alternative Perspective' (1999) 6 *Journal of European Public Policy* 269. See also A Arnull and D Wincott (eds), *Accountability and Legitimacy in the European Union* (Oxford, Oxford University Press, 2002); P C Schmitter, *How to Democratize the European Union... And Why Bother?* (Maryland, Rowman and Littlefield, 2000); J Habermas, 'Toward a Cosmopolitan Europe' (2003) 14 *Journal of Democracy* 86.

proved to be the case in practice. The EU's constitutionalisation process,[4] of which the European Convention is but one 'constitutional moment',[5] is characterised by the multi-dimensional aspects of EU policy-making as part of the constitutional settlement[6] or the 'mixed constitution'.[7] Notwithstanding, however, much of the debate concerning political rights in the EU and democratic legitimacy has tended to emphasise the identity nexus of political rights and in particular, the absence of a European demos,[8] which is perceived as a hurdle to Pan-European political participation. In effect, this has masked the de facto implementation of political rights in a number of ways and at a number of levels.

Indeed, the Convention's work is a useful illustration of political participation which is framed across national, transnational and supranational lines across a number of levels[9] and by a variety of actors.[10] Further examples of the extent to which traditional hierarchical channels of representation have been modified[11] include the representation of sub-nation interests

[4] See J Shaw, 'Process, Responsibility and Inclusion in EU Constitutionalism' (2003) 9 *European Law Journal* 45. J Shaw, P Magnette, L Hoffmann and A Vergés Bausili, *The Convention on the Future of the Union: Working Towards an EU Constitution* (London, Federal Trust/Kogan Page, 2003).

[5] Though there is some dispute as to how this moment should be viewed. Weiler, for example, argues that the Laeken Convention should not be regarded as a formal constitutional moment on the basis of 'constitutional tolerance' and supranationalism. See JHH Weiler, 'A Constitution for Europe? Some Hard Choices' (2003) 40 *Journal of Common Market Studies* 563. Similar concerns have also been voiced by other commentators who are uneasy with the concept of a European Constitution. See R Dahrendorf, 'The Challenge for Democracy' (2003) 14 *Journal of Democracy* 102.

[6] See C Closa, 'Improving EU Constitutional Politics? A Preliminary Assessment of the Convention' (2003) Constitutionalism Web-Papers, ConWEB: <http:les1.man.ac.uk/conweb 1>.

[7] A term favoured by Neil MacCormick to describe the sharing of legislative authority between the European Parliament, the Council and the Commission in the EU. See N MacCormick, *Questioning Sovereignty: Law, State and Nation in the European Commonwealth* (Oxford, Oxford University Press, 1999).

[8] See D Grimm, 'Does Europe Need a Constitution?' (1995) 1 *European Law Journal* 282.

[9] See G Marks, L Hooghe and K Blank, 'European Integration from the 1980s: State-centric v Multilevel Governance' (1996) 34 *Journal of Common Market Studies* 341. See also I Pernice, 'Multilevel Constitutionalism and the Treaty of Amsterdam: European Constitution-making Revisted?' (1999) 36 CML Rev 703. See also J Greenwood, *Representing Interests in the European Union* (London, MacMillan Press, 1997). A Warleigh, 'The Hustle: Citizenship Practice, NGOs and "Policy Coalitions" in the European Union: The Cases of Auto Oil, Drinking Water and Unit Pricing' (2000) 7 *Journal of European Public Policy* 229 and also DM Curtin, "Civil Society" and the European Union: Opening Spaces for Deliberative Democracy?' in P Alston, C de Búrca and B de Witte (eds) *Collected Courses of the Academy of European Law* (Florence, European University Institute, 1999), 185

[10] See also G de Búrca and N Walker, 'Law and Transnational Civil Society: Upsetting the Agenda?' (2003) 9 *European Law Journal* 387.

[11] See generally A Scott, J Peterson and D Millar, 'Subsidiarity: A "Europe of the Regions" v the British Constitution?' (1994) 32 *Journal of Common Market Studies* 1. See also E Bengoa, R Arantzazu and F Tapia, 'The Principle of Subsidiarity and the European Union: A New Political Sphere for the Basque Government' (1995) International Institute for Sociology of Law, Oñati Unpublished Paper and Castro Ruano, JL de, *La emergente participación*

in the Committee of the Regions[12] and the emergence of the Open Method of Co-ordination (OMC) as an alternative to the Community method.[13] Mitigating the Union's democratic deficit has also been effected through the judicial process,[14] accompanying other forms of participatory democracy in other spheres of legislative and administrative decision-making[15] facilitated by the Community's legal order which has provided a source of individual rights.[16] The emergence of 'transboundary participatory rights' in the context of EC law on the environment is indicative of this trend,[17] an era ushered in by the inclusive credentials of the Directive on Environmental Impact Assessment.[18] However, participation has tended to be split along sectoral lines. In short, it is the 'repeat players'[19] or interest groups who tend to make use of the participatory rights which, in the case of the EU, are predominantly corporate.[20] Thus, it is possible for certain individuals to influence policy-making through the judicial process, acting alone, or alternatively acting as a group. This right is, however, somewhat constrained by national procedural rules governing access to national courts which limit the ability of the individual to enforce Community law.[21]

política de las regiones en el proceso de construcción europea ([Oñati], Instituto Vasco de Administratión Pública-Herri-Arduralaritzaren Euskal Erakundea, 1994).

[12] See D Curtin, *Postnational Democracy, The European Union in Search of a Political Philosophy* (The Hague, Kluwer, 1997).
[13] Which was codified at the Lisbon Summit in March 2000. See the Presidency Conclusions, Lisbon European Council, 23 and 24 March 2000. See E Szyszczak, 'Social Policy in the Post-Nice Era' in A Arnull and D Wincott (eds) *Accountability and Legitimacy in the European Union* (Oxford, Oxford University Press, 2002), 329 at 331ff.
[14] See generally C Harlow and R Rawlings, *Pressure through Law* (London, Routledge, 1992).
[15] See HP Nehl, *Principles of Administrative Procedure in EC Law* (Oxford, Hart Publishing, 1999), 61ff.
[16] Within the context of enforcement proceedings which are decentralised courtesy of the preliminary reference procedure (Art 234 EC). See generally R Dehousse, 'The Juridification of the Political Process' in F Snyder (ed) *The europeanisation of Law: The Legal Effects of European Integration* (Oxford, Hart Publishing, 2000), 15
[17] R Macrory and S Turner, 'Participatory Rights, Transboundary Environmental Governance and EC Law' (2002) 39 CML Rev 489.
[18] Dir. 85/337/EEC [1985] OJ L175/40, Art 6(2) as amended by Dir. 97/11/EC [1997] OJ L73/5, Art 1(8). See generally D Chalmers, 'Inhabitants in EC Environmental Law' in P Craig and G de Búrca (eds) *The Evolution of EU Law* (Oxford, Oxford University Press, 1999), 653.
[19] Term used by Galanter. See M Galanter, 'Why the "Haves" Come Out Ahead: Speculations on the Limits of Legal Change' (1974) 10 *Law and Society* 95.
[20] H-W Micklitz and N Reich (eds), *Public Interest Litigation before European Courts* (Baden-Baden, Nomos Verlag, 1996). See also C Harding, 'Who Goes to Court in Europe? An Analysis of Litigation against the European Community' (1992) 17 ELR 105. A similar argument may also be made vis-à-vis the activities of Non-Governmental Organisations (NGOs). In particular, it is debatable whether they can be regarded as representing the concerns of civil society as a whole, given that they tend to be 'single issue' organisations. See PC Schmitter, 'Democracy in Europe and Europe's Democratization' (2003) 14 *Journal of Democracy* 71 at 82.
[21] F Snyder, 'The Effectiveness of European Community Law' (1993) 56 MLR 19. See also C Harlow, 'Towards a Theory of Access for the European Court of Justice' (1992) 12 *Yearbook of European Law* 213.

The procedural barriers to access operate in different ways given the respect for the diversity of legal systems of the Member States.[22] As regards Community law, rules governing standing[23] and legal aid are more restrictive than in other countries such as the United States, thereby limiting the use of litigation as a politically effective lever.[24]

I will not attempt to develop all of the issues mentioned above. The purpose of this chapter is to address the legacy of state building and the emphasis on demos which has framed the debate concerning European political rights. In so doing, I aim to challenge this framework by exploring the impact on state sovereignty provoked by political rights by addressing the *sui generis* nature of the European polity as well as the innovative nature of political participation in the EU. It will be argued that EU citizenship is inappropriate as the basis for political rights in the EU. The implications for the purposes of this chapter are mainly threefold. First, the actors engaged in political participation in the EU include, de facto, EU citizens and non-EU citizens. Secondly, the forms of participation are more innovative than classical conceptions of representative democracy allow. Indeed, in practice, political rights in the EU are framed more widely than the EU citizenship provisions contained in the Treaties.[25] Political participation through judicial activism has rendered the distinction between political rights *stricto sensu* and rights or interests with a political dimension ambiguous. Thirdly, the realisation of de facto political rights in the EU is heavily dependent on national elites and in particular, public authority officials and judges. Their compliance is essential. Member States have been exceedingly defensive in ring fencing areas of their competence where EU-wide political rights would be infringing on their sovereignty in ways that they deem unacceptable. A useful example is provided by the exclusions to public service employment under the free movement provisions. Indeed, it is here that the impact on state sovereignty provoked by European political rights is at its most dynamic and indeed at its most acute, giving rise to implications which are more considerable than those provoked by the EU citizenship provisions in relation to political rights at a first glance.

[22] See *Implementing Community Environmental Law* COM (1996) 500 final, pp 11–13.
[23] Through Art 230 and 232 EC.
[24] Indeed, voluntary political associations greatly influenced the substance of policies by resorting to litigation. The National Association for the Advancement of Colored People, the American Civil Liberties Union, the American Bar Association and the American Jewish Congress were particularly proactive in making the most of the Supreme Court's willingness at times to put rights on the national agenda. This was particularly the case in the period of the Warren Court of 1953 to 1969, a crucial period for the civil rights movement. See M Schudson, *The Good Citizen. A History of American Civic Life* (New York, The Free Press, 1998).
[25] Art 19 EC.

Generally speaking, the introduction of EU citizenship[26] in the Maastricht Treaty restated the *who* and *how* of political rights in a way which least threatened the sovereignty of the Member States whilst omitting to address the fact that de facto, both *who* and *how* had long since reconfigured state sovereignty, albeit in an incremental and selective fashion. In other words, 'all those affected', for all intents and purposes of political rights articulated through the medium of the citizenship provisions, referred to nationals of Member States only. However, 'all those affected', seen through the prism of political rights in the Union includes citizens and non-citizens and spheres of belonging and participation which sometimes overlap, a phenomenon which sits uneasily with state sovereignty not to mention identity.

Political Rights and European Union Citizenship

From the outset, the political rights which attached to EU citizenship constituted a symbolic attempt to contain the Union's democratic deficit by endorsing rights which signalled taking the idea of a 'People's Europe' seriously.[27] It was framed within the mandate of:

> Creating an ever closer Union among the peoples of Europe in which decisions are taken as openly as possible and closely as possible to the citizen.[28]

For many commentators, the Maastricht mandate was overly ambitious.[29] The initial critique was that EU citizenship was sufficiently nebulous to affect a pro-democratic stance whilst remaining ineffectual in practice.[30] However, the litmus test tended, more often than not, to be framed in terms of classical conceptions of representative democracy.

[26] S O'Leary, *The Evolving Concept of Community Citizenship: From the Free Movement of Persons to Union Citizenship* (The Hague, Kluwer Law International, 1996). Note that the idea of Community citizenship was first mentioned in 1976 in the Tindemans Report in relation to social rights for EC nationals residing in Member States other than their own. See Bulletin of the European Communities, Supplement 1/76. See also the Adonnino Report, Bulletin of the European Communities, Supplement 7/85.

[27] See European Commission (1975) *Towards a Citizen's Europe*, Bulletin of the European Communities 7/75,11; European Commission (1984) *A People's Europe* COM (84) 446; European Commission (1993) *First Report on Citizenship* COM (93) 702 final.

[28] Art 1 TEU.

[29] The literature on EU citizenship is vast. I have elected to confine myself to an analysis of the response to the citizenship provisions regarding political rights only. Here also, it is impossible to provide an analysis which is exhaustive. The references which are made are for the purposes of the current argumentation only. See C Lyons, 'Citizenship in the Constitution of the EU: Rhetoric or Reality?' in R Bellamy (ed) *Constitutionalism, Democracy and Sovereignty: American and European Perspectives* (Aldershot, Avebury, 1996),

[30] R Bellamy, 'Citizenship and Rights' in R Bellamy (ed) *Theories and Concepts of Politics* (Manchester, Manchester University Press, 1993), 43. See C Closa, 'The Concept of Citizenship in the Treaty on European Union' (1992) 29 CML Rev 1137.

Indeed, the debates on EU citizenship were as state fixated as the Treaty provisions appeared to be, particularly as regards those by political theorists, many of whom sought to advance the cause of political rights through republican conceptions of citizenship.[31] Accordingly, they tended to frame the criteria in classical terms, where the relationship between the citizen and the state was one based on hierarchy and where democratic legitimacy was best served through widening the circle of political participants in a vertical manner. The response to EU citizenship by republicanism has been dealt with elsewhere and I am, to some extent, doing it some disservice by attempting to distil my critique in but a few lines. However, the constraints which limited its response to EU citizenship along statist lines were experienced both within and outwith the confines of *teoria*, not to mention *praxis*.[32]

Given that the definition of EU citizenship granted only nationals of Member States political rights, the concept was viewed more in terms of the glass half empty of failure. Critics of EU citizenship tended to adopt the strict reading of political participation which the Treaty provided, namely, active and passive electoral rights[33] and the power to petition the Parliament.[34] For some, however, even failure was legitimate, if the nation-state was to

[31] cf D Miller, 'Citizenship and Pluralism' (1995) 43 *Political Studies* 432.

[32] I have used the term 'republicanism' somewhat indiscriminately in this section. There are, of course, as with any 'school of thought', many strands to the debate. Thus, for example, the communitarian/civic humanist version emphasises the need for a homogeneous demos, which exists at the level of the nation-state but not as yet at the level of the EU. David Miller has, for example, used this argument as has Claus Offe. Neo-roman republicans, like Phillip Pettit and Richard Bellamy adopt a view which is more complex. Accordingly, the deliberative community need not be homogeneous. Indeed, it is preferable that it is not, as different sub communities are thereby able to balance each other out through a form of equilibrium. The source of this equilibrium creates a space for rights. They do, however, require a community of interest at some level. The EU is likely to be less than that as compared to a more established demos. Thus, for example, Bellamy and Castiglione argue that civic humanist republicanism assumes that a cosmopolitan demos requires a global community which is, in effect, a form of communitarian version of cosmopolitanism in which interaction between communities can create cosmopolitan elements. I am indebted to Richard Bellamy for his points of clarification regarding this matter. See C Offe, 'Demokratie und Wohlfahrtsstaat' in W Streeck (ed) *Internationale Wirtschaft und nationale Demokratie. Herausaforderung für die Demokratietheorie* (Frankfurt am Main, Campus, 1998), 99; P Pettit, *Republicanism: A Theory of Freedom and Government* (Oxford, Clarendon Press, 1999). See also R Bellamy, 'The "Right to have Rights": Citizenship Practice and Political Constitution of the EU' in A Warleigh (ed) *Citizenship and Governance in the European Union* (London, Continuum Press, 2001), 41.

[33] Arts 19 and 20 EC.

[34] Art 21 EC in conjunction with Art 194 EC. Every citizen also has the right to apply to the Ombudsman established in accordance with Art 195 EC. The Treaty of Amsterdam elaborated the rights of the EU citizen only in respect of the right to petition any of the institutions or bodies of the Union in any of the twelve official languages of the Treaties. The new subparagraph to Art 194 of the EC Treaty now reads:

> Every citizen of the Union may write to any of the institutions or bodies referred to in this Article of Article 4 in one of the languages mentioned in Article 248 (1) and have an answer in the same language.

remain the definitive framework for its articulation,[35] a tone arguably set by the fable of citizenship as recounted by TH Marshall in the 1950s,[36] the time before the 'selling of the family silver' of public services[37] and where the state seemed relatively immune from the 'threat' of supranational and international organisations and the 'evil' forces of globalisation.

Once upon a time, political rights existed as part of the exclusive relationship between the state and its subjects. Moreover, once upon a time, rights could be neatly compartmentalised in terms of 'political', 'social' and 'civil' rights.[38] With the rise of globalisation and the growth of supranational and international organisations, both were called into question. However, it was not so much a case of being confined to the annals of history, but rather, both were recalibrated as part of the overall process of the reconfiguration of state sovereignty.

The amendments introduced as part of the Maastricht Treaty did, however, usher the concept of rights back into the fray of European integration, rather like a phoenix which rose from the ashes of a citizenship debate which had been crippled by years of theoretical exhaustion. An implication of the rights critique developed by inter alia the Critical Legal Studies movement[39] was that exhaustion very soon developed into a state of chronic fatigue, for which there was very little motivation to snap out of until the 1980s.[40] The return of rights from exile from the common fray of the pursuit of ideas meant that citizenship was also, to some extent, rehabilitated and viewed not only in a more favourable light[41] but also as having potential,[42] albeit for citizens only. This served to perpetuate the perennial link between citizenship and rights forged foremost during the era of state formation. This 19th century legacy has also influenced the ways in which rights are both conceived and perceived. Thus, for example, the influence of classical state theory informed much of the initial response to EU citizenship.

35 Se UK Preuß, 'Problems of a Concept of European Citizenship' (1995) 1 *European Law Journal* 267.
36 TH Marshall, *Citizenship and Social Class and Other Essays* (Cambridge, Cambridge University Press, 1950).
37 As Harold MacMillan viewed the privatisation of public services.
38 See Marshall, n 36 above.
39 See A MacIntyre, *After Virtue:A Study in Moral Theory* (London, Duckworth, 1981). See generally RM Unger, 'The Critical Legal Studies Movement' (1983) 3 *Harvard Law Review* 563 and also A Carrino, *Ideologia e coscienza. Critical Legal Studies* (Napoli, ESI, 1992).
40 See C Shore, *Building Europe. The Cultural Politics of European Integration* (London and New York, Palgrave, 2000) 70ff.
41 As in the case of the Citizen's Charter in the United Kingdom. See *The Citizen's Charter*, Cm 1599 (HMSO, 1991). See generally C Barron and J Scott, 'The Charter Programme' (1992) 55 MLR 526.
42 See H D'Oliveria, 'European Citizenship: Its Meaning, its Potential' in J Monar, W Ungerer and W Wessels (eds) *The Maastricht Treaty on European Union: Legal Complexity and Political Dynamic* (Brussels, Interuniversity Press, 1994), 43.

Indeed, initial responses to the concept tended to focus on the transposition of national experiences not to mention intellectual traditions of state theory[43] which was perhaps less appropriate than was originally assumed.[44] The respective national experiences of citizenship seemed unable to measure up to its EU derivative. Not only were many attempts which were made to think 'beyond the state' still very much influenced by the tradition of state theory, despite appearances to the contrary, but many tended to lack feasibility. Conceptualisations based on post-nationalism[45] or cosmopolitanism[46] were irreconcilable with the fact that legal recognition of EU citizenship rights remain dependent on the institutions of the Member States. In other words, Kant's citizen of the world or *Weltbürger*[47] had very little in common with the *EU-Bürger*.

As regards democratic legitimacy, many commentators argued that EU citizenship provided a distraction from where real power resides in the Union given its fragmented distribution through comitology and otherwise.[48] If the litmus tests for the EU citizenship provisions is whether they may be described as effectively transforming power structures, then, on the face of it, they fail to deliver in terms of what Scharpf has termed 'input legitimacy'.[49] They may, however, deliver in terms of 'output legitimacy'.[50] Moving away from classical definitions of democratic legitimacy, however, the indictment is arguably less damning.[51] For many, not only is the 'democratic deficit' in the EU legitimate but the standards according to which it is

[43] See Preuß, n 35 above.

[44] See 'European Citizenship and the Social and Political Integration of the European Union' (EURCIT: Contract Number: SOE2-CT97–3056. Final Report reproduced at <http://www.reading.ac.uk/AcaDepts/ce/GSEIS/GSEISframeP.html>. This statement is by no means intended to criticise the principal scientists in charge of this project but is in fact generated by a sense of *mea culpa* in view not only of my involvement in the project but also of the fact that I initially adopted a statist approach to EU citizenship.

[45] See Y Soysal, *Limits of Citizenship: Migrants and Postnational Membership in Europe* (Chicago, Chicago University Press, 1994).

[46] See A Linklater, 'Cosmopolitan Citizenship' (1998) 2 *Citizenship Studies* 23; D Held, *Democracy and the Global Order: From the Modern State to Cosmopolitan Governance* (Cambridge, Polity Press, 1995); D Archibughi, D Held and M Kohler (eds), *Reimagining Political Communities* (London, Polity Press, 1998).

[47] See I Kant, *Die Metaphysik der Sitten, Rechtslehre* (Frankfurt am Main, Suhrkamp, 1977) at § 62. See also I Kant, *Political Writings* (Cambridge, Cambridge University Press, 1991) at Section III: Cosmopolitan Right reproduced at pp 172–73.

[48] See R Dehousse, 'Towards a Regulation of Transitional Governance? Citizens' Rights and the Reform of Comitology Procedures' in C Joerges and E Vos (eds) *EU Committees: Social Regulation, Law and Politics* (Oxford, Hart Publishing, 1999), 109.

[49] See F Scharpf, *Governing in Europe: Effective and Democratic?* (Oxford, Oxford University Press, 1999).

[50] See M La Torre, 'Legitimacy for a Supranational European Political Order — Derivative, Regulatory or Deliberative?' (2002) 15 *Ratio Juris* 63 at 79.

[51] See O Gerstenberg and C Sabel, 'Directly-Deliberative Polyarchy: An Institutional Ideal for Europe?' in C Joerges and R Dehousse (eds) *Good Governance in Europe's Integrated Market* (Oxford, Oxford University Press, 2002), 289.

judged ought to be both articulated and framed differently. The efficient delegation of tasks to specialised agencies, or what has been referred to in the case of the United States as the 'fourth branch' of government is a case in point.[52]

Even if we accept Majone's invitation to accept this regulatory model of the EC, however, the benefits of the 'new medievalism' premised on '[o]verlapping jurisdictions, legal pluralism, extensive delegation of powers to transnational organisations',[53] bring with them burdens which even reconfigured notions of democratic legitimacy may be unable to carry. In other words, Majone may be right in qualifying the concept of hierarchy and in recognising the existence of overlapping regulatory spheres in relation to the EU's institutional architecture and legitimacy, but this may in effect mean that the democratic deficit runs deeper than was originally presumed. Transparent and accountable decision-making becomes even more important in a system which operates within and outwith the state's institutional boundaries given that they are harder to monitor.[54]

Public law can do very little to sufficiently 'claw back' its authority in a world order which is increasingly beyond its grasp given that it has traditionally been framed in terms of hierarchy underpinned by the moving target of the public/private divide.[55] The evolution of judicial review in the domestic legal systems of some Member States serves as a useful reminder that even broad interpretations of the rules on standing can only go so far in asserting their authority over principles of natural justice.[56] Whereas it is arguable that classical understandings of public law ought to be reconfigured,[57] it is doubtful whether the principles contained therein are reduced to being redundant pieces of semantics. The issue at

[52] See G Majone, 'Europe's 'Democratic Deficit': The Question of Standards' (1998) 4 *European Law Journal* 5. See also G Majone, 'Delegation of Regulatory Powers in a Mixed Polity' (2002) 8 *European Law Journal* 319.

[53] *Ibid* at 27.

[54] See C Harlow, 'Codification of EC Administrative Procedures? Fitting the Shoe to the Foot' (1996) 2 *European Law Journal* 3 at 22. See also R Dahl, 'Can International Organizations be Democratic? A Skeptic's View' in C Hacker-Cordón (ed), *Democracy's Edges* (Cambridge, Cambridge University Press, 1999), 19.

[55] D Oliver, *Common Values and the Public-Private Divide* (London, Butterworths, 1999); see also S Millns and N Whitty (eds), *Feminist Perspectives on* PL (London, Cavendish, 1999).

[56] See A Stone Sweet, *Governing with Judges* (Oxford, Oxford University Press, 2000).

[57] See, eg, K-H Ladeur, 'Towards a Legal Concept of the Network in European Standard-Setting' in C Joerges and E Vos (eds), *EU Committees: Social Regulation, Law and Politics* (Oxford, Hart Publishing, 1999), 151 who at p 162 surmises that:

> The State no longer as its place at the centre of society from which the rules for the conservation of the equilibrium of society can be conceived and formulated. Neither inside the public nor the private spheres can order any longer be constructed as hierarchical. The State has to adapt to a new experimental logic of modelling new domains of option beyond experience, and only on the basis of this more general idea is the observation and description of a whole range of different types of public responsibility meaningful.

stake is the extent to which the mandate of public law as a regulatory mechanism must be recalibrated. For Harlow, the alarm signals of accountability and transparency sound far earlier in the face of overlapping jurisdictions and legal pluralism than they do for Majone. According to the latter:

> Independent agencies can indeed be kept politically accountable, but only by a combination of control instruments: clear statutory objectives, oversight by specialised legislative committees, strict procedural requirements, judicial review, appointments of key personnel, budgetary controls, reorganisations, professionalism, public participation, monitoring by interest groups, even inter-agency rivalry. When such a multi-pronged approach is used carefully and fully, no-one controls an independent agency, yet the agency is under control.[58]

Majone's vision of control underplays the role of human agency. Indeed, like systems theory, which shares many characteristics of Majone's concept of regulatory control, human agency appears to be strangely absent in the cluster of regulatory mechanisms which appear, certainly in Majone's view, to be self-executing.[59] Whereas it is virtually impossible to maintain a conspiracy theory of co-ordinated action being at the root of all circumnavigation of control, it would be naive to deny the existence of co-ordination altogether. In other words, the room for manoeuvre with a view to escaping the supervisory jurisdiction of agencies of control can be created by act *and* by omission.

Leaving aside whether Majone's vision *ought* to be adapted to the EU context, it may be that it contains elements which render it descriptively apt; in other words, it may in fact already be taking place in a world in which the 'living law' of legal practice plays its part. The impact on democratic legitimacy and political rights in the EU, within and without those framed in the context of the citizenship provisions is considerable particularly given the evolution of public law. As Harlow argues,

> the 'state' against which the 'citizen' typically merits protection under EC law is, strangely, the Member State, while the wrongful act or illegality in respect of which protection is granted is a disregard of EC law. Alternatively put, the direct interface between the citizen and state is replaced in EC law by a triangular relationship, while the dualist character of the EC legal order,

[58] See Majone, n 52 above at 27. Regarding the issue of agencies in the European Union see MP Chiti, 'The Emergence of a Community Administration: The Case of European Agencies' (2000) 37 CML Rev 309.

[59] Of course, according to systems theory, the idea of self-executing is particularly apt. See N Luhmann, *Das Recht der Gesellschaft* (Frankfurt am Main, Suhrkamp, 1989) and also N Luhmann, *Legitimation durch Verfahren* (Frankfurt am Main, Suhrkamp, 1983); see further G Teubner, *Law as an Autopoetic System* (Oxford, Blackwell, 1993).

> which requires the ECJ to operate through national courts, further transforms the character of administrative adjudications.[60]

It also, however, transforms the character of rights implementation.

Certain forms of political participation exist in the EU which circumnavigate the ballot box in favour of the judicial process. Despite the restrictive rules on standing, some non-EU citizens have been able to make use of this method of participating in the formation of the general will. Political participation has also, however, been achieved in ways which cut across the categories of citizenship and state institutions, a phenomenon which the European Commission has not only acknowledged[61] but also has increasingly sought to encourage. In its White Paper on Governance,[62] it concedes that Non-Governmental Organisations 'often act as an early warning system for the direction of political debate' with their involvement offering a real potential to

> broaden the debate on Europe's role. It is a chance to get citizens more actively involved in achieving the Union's objectives and to offer them a structured channel for feedback, criticism and protest.[63]

It is debatable whether participation of this nature may be viewed in terms of political rights, strictly speaking. However, the inclusion of representatives of civil society as of right in the EU decision-making process, may have caused the concept to evolve so that the methods of their participation are through channels which constitute political rights *by any other name*, bearing in mind, however, that there is a distinction between 'participation' and 'simple consultation'.[64]

Notwithstanding, the instrumentalisation of procedural law may be more effective in influencing the substance of policies than the ballot box as the case of the *Bureau européen des consummateurs* (*BEUC*) illustrates.[65] In the first *BEUC* case, the European Court of Justice upheld the Commission's refusal to supply non-confidential information in anti-dumping proceedings

[60] See C Harlow, 'European Administrative Law and the Global Challenge' in P Craig and G de Búrca (eds) *The Evolution of EU Law* (Oxford, Oxford University Press, 1999), 261 at 270-271.

[61] See, eg, the Communication of the European Commission of 2 December 1992, 'An open and structured dialogue between the Commission and special interest groups' OJ C63 of 5 March 1993.

[62] Commission of the European Communities *European Governance: A White Paper* COM (2001) 428 final Brussels (25 July 2001).

[63] COM (2001) 428 final.

[64] See, eg, the Economic and Social Committee's opinion on 'Organised civil society and European governance: the Committee's contribution to the drafting of the White Paper' CES 535/2001 (25 April 2001) at points 3,4, and 5.

[65] See Case C–170/89 *BEUC v Commission* [1991] ECR 5709 and also Case T–37/92 *BEUC and NCC v Commission* [1994] II–289.

to 'interested parties' not expressly mentioned in a Regulation.[66] The ECJ rejected the applicant's argument as regards the incoherence of the administrative practice on the basis that the practices were not directed at the applicant, which in this case was a consumer's organisation.[67] The impact of the *BEUC* case, however, had implications which were more far reaching, given that despite having lost the battle before the ECJ, they presumably had some part to play in winning the war of securing rights for consumers' organisations to inspect non-confidential files, which was later included in the 1984 GATT Agreements.[68] The significance of *BEUC* must also be viewed within the context of the broader spectrum of the ECJ's and the Court of First Instance's jurisprudence in protecting procedural rights such as the right to be heard and the duty to state reasons, when individual rights are directly affected by Community decisions.[69]

The picture which emerges is one in which the rule of law, traditionally linked to the nation state, is articulated at the level of the EU through a 'functional equivalent'[70] deriving its legitimacy not from the representational character of a directly elected legislature but from the endorsement of methods by which administrative legitimacy can be enhanced.[71] The role of procedure is central in ensuring that rights are not mere rhetoric, a factor which was recognised by many delegates of the European Convention. The attempts to create a right of the citizen to direct application to the ECJ is a case in point.[72]

The significance of the EU citizenship provisions is identifiable only when taken in conjunction with other measures which make up the rich tapestry of the rule of law. This not only includes its formal inclusion in the TEU but also the status which it derived through judicial activism. The case of access to information provides a case in point because although it had existed prior to Maastricht, this was mainly in relation to competition proceedings.[73] Maastricht arguably provided it with its 'constitutional

[66] See Art 7 (4) (a) of Regulation 2423/88 [1988] OJ L209/1.
[67] See *BEUC*, n 65 above at para 21.
[68] Art 6 (7) of the new Basic Regulation 384/96 now provides for a right of 'users and consumers' organisations to inspect non-confidential files.
[69] See Case C–269/90 *Hauptzollamt München Mitte v Technische Universität München* [1991] ECR-5469; Case T-364/94 *France Aviation v Commission* [1995] ECR II–2845.
[70] I am indebted to Professor Roberto Toniatti for bringing my attention to the notion of the rule of law in the EU legal order being referred to as a 'functional equivalent'.
[71] See generally E Vos, 'EU Committees: the Evolution of Unforeseen Institutional Actors in European Product Regulation' in C Joerges and E Vos (eds) *EU Committees: Social Regulation, Law and Politics* (Oxford, Hart Publishing, 1999), 19 and also M Everson, 'Administering Europe' (1998) 36 *Journal of Common Market Studies* 195
[72] See the proposal by Andrew Duff, CONV 57/02. See also submission by António Vitorino, Chairman of the Working Group II, 'Incorporation of the Charter/Accession to the ECHR' on the question of effective judicial remedies and access of individuals to the European Court of Justice. WG II–WD 021.
[73] See Nehl, n 15 above, at ch 5.

moment' given that it was at this time that it came to be viewed as a means whereby the democratic deficit of the Community might also be remedied. This led to the adoption of Regulation No. 17 on transparency which was annexed to the TEU which was subsequently articulated in a Code of Conduct concerning public access to Council and Commission documents[74] which not only inspired a host of Court of First Instance decisions[75] but was also later incorporated into the EC Treaty through the amendments introduced by the Treaty of Amsterdam.[76] Article 255 (1) is particularly instructive as inter alia its addressees are both EU citizens and any natural or legal person residing or having its registered office in a Member State'.[77] This goes some way towards qualifying the accusations originally made as regards the exclusionary nature of the EU citizenship provisions. Many would no doubt argue, however, that they do not go far enough.

Maastricht created a vehicle of rights which was by definition exclusionary, thereby overlooking other individuals resident in the EU as potential rights holders who are not nationals of a Member State. There is nothing curious about limiting the scope of rights to certain groups of addressees. By definition, citizenship includes at the price of exclusion. Morally speaking, the position that rights ought to go to all is no doubt defensible.[78] The law, however, tries to keep an eye on practice, which tends to contain the good intentions of the former. In the case of political rights, EU citizenship excludes those who do not benefit from nationality of an EU Member State. Thus, it is associative for nationals of Member States but disassociative for non-nationals. In the case of social rights, as the next chapter will show, the criteria of association are interpreted more widely. In other words, they are still associative and disassociative but in a different way giving rise to different *spheres of belonging* and *spheres of political participation* which sometimes overlap. The binary model of 'insiders' and 'outsiders' in a 'Fortress Europe' fails to adequately account for the *status quo* in the Union

[74] 93/730/EC [1993] OJ L340/41 implemented by Council Decision 93/731 and Commission Decision 94/90 [1994] OJ L46/58.

[75] See Case T–194/94 *Carvel v EU Council* [1995] ECR–II–2765; Case T–174/95 *Tidningen Journalisten v Council* [1998] ECR II–2289; Case T–14/98 *Hautela v Council* [1999] ECR II–2489 and also Case T–188/97 *Rothmans International v Commission* [1999] ECR I-19 July, 1999.

[76] See generally DM Curtin, 'Citizens' Fundamental Right of Access to EU Information: An Evolving Digital Passepartout?' (2000) 37 CML Rev 7.

[77] See art 255 (1) which provides that:

> Any citizen of the Union, and any natural or legal person residing or having its registered office in a Member State, shall have a right of access to European Parliament, Council and Commission documents, subject to the principles and the conditions to be defined in accordance with paragraphs 2 and 3.

[78] I Kant, *Die Metaphysik der Sitten, Rechtslehre* (Frankfurt am Main, Suhrkamp, 1977). For a modern restatement of Kant's categorical imperative, see J Habermas, *Between Facts and Norms* (Cambridge, Polity Press, 1997).

and the spheres of belonging which, to some extent, make a mockery of vertically defined hierarchical interpretations of citizenship, not to mention understandings of political participation which fail to recognise the existence of a public sphere carved out by political actors across state boundaries as part of the EU's civil society.[79] The example of medieval city-states serves provides a useful analogy, albeit its application in relation to the EU must be qualified.

CITIZENSHIP AND SPHERES OF BELONGING AND PARTICIPATION

It is sometimes the case that non-EU citizens benefit from certain citizenship rights which are not intrinsically linked to nationality of a Member State. Thus, it is incorrect to say that they are outside 'Fortress Europe', so to speak. Consider the Turkish residents in Germany, who work, pay taxes but who are still unable to vote in local or national elections.[80] They may, however, benefit from social security rights.[81] Thus, they are not entirely outside Fortress Europe, neither are they, however, entirely inside it. They are, to draw from a title of a book by Peter Schuck, 'in-betweens'.[82] It is submitted that the model of the medieval city must not be overlooked as an analytical tool for understanding the debate concerning political rights in the EU.

The Analogy of the Medieval City-States

Medieval city dwellers were protected by the city walls. There were, however, also settlements outside the city limits which were of strategic importance in protecting the city from what the citizens perceived as threats to the outside. Further groups living on the outside of the city walls were allowed entrance into the city to perform essential functions, namely, they were part of the labour force but they were not allowed to reside in the city. The medieval city-states were pivotal in the industrialisation process. At the heart of the functionalist definition of the city-state lies the market. Accordingly, like the EU, they were invented to help solve the problem concerning the division of labour in the economy. This made it possible for

[79] See O De Schutter, 'Europe in Search of its Civil Society' (2002) 8 *European Law Journal* 198.
[80] See WW Barbieri, *Ethics of Citizenship: Immigration and Group Rights in Germany* (Durham INC, Duke University Press, 1998).
[81] This must, however, be qualified by the fact that Turkey has an association agreement with the EU.
[82] PH Schuck, *Citizens, Strangers and In-Betweens: Essays on Immigration and Citizenship* (Boulder, Westview Press, 1998).

producers in the secondary and tertiary sectors to reach high levels of specialisation.[83]

There is a further example of the permeability of the city walls and that is the notion of a wall within a wall which is provided by the example of the changing contours of the former Byzantine-Arab city. Crusaders settled next to the city and built a new wall *intra muros* to protect themselves. Thus, for example, the Caesarea built over or alongside fortifications of Qaisārīya. Archaeological investigations revealed that different elements were caught up in city walls, namely, the wall inside was made of Herodian and Byzantine columns and capitals.[84]

An example from the medieval city which highlights the appropriateness of the analogy of the city-state is the *Podestà*, which was an office which existed in the 13th century in city-states whereby a foreigner was designated as an executive, legislative and judicial authority over a commune. He had to be an outsider so that he would not be 'tainted' by familial and factional parties within the cities; thus, he was chosen from another city.[85] The *Podestà* acted as an arbiter between factious townspeople. He took part in the civic rituals of the state. He held the post for 6 months to a year. In effect, this is an example of aliens administering the law.[86] The importance of the analogy of the medieval city-state is mainly twofold. First, it is an illustration of non-citizen actors carrying out state functions. Secondly, these functions contributed to the political life of the city-state, though not through customary channels of political participation.

However, care must be taken when applying the model of the city-state to the European Union, not least because of the feudal base of the former which is distinct from the base of the latter. However, the city-state model exposes the weaknesses of the Fortress Europe model, which fails to account for the exchange between the centre and the periphery of the EU defined by the Association Agreements[87] which exist between the EU and states which are not members of the EU. Thus, the ECJ has referred to association agreements between the EU and non-Member States in ruling that Turkish workers and their families in the Community enjoy certain rights to equal treatment in social security.[88] The position of third-country nationals resident in the Union

[83] See E Ennen, *The Medieval Town* (Amsterdam, North-Holland, 1979). Note that in Ennen's book which is translated from German, the translator has elected to translate the word '*Stadt*' as town which is unfortunate as what is clearly meant is the city-state.

[84] J Prawer, 'Crusader Cities' in HA Miskimin, D Herlihy and UL Udovitch (eds) *The Medieval City* (New Haven, Yale University Press, 1977).

[85] See K Pennington, *The Prince and the Law 1200–1600. Sovereignty and Rights in the Western Legal Tradition* (Berkeley, University of California Press, 1993), 38.

[86] See Ennen, n 83 above, at 22.

[87] T Faist, 'A Medieval City: Transnationalizing Labor Markets and Social Rights in Europe' (1994) 9/94 *ZeS* — Arbeitspapies (Universität Brenen) at p 7.

[88] S Peers, 'Equality, Free Movement and Social Security' (1997) 22 ELR 342.

who benefit from association agreements represents a special case and must be distinguished from other third-country nationals. The reference to 'other third-country nationals' would seem to suggest that there is such a thing as a uniform Community policy towards third-country nationals, which is far from being the case.[89] What all third-country nationals have in common is that their legal status is unclear. Furthermore, this uncertainty is further amplified by the presence of a multitude of legal spheres in which their rights are articulated. A consequence of the varying degrees of legal protection of third-country nationals is, however, that this gives rise to a challenge to state sovereignty which also operates in varying degrees.

EU Citizenship and the Sense of Belonging

There is a divide which exists in the European Union between a political community defined in national terms and a transnational economic and social community. Migrants or *denizens*, as Locke referred to them,[90] find themselves belonging to the latter and benefit from the protection of human rights enshrined in international treaties and also enjoy rights associated with European Union (EU) citizenship, such as social rights, but are excluded from political citizenship.[91] The people, according to classical definitions of democratic legitimacy, are the authors of the normative framework in which they live. Historically speaking, the link forged between citizenship and political rights has provided a method according to which the nature of the polity may be identified, a perennial link which arose as part of the historical legacy of state building. Indeed, the modern history of citizenship is deeply rooted in the history of state formation[92] in which the state is characterised by the idea of the nation, of belonging to the *Patria*.[93] Whereas the history of citizenship, seen from

[89] Indeed, any social or economic rights they may vary according to whether an agreement between the Union and a particular third-country exists. At the end of 2000, approximately thirty association and co-operation agreements had been concluded between the European Community, its Member States and third countries which had implications regarding the legal status of third-country nationals in varying degrees. See M Hedemann-Robinson, 'An Overview of Recent Legal Developments at Community Level in Relation to Third-Country Nationals Resident within the European Union, with Particular Reference to the Case Law of the European Court of Justice' (2001) 38 CML Rev 525 at 527.

[90] Which has been revived in the literature on citizenship and immigration policy. See T Hammar, *European Immigration Policy: A Comparative Study* (Cambridge, Cambridge University Press, 1983).

[91] V Guiraudon, 'The Marshallian Triptych Re-Ordered: The Role of Courts and Bureaucracies in Furthering Migrant Social Rights' (1998) European University Institute Working Paper 98/4.

[92] R Debray, *L'État séducteur, les révolutions médiologiques du pouvoir* (Paris, Gallimard, 1993).

[93] See M Onaindía, *La Construción de la nación española* (Barcelona, Bailén, 2002), 100ff.

a modern perspective, is characterised by the idea of the nation, of belonging, the idea behind the concept predates the nation-state.[94] Historians would no doubt object to the use of the word 'deeply' in view of the fact that as regards the history of citizenship, state formation was a relatively recent phenomenon. Even though it appeared as late as the 19th century, however, its legacy has been such that it has become so deeply interwoven into the fabric of the citizenship debate that it is difficult to imagine a time when this was not the case. *Indeed, one wonders, how did people do without it?*

Many people, namely non-citizens, did 'do without it'. The history of citizenship is also characterised by a sense of *not* belonging. Indeed, this is the *untold history of citizenship*. 'Doing without' is also used to acknowledge that the process of belonging was in many respects a 'forced' concept. Thus, it was used by rulers in order to rally support on behalf of their subjects in the face of a military threat or of the need to boost economic production. Achieving social and political cohesion through a notion of belonging was, however, predicated on territory. Arguably, the idea of a state provided a way in which the subjects could be controlled. Control is, however, far more effective if it is subtle, even to the extent of ensuring that the controlled rarely notice its presence as part of the 'mobilisation of bias'.[95] The sense of belonging which nationalism instils is particularly persuasive if it is underwritten by cultural politics.[96] The law can play an instrumental role in 'organising culture'.[97] In other words, it can, through the adoption of certain values over others inform its content. Seen through the prism of state building, this content may serve to underpin the idea of certain essentialistic characteristics of the state through the promotion of a 'leading culture' or *Leitkultur*. In the case of the EU, references to a dominant identity are subsumed[98] under

[94] See P Costa, *Civitas. Storia della cittadinanza in Europa. 1. Dalla civilità comunale al Settecento* (Roma and Bari, Laterza, 1999), B Louis, 'Une distinction nécessaire dans L'État nation: la Communauté-nation et l'État-citoyenneté. L'Identité des sociétés occidentales modernes face à l'immigration musulmane' (1993) 31 *Revue Interdisciplinaires d'Études Juridiques* 25.

[95] See S Lukes, 'Political Ritual and Social Integration' (1975) 9 *Sociology* 289 and also Shore, n 40 at 29.

[96] See E Gellner, *Nationalism* (London, Phoenix, 1997).

[97] See T Adorno, *The Culture Industry* (London, Routledge, 1991) who is worth quoting on this issue even though he was not specifically addressing the role of law:

> Whoever speaks of culture speaks of administration as well, whether this is his intention or not. The combination of so many things lacking a common denominator — such as philosophy and religion, science and art, forms of conduct and mores — and finally the inclusion of the objective spirit of an age in the single word 'culture' betrays from the outset the administrative view, the task of which, looking down from on high, is to assemble, distribute, evaluate and organize. (See p 107.)

[98] See R Prodi, *Europe as I See It* (Cambridge, Polity Press, 2000), 5.

the Union's diversity as a whole.[99] Notions of what makes up the European *Leitkultur*, do, however, exist. The debates surrounding the European Convention are a better indication of the existence of assumptions concerning what makes a good European than the actual Draft Constitutional Treaty itself. Religion is a useful case in point. Thus, for example, the latter's nuanced references to Europe's 'cultural, religious and humanist inheritance' in the Preamble[100] reveal little of the contentious discussions over whether references ought to be made to Christianity in the Constitutional Treaty. Be that as it may, the dissemination of the European *Leitkultur* is achieved differently.[101] Unlike states, the EU has been unable to rely on the customary tools used to engender and indeed 'engineer' social cohesion through, for instance, education, conscription and a common language. Although as regards education, europeanisation has been to some extent achieved through educational exchange programmes (SOCRATES) and youth training programmes (LEONARDO). However, these efforts are hardly comparable to the pervasive effects of social cohesion achieved by national curriculae in the Member States.[102] The benefits of engendering social cohesion though culture in the EU was, as the next section will show, recognised from the outset. Implementation was, however, achieved in a different manner.

The Good European

Most people engaged in researching European integration have at one time or another come across the postcard entitled the 'Perfect European'. According to this image, the Perfect European should be, 'cooking like a Brit, driving like the French, available as a Belgian, talkative as a Finn, humorous as a German, technical as a Portuguese, flexible as a Swede, famous as a Luxembourger, patient as an Austrian, controlled as an Italian,

[99] *Ibid.* at ch 3, 'In search of Europe's Soul', pp 40–49. See also Art 128 of the EC Treaty which provides that:

> The Community shall contribute to the flowering of the cultures of the Member States while respecting their national and regional diversity and at the same time bringing the common cultural heritage to the fore.

See also the *First Report on the Consideration of Cultural Aspects in European Community Action* (Brussels, the European Commission, 1996).

[100] CONV 850/03.

[101] Indeed, as Weatherill points out, broadcasting is an example of the 'entanglement of cultural policy with trade policy'. See S Weatherill, 'Finding Space for Closer Cooperation in the Field of Culture' in G de Búrca and J Scott (eds), *Flexibility and Models of Governance for the EU* (Oxford, Hart Publishing, 2000), 237 at 245.

[102] See Shore, n 40 above, at 57 and J Shaw, 'From the Margins to the Centre: Education and Training Law and Policy' in P Craig and G de Búrca (eds) *The Evolution of EU Law* (Oxford, Oxford University Press, 1999), 555. See also A Castro Jover (ed), *Educación como transmisión de valores* (Oñati, The Oñati International Institute for the Sociology of Law, 1995).

sober as the Irish, humble as a Spaniard, generous as a Dutchman, organised as a Greek and discreet as a Dane'. The 'joke' is to be found in the inversion of these categories as the accompanying cartoons show. Thus, the Brits cannot cook, the French drive badly, the Belgians are never available, the Finns are far from talkative and so on. National stereotypes are not, however, only found in the exclusive domain of popular culture.[103]

Walter Hallstein, the first President of the European Commission, originally spoke of a European Community in terms of universals of European heritage such as inter alia Greek philosophy, ancient Rome, Christianity, Judaism, Kant, Hegel, Locke, Beethoven, Shakespeare, Dante, Goethe, Pascal and so on,[104] a position which has also found favour amongst some lawyers.[105] However, Goethe may not necessarily be meaningful to every German. Secondly, Goethe may not be meaningful to the average German. Lastly, Goethe may also not be meaningful to 'outsiders'. In other words, Elvis Presley or Coca-Cola may be more meaningful to the average German than Goethe.

The role of culture in the construction of identity has been acknowledged, with particular reference to what is referred to as the 'Other'. Accordingly, the European heritage seen through the lens of what is *not* deemed to be 'European,' as in, for example, Islam, Buddhism, Sufi-ism, Omar Kayam, Rumi. Not only does this draw attention to the presence of 'other Europes'[106] but it also forms the basis of what has been referred to as the two basic human strategies of dealing with the 'alien'.[107] One strategy is to remove boundaries by inviting the 'Other' to assimilate to the dominant identity. The other strategy is to acknowledge the validity of certain forms of bounded identity but to reach across differences in recognition of our essential humanity. To reformulate Lord Atkin's phrase in *Donoghue v Stevenson*[108] somewhat: *who then, in law, is my Other?* The question has framed discussions concerning political democracy which it owes to the legacy of state formation.

[103] See S Puntscher Riekmann, 'The Myth of European Unity' in G Hosking and G Schöpflin (eds) *Myths & Nationhood* (New York, Routledge, 1997), 60, A-M Thiesse, *La Création des identités nationales. Europe XVIII–XX siécle* (Paris, Seuil, 2001).

[104] W Hallstein, *Der unvollendete Bundesstaat* (Düsseldorf, Wien, 1969) at ch 1. See also A Smith, *National Identity* (Oxford, Clarendon Press, 1991), 119 whose list includes:

> Roman law, Judeo-Christian ethics, Renaissance humanism and individualism, Enlightenment, rationalism and science, artistic classicism and romanticism, and above all, traditions of civil rights and democracy.

This is discussed by Jo Shaw in J Shaw, 'The Many Pasts and Futures of Citizenship in the European Union' (1997) 22 ELR 554.

[105] See P Häberle, *Europäische Rechtskultur: Versuch einer Annährung in zwölf Schriften* (Baden-Baden, Nomos Verlag, 1994).

[106] G Delanty, *Inventing Europe. Idea, Identity, Reality* (London, Macmillan Press, 1995).

[107] JHH Weiler, 'Forward' in Eric Stein, *Thoughts from a Bridge: A Retrospective of Writings on New Europe and American Federalism*, (Ann Arbor, University of Michigan, 2000), xiv.

[108] [1932] AC 562 at 580.

The 'Other' customarily refers to non-nationals or non-citizens. They need not be regarded in terms of friend or enemy, or what Schmitt referred to as *Freund / Feind*, but the delineation serves to protect the continuity of ethnic units through the maintenance of a boundary. For Schmitt, political democracy is anchored in belonging to a particular people or *Volk*. In other words, the state form of democracy can only be grounded in a specific and substantive conception of equality.[109] Thus, equality is only bestowed on members of a state.[110] Schmitt regards treating foreigners or *Fremde* equally as a matter of liberal rights to freedom, which he does not classify as being political considerations. Thus, equality is not defined legally, politically or economically but belongs, as far as constitutional theory is concerned, to liberal individualism and the principle of basic rights.

Generally speaking, the writings of Schmitt are of limited relevance to the process of European integration as a whole despite the fact that his spirit lives on in some select academic circles[111] not to mention in a handful of judicial decisions. A notable example, the *Maastricht* decision by the German constitutional court[112] was referred to in the previous chapter in relation to fundamental rights. The basis of the claim, however, was one which was framed in terms of democratic legitimacy by a plaintiff who viewed Germany's membership of the EU as a violation of his right to vote as contained in article 34 of the German Basic Law. The 'democratic legitimacy' audit by the German Constitutional Court is notable, not because of its 'ethnic' definitions of the people, as has been suggested by some,[113] but rather by virtue of its illustration of the indelible link between political rights, citizenship and demos as well as the lengths to which courts will protect what they see as integral parts of state sovereignty, taking their cue from classical state theory in which the state is sovereign over both its territory and people.[114]

Schmitt usefully illustrates the tradition in state theory of excluding individuals from the 'inner circle' of political participation by virtue of nationality predicated on an a priori metaphysical notion of a *Volk*.

[109] C Schmitt, *Verfassungslehre* (Berlin, Duncker & Humblot, 1928), 226.

[110] '[w]er nicht Staatsangehöriger ist, kommt für diese demokratische Gleichheit nicht in betracht.' *Ibid* at 227.

[111] See P Zumbansen, 'Carl Schmitt und die Suche nach politischer Einheit' (1997) 30 *Kritische Justiz* 63.

[112] See M Zuleeg, 'The European Constitution under Constitutional Constraints: The German Scenario' (1997) 22 ELR 19.

[113] See JHH Weiler, 'Does Europe Need a Constitution? Demos, Telos and the German Maastricht Decision' (1995) 1 *European Law Journal* 259.

[114] Thus as Brownlie succinctly notes, the characteristics of sovereignty and equality of states are:
1) jurisdiction, prima facie exclusive, over a territory and the population living there;
2) a duty of non-interference in the area of exclusive jurisdiction of other states; and
3) the dependence of obligations arising from customary law and treaties on the consent of the obligor. (I Brownlie, *Principles of Public International Law* (Oxford, Clarendon Press, 1990), 287.)

Whereas nationality laws need not necessarily draw from a priori notions, they tend to focus on a notion of identity which is homogeneous, static, fixed and which for many is more imagined than real.[115] The presence of a leading culture may, in many cases, mean that 'insiders' may also be 'outsiders'. Following this line of reasoning, the 'Other' may be described as being in all of us. The view of state formation which emerges is one which colonised identity, leading to an indelible link being forged between citizenship and nationality. The rejoinder often made here is that identity is multi-faceted; it is a veritable kaleidoscope of qualities,[116] which are not necessarily bound by a state predicated on national 'essence'. The last point draws from Gellner's position that the state was first created with nationhood and identity predicated on cohesion — affected or otherwise — being a secondary part of the chain of causation.[117] Ordinarily speaking, States have been created in the absence of a political culture. This is not the case as regards the EU, which already has an established political culture, institutionally and ideologically speaking. In other words, it has customarily been a case of making the state and then the citizens. In the case of the EU, however, it has been the other way around.

It is arguable that the central barrier to a unified concept of European citizenship has been the state-centred perspective tension between national and European citizenship.[118] Subsidiarity has avoided a conflict between the two by conceptualising EU citizenship so that it leaves national conceptions of citizenship virtually untouched,[119] despite the European Court of Justice's attempt to interpret this selectively.[120] However, this only accounts for part of the picture, so to speak, as third-country nationals who reside in the Union benefit from social and civil rights.[121] Indeed, the legal position of third-country nationals who are resident in the Union is highly fragmented between the Community level which has yet to adopt a uniform position regarding their rights, and the international level, where their rights are embedded in a plethora of international agreements.[122] The categories of exclusion and inclusion are not as clearly defined as customary understandings of EU citizenship would have us believe. Elements of a

[115] See B Anderson, *Imagined Communities* (London, Verso, 1983).

[116] E Morin, *L'Identité humaine* (Paris, Seuil, 2001), 70.

[117] E Gellner, *Nations and Nationalism* (Oxford, Blackwell, 1983).

[118] J Shaw and A Wiener, 'The Paradox of the European Polity' in M Green Cowles and M Smith (eds) *State of the European Union 5: Risks, Reform, Resistance and Revival* (Oxford, Oxford University Press, 2000), 64.

[119] See CN Kakouris, 'The Case Law of the European Court of Justice on Immigration' in GD Korella and PM Twomey (eds), *Towards a European Immigration Policy* (Brussels, European Interuniversity Press, 1994), 155.

[120] See Case C–369/90 *Micheletti* [1992] ECR I–4239.

[121] See generally E Staples, *The Legal Status of Third-Country Nationals Resident in the European Union* (The Hague, Kluwer Law International, 1999).

[122] See Hedemann-Robinson, n 89 above.

'dominant identity' to which all individuals, including EU and non-EU citizens, must assimilate if they are to be considered 'European' exist. They may, however, in effect exclude those who are de jure on the 'inside' of the Union, that is to say, EU citizens, for whom the underlying assumptions which exist as regards European identity and the cultural heritage of the EU is as remote as it might be for third-country nationals. The German *Leitkultur* debate, which focuses on the Judeo-Christian tradition, the enlightenment and humanism, excludes many of those who reside in Germany, both Germans and non-Germans alike. Though nuanced, the debates concerning the European *Leitkultur* can do little to deny the legacy of market building.[123] Appeals to a European heritage made by *Hallstein*, for example, were made in the context, not of state building,[124] but of the market. It has been argued that EU citizenship illustrates how a narrow notion of citizenship reinforces exclusion. Thus, for example, a narrow concept of social policy tends to reinforce social exclusion particularly vis-à-vis those outside the labour market.[125] The 'Good European' is economically active and uses his or her right to freedom of movement in order to further the cause of European integration. Given the traditional link between political rights and citizenship, the mobile or 'transient' EU citizen is best seen but not heard in matters of political participation where matters of a purely 'national interest' are at stake. Indeed, the political rights which attach to EU citizenship in fact challenge classical state theories of democratic legitimacy which are premised on subjects who form part of a stable community and who remain within a state's borders. An interesting illustration of the influence of this legacy on the legal reasoning behind political rights is provided by decisions of the German Federal Constitutional Court concerning the right of third-country nationals to vote in local elections.[126]

Generally speaking, migrants have been unable to participate in the political processes in Germany.[127] Legislation was enacted in some *Länder*,

[123] See M Everson, 'The Legacy of the Market Citizen' in J Shaw and G Moore (eds) *New Legal Dynamics of the European Union* (Oxford, Clarendon Press, 1995), 73 and also T Downes, 'Market Citizenship: Functionalism and Fig-leaves' in R Bellamy and A Warleigh (eds) *Citizenship and Governance in the European Union* (London, Continuum, 2001), 93.

[124] Despite views of some who have argued that the European integration will probably result in some form of statehood. See GF Mancini, 'Europe: the Case for Statehood' (1998) 4 *European Law Journal* 29.

[125] G Room, 'Social Quality in Europe. Perspectives on Social Exclusion' in W Beck, L Van der Maesen and A Walker (eds) *The Social Quality of Europe* (The Hague, Kluwer Law International, 1997), 255.

[126] See GL Neuman, '"We are the People": Alien Suffrage in German and American Perspective.' (1992) 35 *Michigan Journal of International Law* 237.

[127] There have, however, been exceptions, such as the *Party of Expellees and Deprived* (BHE) which was founded by refugees which at one stage became the second party in Schleswig-Holstein in 1950, polling 23.4 % of the votes. In 1953, a total of 27 members were elected to the *Bundestag* and participated with two ministers in the federal cabinet. However, the participation in the political process was short lived and the party lost its importance by the early 1960s. In the 1970s, however, Germany saw fit to establish the post of a foreigners'

namely, Hamburg,[128] Schleswig-Holstein,[129] and Bremen,[130] at the end of the 1980s to allow third-country nationals to vote in local elections. However, this legislation was held to be irreconcilable with the Basic Law (in particular article 28) by the Federal Constitutional Court.[131] The court's reasoning was somewhat constrained by Article 116 of the Basic Law which defines German nationals. Notwithstanding, the judgment illustrates the challenge of a moveable polity to classical notions of popular sovereignty.

Let us begin with the definition of foreigner advanced in the three legislative documents — given that the definition was by no means universal. In Hamburg, for example, foreigners were defined as being all those who had lived in Germany for least eight years.[132] In Bremen, foreigners entitled to vote in local and municipal elections had to have resided in the city for at least four years.[133] Whilst Schleswig-Holstein's residence provision amounted to five years, it limited its definition of foreigners to a handful of nationalities, namely, Danish, Irish, Dutch, Swedish and Swiss nationals. The justification for limiting the voting rights to these nationalities remains elusive.[134]

In the case of Schleswig-Holstein, it was argued that people allowed to vote in local elections referred to those holding German nationality in other words *das deutsche Volk*. Article 17 (2) sentence 2 of the Weimar Constitution (WRV) was recalled which referred to *reichsdeutschen Männer und Frauen*. Being a member of a state was characterised by an insoluble bond of personal rights between the state and the citizen.[135] It was argued that foreigners could return to their homeland at any time.[136] Moreover, foreigners might also leave the region at any time without having to suffer the consequences of their decision.[137] The fact that a German could do the same does not seem to have troubled the court.

commissioner, a sort of ombudsman (*Ausländerbeauftragter*) to write a report on the situation advising appropriate policy changes. See D Thränhardt, 'Europe — A New Immigration Continent. Politics and Policies since 1945 in Comparative Perspective' in D Thränhardt (ed), *Europe: A New Immigration Continent. Policies and Politics in Comparative Perspective* (Münster, Lit, 1992), 15.

[128] GVBl 1989, Teil 1 S 29.
[129] GVBl 1989, S 12.
[130] GVOBl 1989, S 241.
[131] Case of the Federal Constitutional Court from 31 October 1990, 2 BvF 2/89, 6/89; 2 BvF 3/89. Note that this case was somewhat overtaken by the event of the TEU which provided EU nationals with the ability to vote and stand in local elections (Art 19 EC Treaty).
[132] Art 1 § 6 (2) GVBl. 1989, Teil I, S 29.
[133] § 3 (2) GVBl. 1989, S 241.
[134] See Art 1 § 3 (2), GVBl. 1989, S 12.
[135] This ethnic conception of 'the People' was also followed in the Hamburg case. See 2 BvF 3 /89 at 71.
[136] 2 BvF 3 /89 at 40
[137] *Ibid* at 41.

The arguments in favour of upholding the right to foreigners to vote in local elections were more inclusive. Thus, it was argued that the model for the Basic Law was based on people and not on the notion of a collective nation. Discrimination between people belonging to the state and those outside it (*Untertanen Verband)* was unacceptable. The People or *das Volk* concerned the legitimacy of decision-making and the sovereignty of the people as opposed to a nationalist definition. In short, the people did not necessarily mean the *German* people.[138] The Court placed great emphasis on the people having an effective influence on the power exercised by the state whose acts must be traceable to the will of the people.[139] What if, however, the people are not static?

The judgment preceded the EU citizenship provisions introduced by the Maastricht Treaty which inter alia granted the EU citizen political rights which do not, however, correspond to the political rights of nationals of Member States of the EU. In effect, this gives rise to a hierarchy of rights holders. This hierarchy has, however, tended to be viewed in terms of binary models of reasoning predicated on 'insiders' and 'outsiders', which has been instrumentalised in the debate concerning European integration in terms of 'Fortress Europe'. It is not, as has already been suggested, the most appropriate model for understanding political rights in the EU.

The challenge to state sovereignty is not extensive given that EU citizenship appears to leave state competence concerning the definition of the state's polity untouched, relatively speaking.[140] Be that as it may, EU citizenship, not to mention the development of an EU immigration and asylum law and policy[141] has had considerable consequences for the Member States' capacity to define their polities given that they are faced with the moveable polities of EU citizens and third-country nationals caused by free movement and migration respectively. The challenge is more discernible by focusing on the role of elites who have, traditionally speaking, acted as the interlocutors in the process of state formation.[142] Elites have been crucial in 'bringing the nation

[138] See Weiler, n 113 above.

[139] BVerfGE 83, 60–81 at 72.

[140] Thus Art 17 of the EC Treaty provides that:

> Citizenship of the Union is hereby established. Every person holding the nationality of a Member State shall be a citizen of the Union. Citizenship of the Union shall complement and not replace national citizenship.

[141] See generally J Monar, 'Justice and Home Affairs in the Treaty of Amsterdam: Reform at the Price of Fragmentation' (1998) 23 ELR 320; K Hailbronner and C Thiery, 'Asylrecht und Einwanderung sowie Überführung des Schengen-Besitzstands aud EU-Ebene' (1998) 5 *Europarecht* 583; B Marschang, 'Mißtrauen, Abschottung, Eigensinn — Entwicklungslinien der europäischen Asylrechts <harmonisierung> bis zum Amsterdamer Vertrag' (1998) 69 *Kritische Justiz* 69 and also E Guild, *The Developing Immigration and Asylum Law of the EU* (The Hague, Kluwer Law International, 1995).

[142] See generally R Bendix, *Nation-building & Citizenship* (New Brunswick, Transaction Publishers, 1996) at ch 4, 'Administrative Authority in the Nation-State', 127–72.

home to the people' through the mediums of race, territory and language and a sense of common history. They have also been crucial in recognising and implementing rights and policies which mediate the relationship between the citizen and the state. Indeed, their co-operation is crucial as rights mean very little if they are not implemented. The forms of political participation in the EU are facilitated by elites such as judges and public authority officials. The policy of the Member States has tended to be one of resistance in the face of the challenge posed by European political rights, not in relation to the provisions contained in the Treaties per se, but in relation to their impact on the national constitutional orders and cultures. The process of constitutional adjustment is, as the Member States have long since recognised, where the tension between state sovereignty and a supranational organisation is most acute. It is of little surprise that in its final report to the members of the European Convention, Working Group V recommended redrafting article 6 (3) TEU in such a way as to clarify what was meant by essential elements of national identity. These included inter alia political and constitutional structure, regional and local self-government, choices regarding languages, national citizenship and territory.[143] Article 6 (3) TEU protects diversity to the extent that, 'The Union shall respect the national identities of its Member States.' The Draft Constitutional Treaty provides that respect of the national identities of the Member States includes respect of what is

> inherent in their fundamental structures, political and constitutional, inclusive of regional and local self-government. It shall respect their essential State functions, including those for ensuring the territorial integrity of the State, and for maintaining law and order and safeguarding internal security.[144]

There are no references to national public services although they fall under fundamental structures and essential elements of national identity. The case law regarding access to public service employment under article 39 (4) provides a useful example of where the challenge a Member State's sovereignty regarding the definition of polity definition is actually located which sheds considerable light on the inherent tension between sovereignty and identity which underwrites the notion of European political rights.

Access to Public Service Employment

Generally speaking, the exclusion of non-nationals from employment in the public service has been widely accepted both under international and

[143] CONV 375/1/02.
[144] See Art 5 (1) of the Draft.

European law[145] on the basis of loyalty and special allegiance existing between public sector employees and the state.[146] This notion is articulated in the EC treaty courtesy of article 39 (4) which provides that the free movement provisions do not apply to employment in the public service.[147] The assumption which exists is that non-nationals cannot be trusted to serve the state as loyally as the state's nationals. This explains why Member States have been so willing to define those public service positions which qualify as an exception to the freedom of movement as widely as possible.[148] This is in contrast to the European Court of Justice, which has repeatedly attempted to define the exceptions to the free movement provisions as narrowly as possible, showing a slight inconsistency in its approach given that it has done precisely the opposite in relation to the direct effect of directives.[149] Indeed, there, the ECJ has elected to define 'the State' very widely, thereby illustrating the *effet utile* which underlines its decisions.[150] In *Marshall*, the State was taken to include all organs of the state and not just the central civil service. In *Costanzo*, the State was held to include all organs of administration, including decentralised authorities such as municipalities.[151] In *Foster*, the state was held to include those bodies which provided a public service under the control of the State.[152] As regards the public service exception, however,

[145] See generally N Beenen, *Citizenship, Nationality and Access to Public Service Employment: The Impact of European Community Law* (Groningen, Europa Law Publishing, 2001) particularly at pp 72–73 and also D O'Keefe, 'Judicial Interpretation of the Public Service Exeption in Article 48, paragraph 4 of the EEC Treaty' in D Curtin and D O'Keefe (eds) *Constitutional Adjudication in European Community and National Law* (Dublin, Butterworths, 1992), 89.

[146] See, eg, para 4.I.I. of the UK Civil Service Management Code which provides that civil servants owe a duty of loyal service to the Crown as their employer. See generally C Demmke and U Linke, 'Who's a National and Who's a European? Exercising Public Power and the Legitimacy of Art 39 4 EC in the 21st Century' (2003) 2 *EIPAscope* 2.

[147] In some Member States, loyalty is not only presumed but in some cases, is explicitly called upon as an essential element of the job description. Thus, Art 33 of the German Basic Law, for example, not only upholds a nationality requirement for certain posts in the public service but it also includes a stipulation as to loyalty between members of the public service and the State.

> Die Ausübung hoheitsrechtlicher Befugnisse ist als ständiger Aufgabe in der Regel Angehörigen des öffentlichen Dienstes zu übertragen, die in einem öffentlichrechtlichen Dienst — und Treueverhältnis stehen. (Art 33, para 4).

[148] The Commission decided in 1988 that Art 39 (4) covered specific functions of the state such as inter alia the armed forces, the police, the judiciary, tax authorities and the diplomatic corps. See Communication 88/c72/02: Freedom of Movement of Workers and Access to Employment in the Public Service of the Member States. Commission Action in Respect of the Application of Article 39 (4) of the EC Treaty (OJ 1988 C72/2). However, the Commission also clearly stated that not all jobs exercising state functions fall within the scope of article 39 (4). See Communication from the Commission, COM (2002) 694 final, 11 December 2002.

[149] See Case C–152/84 *Marshall v Southampton and South-West Hampshire Health Authority* [1986] ECR 723. See generally S Prechal, *Directives in European Community Law* (Oxford, Clarendon Press, 1995).

[150] Presumably to mitigate the absence of horizontal direct effect. See Case C–91/92 *Faccini Dori v Recreb Srl.* [1994] ECR I–3325.

[151] See Case C–103/88 *Fratelli Costanzo v Commune di Milano* [1989] ECR 1839.

[152] See Case C–188/89 *Foster and others v British Gas Plc* [1990] ECR I–3133.

the Court has concentrated not on who controls the body, but on the duties and tasks performed by it.[153] The test it outlined in *Commission v Belgium* seems innocuous enough as regards constituting a challenge to state sovereignty given that the sector involved was advertisements by the Belgian national railways and certain posts advertised by the City of Brussels.[154] Moreover, the Court acknowledged the importance of loyalty for those posts which

> involve direct or indirect participation in the exercise of powers conferred by public law and duties designed to safeguard the general interests of the state or other public authorities.[155]

It stated that such posts presumed a 'special relationship of allegiance to the state and reciprocity of rights and duties which form the foundation of the bond of nationality'.[156] The ECJ has also created several inroads into other areas which have been traditionally regarded as belonging to the exclusive competence of the state.

As regards health, for example, the posts of nurses in public hospitals were not construed as constituting employment in the public service within the meaning of article 48 (4) of the Treaty.[157] As regards education, the post of a trainee teacher was held not to involve direct or indirect participation in the exercise of official powers conferred by public law and did not thereby qualify as a legitimate exception for the purposes of article 39.[158] The policy of the Italian National Research Council (Consiglio Nazionale delle Ricerche (CNR)) is to grant non-national researchers working for the Council fixed-term. The Court held that this could not be justified in view of the fact that the researchers were not responsible for managerial duties in the laboratories or for advising the State regarding scientific questions. Education is an interesting example because even though the Court held that the protection of national identity was a legitimate aim, is could not be used to justify the use of a nationality requirement in matters relating to education.[159] The reticence exhibited towards including non-nationals in posts of public service is premised on a fundamental *malaise* which state institutions have concerning a moveable polity. In other words, trust is best

[153] See Case C–149/79 *Commission v Belgium* [1980] ECR 3881 and [1982] ECR 1845.
[154] Such as night-watchmen, plumbers and gardeners.
[155] See Case C–149/79 *Commission v Belgium* [1980] ECR 3881 and [1982] ECR 1845 para 10
[156] *Ibid*
[157] Case C–307–84 *Commission v France* [1986] ECR 1725, para13.
[158] Case C–66/85 *Lawrie-Blum v Land Baden-Württemburg* [1986] ECR 2121. See also Case C–33/88 *Allué v Coonan* [1989] ECR 1591 and Case C–4/91 *Bleis v Ministère de l'Éducation Nationale* [1991] ECR I–5627.
[159] See Case C–473/93 *Commission v Luxembourg* [1996] ECR I–3207.

vested in representatives of the static polity where matters pertain, to paraphrase the Draft Constitutional Treaty, 'essential State functions'.[160]

CONCLUSION

It is clear that in order to assess the extent of the 'evolving concept of EU citizenship', to paraphrase the words of the Spanish presidency,[161] the parameters of the enquiry must be framed more broadly in order to accommodate the development of rights both within and outwith its confines. EU citizenship may be merely symbolic. Symbolism, however, is important. Indeed, during the deliberations of the European Convention amendments were suggested to include references to both the citizens *and* the peoples of Europe in article 1 which governs the establishment of the Union,[162] a move which was fiercely resisted by some delegates.[163] The final Draft Constitutional Treaty refers to the peoples of Europe in the preamble but provide that the will to build a common future is one which is of the citizens and States of Europe.[164]

Political rights in the EU illustrate how far they have evolved both in conceptual and in structural terms, an issue which is not apparent on a strict reading of the citizenship provisions contained in the EC Treaty which are framed in classical terms of political legitimacy. The symbolism with which the Maastricht provisions were vested, however, was not only directed at the citizens of Europe but was also an attempt to symbolise that the sovereignty of the Member States had remained intact as regards not only citizenship and nationality but also the methods by which those citizens could influence the process of will formation. The rhetoric of policy makers emphasises uniformity and homogenisation which is at odds with the cold light of day of legal practice in the EU. In other words, the former continue to both deliberate and operate within a context, or paradigm, which bears little resemblance to the context of flexibility, in a polity which is framed by an overlap of national and supranational spheres underwritten by multi-level forms of governance. As the previous chapter showed, judges also conceive of their role as being one which is predicated on uniformity and homogenisation. They have, however, as this Chapter has shown, played an instrumental role in framing the articulation of political rights in a broader sense, albeit unwittingly, rather like Chaplinesque figures who

[160] See Art 5 of the Draft Constitutional Treaty (CONV 850/03).
[161] See generally Closa, n 30 above.
[162] See CONV 574/1/03 REV 1 and in particular the amendments proposed by Fischer, Palacio et al.
[163] Notably by Badinter, Hain *et al*. See CONV 574/1/03 REV 1.
[164] See CONV 850/03.

are unaware of the 'bigger picture' of *Modern Times*. Their attempts to resolve the tricky relationship between people, territory and the state illustrates that the tensions caused by the transfer of sovereignty to a supranational organisation such as the EU have culminated in a reconfiguration of the concept of political rights which exist within the legal cultures of the Member States both in principle and as regards implementation. Social rights provide a further case in point.

4

Social Rights

INTRODUCTION

SOCIAL RIGHTS HAVE emerged in a variety of policy contexts, most of which have been taken up in legislation and have been enforced under the auspices of the Charter of Fundamental Rights. Most importantly, this is the case in the areas of social policy and labour[1] but it is also relevant to housing, discrimination (racial, ethnic, sex),[2] equal treatment for EU migrants, co-ordination of social security entitlements and the impact of free movement of services and entitlements to health care in the context of the internal market.[3] Consequently, social rights provide a useful case study of the challenge posed by European rights to legal cultures of the Member States. Questions of social security have customarily been regarded as being within the exclusive competence of the Member States, though the word 'exclusive' is somewhat misleading as it tends to ignore the impact of europeanisationon the Member States' legal cultures not to mention their administrative and bureaucratic structures and decision-making in a variety of areas. In order to examine the issue of europeanisation, I shall concentrate on the policy of cross-border access to health care. Free movement of this kind is arguably not the most appropriate test for social rights *stricto sensu*. It does, however, reveal the tension between social rights *stricto sensu* and economic rights with a social dimension.[4] It is this competitive tension which gives rise to an ambiguity

[1] See generally A Lo Faro, *Regulating Social Europe: Reality and Myth of Collective Bargaining in the EC Legal Order* (Oxford, Hart Publishing, 2000).
[2] See, eg, Art 13 EC taken in conjunction with Art 3 of the anti-racism directive which includes the prohibition of discrimination in relation to social protection, health care, housing and education. See Directive 2000/43 [2000] OJ L180/22. See generally M Bell, *Anti-discrimination Law and the EU* (Oxford, Oxford University Press, 2002).
[3] AP van der Mei, 'Cross-border Access to Medical Care within the European Union: Some Reflections on the Judgments in Decker and Kohll' (1998) 5 *Maastricht Journal of European and Comparative Law* 277.
[4] For an illustration of the social dimension of the free movement provisions see C 286/82 & 26/83 *Luisi & Carbone v Ministero del Tesoro* [1984] ECR 377. As for the gradual incorporation of social and economic objectives under the aegis of social policy compare Case 80/70 *Defrenne v Belgium* [1971] ECR 455 and Cases C–270/97 & C–271/97 *Deutsche Post v Sievers and Schrage* [2000] ECR I–929.

at both the policy making stage and at the level of implementation leading to a certain overlap of EU competences. Much of the policy measures regarding health, for example, have been developed under the aegis of social protection.[5]

I begin by examining the case law of the European Court of Justice in the light of the Charter of Fundamental Rights and the Draft Constitutional Treaty. I shall then move on to discuss the ECJ's most recent ruling in this area, the *Müller-Fauré* case, which raises a number of salient issues as regards future policy practice in this area. Cross-border access to health care has three important implications for the development of a social rights agenda in EU constitution-making. First, it illustrates the increasing trend towards the adoption of the language of rights and fundamental freedoms, albeit through the prism of the internal market. Secondly, it illustrates the importance of policies through which rights can be articulated. Thirdly, policies mean very little if there is no effective implementation in practice, that is to say, the realisation of rights is heavily dependent upon national elites — in this case of ministry of health officials and their local counterparts, medical professionals, hospital administrators and insurance brokers. Indeed, it is here that the impact is particularly acute yet the lack of empirical work means that we know very little of practice in this area. Health economics as a discipline is in its infancy in the EU, if not non-existent as compared with the United States, Canada, Australia and New Zealand. Studies which have been conducted within the EU have addressed the issue of capacity by national health care systems vis-à-vis cross-border access to health care as well as compliance by medical professionals to enable patients in the EU to activate their rights. Their co-operation is essential. In one study, some doctors involved in a National Health Service (NHS) pilot scheme[6] knew very little about cross-border access or did not agree with it in principle on the grounds of value for money for the tax payer and moreover were uneasy about patient care being fragmented along supranational lines, particularly in relation to reintegrating patients into the national health-care system once they had been treated in another Member State.[7] Thus, capacity for implementation depends on knowledge of the relevant professionals, values (do they believe in the european social rights' agenda?), functional adaptiveness (can health care cope with such patients and practices?), and resources (do they have the money to support it?).

[5] Indeed, it is of interest to note the inclusion of health in policy co-operation initiatives under the aegis of social protection. See COM (2003) 261 final, *Strengthening the Social Dimension of the Lisbon strategy: Streamlining Open coordination in the Field of Social Protection* at p 15. See also COM (2003) 57 final, *Scoreboard on Implementing the Social Policy Agenda* at p 20.

[6] YHE Consortium, *Evaluation of Treating Patient's Overseas* (York, The University of York, 2002).

[7] *Ibid* at p 86.

Lawyers tend to be more reluctant to frame the debates on social welfare in terms of rights.[8] Part of the reason is that legal reasoning tends to act in such a way so as to enforce the need to qualify the use of the language of rights. At least, legal reasoning constrains lawyers in such a way so as to preclude referring to certain claims in terms of rights. Moreover, lawyers tend to be more sceptical as to the effectiveness of rights vis-à-vis questions of social welfare. As it has been argued, there is no tight connection between social rights in a constitution and the benevolence of social welfare policy.[9] Rights have, however, acted as symbolic and ideological covenants in order to generate the idea of 'national' social cohesion, whether 'civic' or 'ethnic'. The intrinsic link between rights and welfare was pivotal to the development of the modern European nation-state between 1870–1970. By the third quarter of the 20th century, European states were as much recognised as being 'welfare states' as 'nation-states'.[10] The role of rights as an instrument for underwriting socio-economic minimum standards was central to the process of state formation through the cohesive link between the state, its people and welfare.[11] The 'sense of belonging' referred to in the previous chapter in relation to political rights was generally articulated through principles and concepts such as solidarity, community and the right to existential minimums which were instrumentalised to engender loyalty to the state.[12] The enjoyment of existential fundamental rights was a key basis for the capacity to enjoy 'full membership'[13] of society,[14] at least symbolically speaking.

[8] Although they may do so as regards public international law. See generally A Eide, C Krause and C Rosas (eds), *Economic, Social and Cultural Rights: A Textbook* (Dordrecht, Kluwer, 1995).

[9] See W Sadurski, 'Postcommunist Charters of Rights in Europe and the U.S. Bill of Rights' (2002) 65 *Law and Contemporary Problems* 223 at 229.

[10] See, eg, DE Ashford, *The Emergence of the Welfare States* (Oxford, Blackwell, 1986), GV Rimlinger, *Welfare Policy and Industrialization in Europe, America and Russia* (New York, Wiley, 1971) and also KG Banting, 'The Welfare State as Statecraft: Territorial Politics and Canadian Social Policy' in S Leibfried and P Pierson (eds) *European Social Policy: Between Fragmentation and Integration* (Washington DC, Brookings Institute, 1995), 269.

[11] See generally J Fink, G Lewis and J Clarke (eds), *Rethinking European Welfare* (London, Sage, 2001). The concept of social rights may be traced back to the 1793 French Constitution (Art 21). The German *Weimar* Constitution contained social basic rights such as, for example, the right to work (Art 163 II), the care for illness, accidents and age (Art 161) and the care for accommodation (Art 155). Early conceptions of the role of the State were based on the individual's freedom from the State. Accordingly, society was able to pursue economic and cultural objectives on its own, needing the State only to defend the security of the individual through the army, the police and the justice system. This conception evolved, particularly in the post-war period where, in States such as Germany, for example, the State was viewed as having a duty to both guarantee and enable the individual to realise his rights. See EW Böckenförde, 'Die sozialen Grundrechten im Verfassungsgefüge' in EW Böckenförde, J Jekemitz and T Ramm (eds), *Soziale Grundrechte: Von der bürgerlichen zur sozialen Rechtsordnung* (Heidelberg, CF Müller, 1981), 7.

[12] See M Hechter, *Containing Nationalism* (Oxford, Oxford University Press, 2000).

[13] See TH Marshall, *Citizenship and Social Class and Other Essays* (Cambridge, Cambridge University Press, 1950).

[14] See generally R Burrows and B Loader (eds), *Towards a Post-Fordist Welfare State?* (London, Routledge, 1994), G Esping-Anderson, *The Three Worlds of Welfare Capitalism* (Princeton, Princeton University Press, 1990).

The last quarter of the 20th century saw a gradual shift away from the shared heritage in Europe where the state was the sole guarantor of social welfare which, together with the concomitant impact of globalisation,[15] has reconfigured the European state, both structurally and conceptually speaking.[16] The state no longer remains the sole guarantor of social entitlements. In this period the concept of government has increasingly lost ground to the concept of governance,[17] which permeates the borders of the nation-state. Social welfare is one of the policy areas where the rise of EU governance has created an immense challenge to the traditional territoriality of government states. Classical understandings of citizenship are situated at the axis of the individual and the state. The vocabulary of citizenship is the vocabulary of the state. The language of social rights is also statist.[18] This is somewhat problematic when we speak of social rights in the EU given that classical understandings of citizenship are situated at the axis of the individual and the state. Social rights in the EU are linked with an EU polity which is not territorially bound, and yet, as a consequence of EC law and the free movement provisions contained therein, citizens are able to make claims to social welfare in Member States other than their own. It is not, however, only the addressees of social rights who cut across the borders of the nation-state. The key actors who shape social policy are also drawn from a wider pool of participants. The role of civil society has also increased exponentially[19] along with methods of policy-making which cut across state hierarchies. The emergence of the Open-Method of Co-ordination (OMC) is a case in point,[20] particularly as it introduces the concept of

[15] Which some have elected to refer to in terms of the shift from the welfare state to the welfare society. See P Donati, *Riposte alle crisi dello stato sociale*: *Le nuove politiche sociali in prospettiva sociologica* (Milano, Franco Angeli, 1984), 261ff. See also R Sykes, B Palier and PM Prior (eds), *Globalization and European Welfare States* (London, Palgrave, 2001).

[16] See generally M Rhodes, M Ferrera and A Hemerijck, 'The Future of the European "Social Model" in the Global Economy' (2001) 3 *Journal of Comparative Policy Analysis* 1.

[17] As regards the latter see C Barnard and S Deakin, 'Corporate Governance, European Governance and Social Rights' in B Hepple (ed), *Social and Labour Rights in a Global Context*: *International and Comparative Perspectives* (Cambridge, Cambridge University Press, 2002), 122.

[18] Which is particularly problematic in the case of the determination of social policies at the global level which are framed in the realm of foreign and commercial policy. See M Poiares Maduro, 'Is There Any Such Thing as Free of Fair Trade? A Constitutional Analysis of the Impact of International Trade on the European Social Model' in G de Búrca and J Scott (eds), *The EU and the WTO*: *Legal and Constitutional Issues* (Oxford, Hart Publishing, 2001), 257 at 267.

[19] See Commission of the European Communities *European Governance: A White Paper* COM (2001) 428 final Brussels (25 July 2001).

[20] Which was codified at the Lisbon Summit in March 2000. See the Presidency Conclusions, Lisbon European Council, 23 and 24 March 2000. See M Télo, 'Governance and Government in the European Union: The Open Method of Co-ordination' in MJ Rodrigues (ed), *The New Knowledge Economy in Europe*: *A Strategy for International Competitiveness and Social Cohesion* (Cheltenham, Edward Elgar Publishing, 2002), 242. See also A Héritier, 'New Modes of Governance in Europe: Increasing Political Efficiency and Policy Effectiveness?' in T Boerzel and E Chicowski (ed) *State of the European Union* (Oxford, Oxford University Press, 2003).

'variable forms of partnership'[21] though it is debatable whether this in effect opens up the debate to civil society as a whole.

Furthermore, in the EU, the broad granting of social welfare rights results in a tension between the polity as politically exclusive and the welfare state as socially inclusive. Whereas the polity carves its borders through markers of political inclusion, namely, the legal and political benefits which a polity attributes to the members of the political system (right to vote, right to stand for election etc), in contrast the welfare state is a key vehicle for inclusion as it provides for 'residents' as opposed to 'citizens'. Whilst civil rights are enjoyed by all, the territorial base of the nation-state and transnational scope of welfare provisions generate a permanent — and to some extent conflicting — tension between different types of inclusion or spheres of belonging.

Moreover, some spheres in which social rights have been articulated are more developed than others. Indeed, as has been acknowledged, EU social policy represents a 'microcosm' of the flexibility debate in the sense envisaged in article 11 of the EC Treaty.[22] It is a microcosm within which the respective traditions amongst the Member States as regards social rights and policy are reconfigured, and considerably so, thereby recalibrating their sovereignty and by implication their identity. Whereas the requirement to respect the Member States' identity is upheld by the Treaty of European Union (article 6 (3)), it is clear that the protection of diversity envisaged is subject to the qualifications imposed by European integration.

EMBRACING DIVERSITY

Social rights in the EU are shaped by two fundamental realities: first, the existing diversity of Member States, and secondly, the underlying impetus of convergence pressures. The experiences amongst the Member States regarding welfare differ markedly.[23] In Spain, for example, they constitute interests due to the fact that their constitutionality cannot be challenged by way of a constitutional complaint.[24] The 1937 Irish Constitution refers to social policy and makes whole areas of social policy part of the constitutional order of

[21] See the Presidency Conclusions, Lisbon European Council, 23 and 24 March 2000, para 38. See also COM (2000) 379 at p 8.

[22] See C Barnard, 'Flexibility and Social Policy' in G de Búrca and J Scott (eds) *Flexibility and Models of Governance for the EU* (Oxford, Hart Publishing, 2000), 197.

[23] See, eg, P Guibentif and D Bouget, *Minimum Income Policies in the European Union* (Lisbon, União das Mutualidades Portuguesas, 1997).

[24] See generally C Villiers, *The Spanish Legal Tradition* (Dartmouth, Ashgate, 1999). See also E Bandrés Moliné, G Fernández and F C García-Moreno (eds), *Derecho, economía y sociedad en España* (Madrid, Escuela Libre Editorial - Las Estructuras del Bienestar, 1997) and also JA Garde (ed), *Políticas sociales y estado de bienestar en España* (Madrid, Trotta, 1999).

the state (family, marriage, etc).[25] In the case of Germany, article 20 (1) refers to a 'social Federal State' and article 28 (1) refers to a '*sozial Staat*' of the Basic Law. The State's legal obligation, however, does not translate into justiciable individual rights.[26] Social rights are programmatic to the extent that they are aimed at guaranteeing an existential minimum.[27]

For many EU Member States, social components are framed by the constitution and the values which are established as part of the constitutional order set out therein.[28] These basic constitutional values are a vital mechanism for underpinning a state's identity. The issue of the relationship between the EU's 'identity' and 'social rights' has been confronted in the context of free trade and globalisation in which the EU has been described as having to face the identity of its social policy.[29] It was also an issue which was addressed by the European Convention. Indeed, those who favoured references to the Union as a 'social market economy' as opposed to the current Treaty reference to an open market economy[30] eventually won the day.[31] Be that as it may, it is a social market economy which is characterised by diversity given the different legal frameworks and indeed capacity to pursue social policies in the Member States. This will be further amplified by EU enlargement given that the legacy of socialism and the problems of transition continues to inform the respective approaches to questions of social welfare by the new Member States.[32] One of the significant consequences of

[25] See Art 45 (1) which provides that:

> The State shall strive to promote the welfare of the whole people by securing and protecting as effectively as it may a social order in which justice and charity shall inform all the institutions of the national life.

Note that the directive principles are unenforceable in the courts.

[26] BVerfGE 39, 302, 315.

[27] See R Alexy, *Theorie der Grundrechte* (Frankfurt am Main, Suhrkamp, 1996).

[28] See EW Böckenförde, 'Grundrechtstheorie and Grundrechtsinterpretation' (1974) *New Juristische Wochenschrift* 1529 who distinguishes between a liberal model, an institutional model, a value systematic model, a democratic-functional model and a social welfare model. The focus of the Art is the German constitutional context. The issue of values was also addressed in the final report submitted by Working Group V chaired by Mr Henning Christopherson to the European Convention at its plenary session on 7 and 8 November 2002 on Complementary Competencies. See CONV 375/1/02 REV 1 at p 11 in which distributive policies concerning income, personal taxes, the system of social welfare benefits, the educational system, the public health care system, cultural preservation development and compulsory military community service are referred to as areas of 'core national responsibilities' and representing basic public policy choices and social values of a Member State. See also the contribution of Mr Spini who refers social matters in the Member States as being marked by different 'philosophical and financing notions'. See the report of the meeting of 10 July 2002 of the Working Group on Economic Governance (WD007 WG VI).

[29] See Poiares Maduro, n 18 above, at 279.

[30] See the final report of Working Group XI 'Social Europe' to the European Convention chaired by Mr Katiforis CONV 516/1/03 REV 1 at p 10.

[31] See Art 3 (3) of CONV 850/03.

[32] The legacy of the transition from planned economies to market economies has also given rise to considerable degrees of poverty which has also contributed to the incorporation of socio-economic rights in the constitutions of the Central East European countries. See Sadurski, n 9 above; see also W Osiatynski, 'Rights in New Constitutions of East Central

the collapse of communism in Europe is that at the level of international political economy, the fragmentation of the post-war consensus of 'embedded liberalism'[33] in the old Member States has spread eastwards to affect the new EU Member States. Values in national legal cultures may be at odds with those contained in other constitutional orders, particularly those which emanate from supranational and international legal fora. How far is state intervention justified in administering social justice, policies for which may differ markedly along party political line's[34] not to mention country and regional lines.[35] After all, diversity of practice is reflected in the language of the law which emphasises the principle of subsidiarity in social policy to soothe Member States' fears that their sovereignty is being impermissibly encroached upon.[36] As we shall see, diversity of state practices is a powerful factor, undermining the uniform application of the law and in particular vis-à-vis the implementation of rights.

It is not so much a case of using terms such as 'strong' or 'weak' states when one evaluates the Member States' traditions regarding welfare but rather the states are not equally capable of intervening in different areas of economic life across the Union.[37] Part of the criteria of differentiation are to be found in the fabric of state construction, such as the distinction between unitary states and federal states. They are also to be found in the values set out in constitutional orders, in party political ideological markers and in legal cultures. In combination these make for a structural differentiation that has obvious consequences for European social rights in principle and as regards implementation.

THE EUROPEAN UNION'S SOCIAL SPHERE

The social nexus of the EU was first mentioned in 1972 in terms of the 'social sphere' which was pivotal in achieving economic and monetary union.[38]

Europe' (1994) 26 *Columbia Human Rights Law Review* 111; G Brunner (ed), *Before Reforms: Human Rights in the Warsaw Pact States 1971–1988* (London, Hurst & Co, 1990).

[33] See JG Ruggie, 'International Regimes, Transactions and Change: Embedded Liberalism in the Postwar Economic Order' (1982) 36 *International Organization* 379.
[34] See generally W Bogdan Sztyber, 'Market and State in Times of Globalisation' (2001) 12 *European Journal of Law and Economics* 145.
[35] See V Vence, 'Riqueza desde la diversidad: disparidades regionales y cohesión en la Unión Europea' in V Vence and JL Outes (eds), *La Unión Europea y la crisis del estado del bienestar* (Madrid, Síntesis, 1998),
[36] See, for eg, S Van Raepenbusch and D Hanf, 'Flexibility in Social Policy' in B de Witte, D Hanf and E Vos (eds) *The Many Faces of Differentiation in EU Law* (Antwerp, Intersentia, 2001), 65.
[37] For an instructive critique of the terms 'strong' and 'weak' state see PB Evans, D Rueschemeyer and T Skopcpol, 'On the Road toward a More Adequate Understanding of the State' in PB Evans, D Rueschemeyer and T Skopcpol (eds) *Bringing the State Back In* (Cambridge, Cambridge University Press, 1985), 347.
[38] Bull EC 10-1972, para 6. See generally D Collins, *The European Communities: The Social Policy of the First Phase* (London, Martin Robertson, 1975) for an historical account of the

Delors' vision during his presidency of the European Commission, was for a European '*Espace social*'.[39] He emphasised overcoming legislative difficulties in the Council by linking social policy to the objectives of realising the internal market by 1992.[40] Given that the historical legacy of European Social Policy was framed in terms of the prevention of 'social dumping',[41] whereby Member States with a lower level of protection could gain a competitive advantage over those with higher levels of protection and the avoidance of the distortion of competition,[42] it is clear that anything emanating under the aegis of social rights was intrinsically linked to single market building.[43] The 'social dialogue' in the EU has traditionally been embedded for the most part in the language of labour,[44] but also has at times been articulated through the language of rights. The period of the *travaux préparatoires* leading up to the adoption of the Social Charter in 1989 is a useful case in point.

Aside from the inclusion of the citizenship provisions in that Treaty, it is significant that the Institutional Affairs Committee of the European Parliament, which was consulted regarding the Draft Social Charter, discussed it in terms of a *Basic Bill of Rights*, stating that the Social Charter ought to provide all citizens with comparable rights and freedoms. Commentators were quick to point out the emergence of a rights nexus, the aim of which was to create a vision of a Community (as it was then) with a 'human face'.[45] Indeed, the role of rights as rhetorical devices were central

development of EU social policy. See further E Vogel-Polsky and J Vogel, *L'Europe sociale 1993. Illusion, alibi ou réalité* (Brussels, Éditions de l'Université libre de Bruxelles, 1991).

[39] European Commission *Growth, Competitiveness, Employment: The Challenges and Ways Forward into the 21st* Century, Bulletin of the European Communities, Supplement, 6 / 93.
[40] See R Nielson and E Syzszczak, *The Social Dimension of the European Community* (Copenhagen, Handelshøjskolens, 1991), 31ff.
[41] Although the existence of this phenomenon is disputed in the context of the European Union. See C Barnard, 'Social Dumping and the Race to the Bottom' (2000) 25 ELR 57.
[42] See H Spaak, *Comité intergouvernmental crée par la conférence de Messine: Rapport des chefs de délégations aux ministères des affaires etrangères* (Messina, 1956) otherwise known as the 'Spaak Report' at p 61. See also C Barnard, 'The Economic Objectives of Art 119' in T Hervey and D O'Keefe (eds) *Sex Equality Law in the European Union* (London, Wiley, 1996).
[43] See C Barnard, 'EC "Social Policy"' in P Craig and G de Búrca (eds), *The Evolution of EU Law* (Oxford, Oxford University Press, 1999), 479 497ff and also generally J Shaw (ed), *Social Law and Policy in an Evolving EU* (Oxford, Hart Publishing, 2000).
[44] Thus, the language of EU Social Policy, so to speak, is framed in terms of inter alia the improvement of living and working conditions, employment, labour law, vocational training, social security, equal pay and so on.
[45] 'In some respects this action, taken together with the Social Charter, complements and applies to the EC many of the rights set down in the Council of Europe's Social Charter (which came into effect in 1965) and its European Convention on Human Rights both of which address social and human rights from welfare to children's rights and those of migrant workers'. See J Lodge, 'Social Europe: Fostering a People's Europe?' in J Lodge (ed) *The European Community and the Challenge of the Future* (London, Pinter, 1989), 303 at 316.

to Delors' vision of the social space. For this reason, Delors' vision was often viewed as a work of fiction[46] from which it would be extremely ill advised to draw conclusions for the advancement of social rights, *stricto sensu*. The insertion of article 118 B, as it was then, (now article 139) into the EC Treaty provides a further case in point. Generally speaking, article 118 B was designed to promote social dialogue between management and labour at the European level. The 'language of the social dialogue' was for all intents and purposes, the language of rights, that is to say, enabling the parties to determine the substantive content of rights which constitute inter alia the rules governing their relationship.[47] Social security matters were never far from the political fray of the social dialogue, though sometimes more by implication.

Generally speaking, EU citizens must not be inhibited from exercising their rights to free movement by the lack of social security protection.[48] Thus, for instance, a German national may receive unemployment benefit in France for a limited period whilst she seeks employment.[49] However, the instrument upon which this principle is based, namely, Regulation 1408/71 which encompasses inter alia sickness, invalidity, unemployment benefit[50] applies to employed or self-employed persons who are nationals of a member state *and* to stateless persons or refugees residing within the territory of one of the Member States. This excludes EU citizens who are not regarded as 'workers'. It also excludes denizens. Thus, a worker of Turkish nationality who has worked in Germany and the Netherlands is not covered and would be penalised for moving to another Member State despite her contributions to the social security system in Germany.[51] It would be erroneous to assume that solidarity is withdrawn completely, in the case outlined above, from those who do not fall under the labour category. International obligations notwithstanding, the level of solidarity is applied in varying substantive degrees and gives rise to new forms of social categories.

[46] See I Ward, *A Critical Introduction to European Law* (London, Butterworths, 1996), 155.

[47] See B Bercusson, 'Fundamental Social and Economic Rights in the European Community' in A Cassesse, A Clapham and JHH Weiler (eds) *Human Rights and the European Community: Methods of Protection* (Baden-Baden, Nomos Verlag, 1991), 207 at 207–8. See also S Clauwert, *Fundamental Social Rights in the European Union: Comparative Tables and Documents* (Brussels, European Trade Union Institute, 1998) and B Hepple, *European Social Dialogue: Alibi or Opportunity* (London, The Institute of Employment Rights, 1993).

[48] See generally M Moore, 'Freedom of Movement and Migrant Workers' Social Security: An Overview of the Court's Jurisprudence 1992–1997' (1998) 35 CML Rev 409.

[49] However, her *eligibility* for and content of this benefit is still assessed by Germany welfare institutions, thereby arguably leaving national sovereignty intact. See Reg (EEC) No 1408/71 of the Council of 14 June 1971 on the application of social security schemes to employed persons, to self-employed persons and to members of their families moving within the Community. See also Reg 574/72 which implements Reg 1408/71. See generally F Pennings, *Introduction to European Social Security Law* (The Hague, Kluwer Law International, 1998).

[50] Other forms of benefit covered include old age benefit, benefit for accidents at work, death grants, family benefit, and benefit for dependents and for orphans.

[51] See Pennings, n 49 above, at 39.

In the case of Regulation 1408/71, that category of citizens who work are given more social rights than others who do not work, or non-citizens who do work. This example illustrates how the project of economic and monetary union gives rise to *spheres of belonging* which cut across the binary delineation between the 'insiders' (EU-citizens) and 'outsiders' (non-EU citizens).

Ultimately, this can be traced back to a finite resources argument which has customarily been employed to justify excluding or limiting access to certain rights on the basis of territoriality, of those who belong to a state and who are therefore entitled to social protection by virtue of their 'statehood' as opposed to universal rights of persons.[52] The addressees of social rights have ordinarily been regarded as remaining within the exclusive competence of the nation-state, a position which has, as we noted earlier, been reconfigured in the face of the gradual erosion of state sovereignty. In particular, social rights in the EU 'qualify' or 'pool'[53] the sovereignty of the nation-state as regards who may benefit from social protection and, by extension, who may be included as the addressees of solidarity. Indeed, as some have pointed out, Europe seen through the prism of social welfare is a 'multiply-bounded constituency of belonging'.[54]

SOCIAL RIGHTS AND SOVEREIGNTY — *EUROPE SANS ET AVEC FRONTIÈRES*

Social rights have traditionally been regarded as existing within the exclusive competence of the state, International and European commitments notwithstanding.[55] Designing the Union's 'human face'[56] by adopting a 'softy, softly' approach has been achieved by creating a link between social policy and rights which has further been instrumentalised as part of the bid to promote the democratic legitimacy at Maastricht.[57] The optimism of the kind contained in *The Report of the Comité des Sages* in its advocation of

[52] See C Offe, 'Demokratie und Wohlfahrtsstaat' in W Streeck (ed) *Internationale Wirtschaft und nationale Demokratie*: *Herausaforderung für die Demokratietheorie* (Frankfurt am Main, Campus, 1998), 99 at 102.
[53] See N MacCormick, 'The Maastricht Urteil: Sovereignty Now' (1995) 1 *European Law Journal* 255.
[54] See Fink *et al*, n 11 above, at 6.
[55] This section draws from a paper I gave at a 'European Citizenship and the Social and Political Integration of the European Union' (EURCIT) Workshop, 9–11 June 2000 at the University of Sassari, in Sardinia. I wish to thank Jo Shaw, Dario Castiglione and Richard Bellamy as well as the other participants to the Workshop for their advice and criticism.
[56] See above.
[57] Indeed, the 'Maastricht' debate on the Treaty of European Union (TEU) in 1992 and 1993 has been referred to in terms of a 'legitimacy crisis'. See G de Búrca, 'The Quest for Legitimacy in the European Union' (1996) 59 MLR 349.

extending social protection beyond the labour category[58] was somewhat curtailed by the 'safety valve' that social protection is a policy area that requires unanimity in the Council. This check precludes too great a threat to state sovereignty being posed. How effective is the safety valve in stemming the flow of the 'irresistible tide of europeanisation'[59] arising as a consequence of day-to-day legal practice?

The effect of europeanisation on the domestic legal orders of the Member States has been so pervasive that it is increasingly becoming difficult to tell them apart from the EU legal order. As I argued in Chapter Two, the European legal order is intertwined with the legal systems of the Member States to such an extent that attempts to consider them as separate legal orders seems, at times, anachronistic. Not only does EC law both inform and form the national law through europeanisation but also convergence between the legal systems of the Member States[60] arises as a consequence of a 'spill over'[61] albeit it in certain sectors of law only. The implications for state sovereignty are considerable.

As regards social policy, an erosion of state sovereignty is provoked by the gradual, incremental expansion of the EU through regulations and court decisions,[62] particularly given the exportability of social benefits, which arises as a consequence of the free movement provisions.[63] One must distinguish between the application of free movement (negative integration) and the harmonisation in the field of social rights (positive integration). It is arguable that europeanisation has only affected social policy issues in a procedural manner. Thus, for instance, a German national may receive unemployment benefit in France for a limited period whilst she

[58] European Commission *For a Europe of Civic and Social Rights* (Report by the *Comité des Sages* chaired by Maria de Lourdes Pintasilgo) (Luxembourg, Office for Official Publications of the European Communities, 1996).

[59] cf D Marquand, 'The Irrestible Tide of europeanisation' in S Hall and M Jacques (eds) *New Times* (London, Lawrence and Wishart, 1991),

[60] See JWF Allison, 'Transplantation and Cross-Fertilisation' in J Beatson and T Tridimas (eds), *New Directions in European Public Law* (Oxford, Hart Publishing, 1998), 169; see B Markesinis, *The Gradual Convergence: Foreign Influences and English Law on the Eve of the 21st Century* (Oxford, Clarendon Press, 1994). Against, P Legrand, 'European Legal Systems Are Not Converging' (1993) 45 *International and Comparative Law Quarterly* 52.

[61] This term draws from Haas but has been transposed to the legal sphere. See generally EB Haas, *The Uniting of Europe: Political, Economic and Social Forces, 1950–1957* (Stanford, Stanford University Press, 1968) and in particular A Stone Sweet and TL Brunell, 'Constructing a Supranational Constitution: Dispute Resolution and Governance in the European Community' (1998) 92 *American Political Science Review* 63.

[62] Thus, social security law cases form a considerable part of the case load of the European Court of Justice. See B Jésus-Gimeno, 'International and Community Obligations of the Member States in the Field of Social Security Schemes: Which Impact for Migrant Workers?' in V Kronenberger (ed) *The EU and the International Legal Order: Discord or Harmony?* (The Hague, TMC. Asser Press, 2001), 297.

[63] Indeed, Art 51 of the Treaty of Rome, as it was then, illustrates the social rights nexus of the European Community from the early stages.

seeks employment.[64] However, her *eligibility* for and content of this benefit is still assessed by German welfare institutions, thereby arguably leaving national sovereignty intact. Thus, the European Court of Justice has repeatedly stressed that it is for the Member States to determine the type and content of the provision of benefits schemes.[65] This deference is also to be found in Commission documents where, for example, 'solidarity with the disadvantaged sections of the population is primarily a matter for the Member States'.[66]

Substantive inroads have also been created by instruments of EC law which have excelled in giving the impression that social welfare is still within the exclusive competence of the state, essentially speaking. For example, the Social Charter for Workers originally referred to 'adequate' social protection and 'sufficient' resources.[67] The Preamble also referred to social consensus which, true to the form of European Social Policy, it linked with the strengthening of the competitiveness of undertakings, which is an essential condition for ensuring sustained economic development. The legal status of the Social Charter was unique in European Union law when it was introduced. In effect, it was declaratory and not a legal instrument in the sense envisaged by article 189 [now article 249] of the EC Treaty, neither was it a convention or a Treaty.[68] It was a political program promulgated by the Council of Ministers, to be taken in conjunction with the Community's general law-making powers and as a means of interpreting both Community and national implementing legislation. It was not legally binding under European Community or Public International Law. This declaratory model was used in the Maastricht Social Agreement and then later during the process of drafting the EU Charter of Fundamental Rights, its lack of a binding nature asuaging Member States' fears that their sovereignty was being encroached upon impermissibly.

However, the Court has striven for uniformity of EC law[69] which also has substantive implications. Thus, it has elected to apply a broad definition of the term 'worker' as regards the free movement of workers.[70] In *Unger*[71]

[64] See Reg (EEC) No 1408/71 of the Council of 14 June 1971 on the application of social security schemes to employed persons, to self-employed persons and to members of their families moving within the Community. See also Reg 574/72 which implements Reg 1408/71.
[65] Case C–41/84 *Pinna* [1986] ECR I–17 and Case C–22/77 *Mura* [1977] ECR I–1699.
[66] COM (92) 562 final.
[67] Art 10 I of the Charter.
[68] See B Hepple, 'The Implementation of the Community Charter of Fundamental Social Rights' (1991) 53 MLR 643.
[69] See *Pinna*, n 65 above, at p 25 para 25:

> It follows that the Community rules on social security introduced pursuant to Art 51 of the Treaty must refrain from adding to the disparities which already stem from the absence of harmonization of national legislation.

[70] See the opinion of Advocate General Geelhoed in Case C–413/01 *Franca Ninni-Orasche v Bundesminister für Wissenschaft, Verkehr und Kunst* of 27 February 2003 at para 25 in which the European Court of Justice's case law relating to the concept of 'worker' is discussed.
[71] Case C–75/63 *Unger* [1964] ECR 177.

a Dutch national was granted sickness benefit and expenses for treatment after falling ill in Germany despite the fact that she was no longer employed and had since the termination of her employment entered a voluntary insurance scheme. She relied on article 19 (1) of the Regulation then in force, which refers to 'insurance on a optional basis' but does not contain a definition of the term 'worker'[72]. The crux of the case was that even though she was not employed, she had assimilated with employed persons under a national social security scheme.

Social Citizenship and the Freedom of Movement

The social nexus of the freedom of movement was recognised almost from the outset to the extent that it was acknowledged that EU migrants and their families would require a certain level of social protection whilst residing in a Member State other than their own.[73] Whereas the Treaties provided a basic framework for social protection, however, it was the European Court of Justice which developed the policies underlying it in a piecemeal and incremental fashion,[74] exemplifying, for some, a shift of power from the 'principal', namely the Commission and the Council to the 'agent', namely the ECJ,[75] a shift which was regarded by some as dubious in terms of democratic legitimacy.[76]

In so doing, the ECJ has been faced with resistance by the Member States who have responded to the implications of the freedom of movement for their social welfare systems by applying and devising policies which are discriminatory despite individual litigation before national courts and occasional actions brought by the European Commission as part of infringement proceedings.[77] Whereas most Member States have tended to amend policies so that they reflect reasoned opinion of decisions by the ECJ, they have generally tended to do this on a case by case basis and have, as part of

[72] Reg 3 which was drawn up in 1958. See OJ 30 of 16 December 1958 which was eventually replaced by Reg 1408/71.

[73] See generally AP van der Mei, *Free Movement of Persons within the European Community: Cross-border Access to Public Benefits* (Oxford, Hart Publishing, 2002).

[74] See Á Castro Oliviera, 'Workers and Other Persons: Step-by-Step from Movement to Citizenship. Case Law 1995–2001' (2002) 39 CML Rev 77.

[75] J-M Josselin and A Marciano, 'Displacing your Principal: Two Historical Case Studies of Some Interest for the Constitutional Future of Europe' (2000) 10 *European Journal of Law and Economics* 217. For a general overview of the economic theory of the principal-agent relationship as applied to the European Court of Justice see M Pollack, 'Delegation, Agency, and Agenda Setting in the European Community' (1997) 51 *International Organization* 99.

[76] See generally TC Hartley, *Constitutional Problems of the European Union* (Oxford, Hart Publishing, 1999) although the point has been made in relation to socio-economic rights as a whole. See M Tushnet, *Taking the Constitution Away from the Courts* (Durham NC, Duke University Press, 1999).

[77] See L Conant, *Justice Contained: Law and Politics in the EU* (Ithaca, Cornell University Press, 2002).

their 'constrained compliance' avoided overhauling or aligning policies in the areas of social security and tax legislation so as to prevent possible infringement in parallel situations.[78]

In *Molenaar*, a retired couple living in France but who had worked in Germany were held to be justified in applying to their German medical insurers for medical care (*pflegeversicherung*) despite the fact that they no longer lived in Germany.[79] A resources argument was more explicit in this case given that the couple in question were retired and could therefore no longer be considered as 'workers'. Notwithstanding, the Court held that they should not lose their social benefits by virtue of having exercised their citizenship rights, much to the consternation of those Member State governments which were represented before the Court. Some commentators view the Court's jurisprudence in relation to free movement as creating functional equivalents of fundamental rights or what is referred to in German public law and theory as *Grundrechtsähnlich* albeit enshrined in an 'economic constitution'.[80] However, this view is embedded in a particular understanding of constitutionalism. Certain strands of German public law are at ease with conceptualising them in terms of basic rights, or what has been referred to as 'ein allgemeines Grundrecht auf wirtschaftliche Freizügigkeit'.[81] This view represents only one strand of German public law, or rather, one strand of German legal theory vis-à-vis the European Community legal order. Other views, in which the EU is viewed in terms of intergovernmentalism beg, or rather demand, the right to differ.[82] Be that as it may, the view of the EC Treaty as an economic constitution is not exclusively a German approach. It is also to be found in academic legal opinion in other Member States[83] inspired by the language of the decisions of the ECJ which has increasingly resorted to the language of constitutionalism which in itself suggests a value-orientated approach by judges which is essentially political.

[78] *Ibid* at 191.
[79] See Case C–160/96 *Molenaar* [1998] ECR I-843. See also C–35/97 *Commission v France* where it was held that cross-border workers (in this case, workers resident in Belgium but working in France) were held to be able to qualify for supplementary retirement pension points after early retirement according to an unemployment insurance scheme which was only open to workers resident in France on the basis of equal treatment which applied because the benefit constituted a social advantage linked to the employment contract.
[80] See generally C Joerges, 'European Economic Law, the Nation State and the Maastricht Treaty' in R Dehousse (ed) *The European Union Treaty* (München, CH Beck, 1994), 29.
[81] K Füßer, 'Grundrecht auf wirtschaftliche Freizügigkeit und Art. 8 a EGV als Auffangbeschränkungsverbot des Gemeinschaftsrechts' (1999) *Die öffentliche Verwaltung* 96 who uses these terms to refer to the decision of the European Court of Justice in *Gebhard*. (See Case C–55/94 *Gebhard v Consiglio dell' Ordine degli Avvocati e Procuratori di Milano* [1995] ECR I-4165). See also M Herdegen, *Europarecht* (München, CH Beck, 1999), 207ff.
[82] M Pechstein and M Koenig, *Die Europäische Union: Die Verträge von Maastricht und Amsterdam* (Tübingen, Mohr, 1998).
[83] See M Poiares Maduro, *We, the Court* (Oxford, Hart Publishing, 1998).

In *Bosman*,[84] the transfer of a football player to a new club was made conditional on the purchasing club having to pay a transfer fee. The UEFA/FIFA regulations also restricted the number of foreigners in the team. Bosman challenged under article 48 [now article 39] of the EC Treaty. The European Court of Justice held that the transfer fee affected the planning of football clubs and restricted the employment opportunities of the football players.[85] In *Bosman*, the ECJ markedly framed its judgment in constitutional terms. It has been argued that:

> The Citizenship provisions of the EC Treaty confirm the Court's case law giving a constitutional character to the free movement of persons, which certainly distinguish them from goods[86]

thereby highlighting the *Grundrechtsähnlichlichkeit* of the four freedoms, particularly given the legal basis of article 48 [39] EC, namely, that of non-discrimination, which goes to the very core not only of the concept of EU citizenship but is the rock upon which the 'church', ie the EU, is founded.[87] However, the language of rights was only used selectively, that is to say that it was addressed to only those rights holders who are economically active or *homo economicus*. According to this critique, EC legal provisions are constructed according to their universalist 'social' function only to the extent that they serve latent market ideology.[88] The same has been argued in relation to the development of fundamental rights in the sphere of sex equality.[89]

The development of social citizenship is, however, constrained by the issue of competences and the 'creative'[90] or 'extensive'[91] jurisprudence of

[84] See Case C–415/93 *Union Royale Belge des Sociétés de Football Association ASBL v Bosman* [1996] 1 CMLR 645.
[85] Thus, Member States could not prohibit or hinder the establishment of one of its nationals or of a company in another Member State. It further held that there was no objective justification to the extent that the rules could only be justified if the rules pursued a legitimate aim compatible with the Treaty and were justified by pressing reasons of public interest. See *Bosman*, n 84 above, at para 104.
[86] E Johnson and D O'Keefe, 'From Discrimination to Obstacles to Free Movement: Recent Developments Concerning the Free Movement of Workers 1989–1994' (1994) 31 CML Rev 1313.
[87] Art 6 [12] EC.
[88] See TK Hervey, 'Migrant Workers and their Families in the European Union: The Pervasive Market Ideology of Community Law' in J Shaw and G Moore (eds) *New Legal Dynamics of the European Union* (Oxford, Clarendon Press, 1995), 110.
[89] See E Ellis, 'Recent Developments in EC Sex Equality Law' (1998) 35 CML Rev 379. See, however, C–249/96 *Grant v South West Trains Ltd* [1998] ECR I–621 and also C–13/94 *P v S & Cornwall County Council* [1996] ECR I–2143.
[90] See generally T Tridimas, *The General Principles of EC Law* (Oxford, Oxford University Press, 1999).
[91] See N Reich, 'Union Citizenship: Metaphor or Source of Rights?' (2001) 7 *European Law Journal* 4.

the ECJ. Social protection through rights is thereby structurally constrained. However, there is an overlap of influence, mainly because jurists, who are the driving force behind the development of rights, are instrumental in 'filling the gaps' between Community law and national law in such a way that the process of 'picking and choosing' legal remedies to represent their clients' interests becomes one which shapes both the production of norms but also the development of policy in a way which cuts across hierarchy. It is, however, not always easy to track the cause and effect of mutual influence in a polyarchical policy and law making process.[92] For its part, the ECJ's attempt to move beyond the 'market citizen' illustrates that whereas the *homo economicus* critique may still be apt, it has undergone a degree of reconfiguration.[93]

In the *Martínez Sala*[94] case, for example, a Spanish national lawfully resident in Germany was able to claim a child raising allowance, a benefit ordinarily granted to all residents in Germany who had a dependent child in their care and were either unemployed or had no full-time employment.[95] The Court held that article 8a of the EC Treaty [now article 18] did not need to be invoked given that the right to reside in Germany was uncontested by the German government. Instead, Ms Sala could rely on article 8 (2) EC which provides that not only are EU citizens subject to the rights and duties contained in the EC Treaties but also they must not be discriminated against on the grounds of nationality,[96] a principle which it had previously outlined in *Cowan*.[97] In *Grzelczyk*,[98] the Court reaffirmed its decision in *Sala*, namely, that an EU citizen who is a legally resident migrant[99] may rely on the principle of equal treatment within the material scope of the Treaty. Rudy Grzelczyk, a French national studying at the University of Louvain in Belgium applied for a non-contributory social benefit designed to ensure a minimum income[100] which was refused on the grounds that he was an EC

[92] An argument which has been made in relation to polyarchical models of law making in general. See L Fuller, 'The Forms and Limits of Adjudication' (1978) 92 *Harvard Law Review* 353.

[93] An argument which can also be extended to the field of sex equality. See C–249/96 *Grant v South West Trains Ltd* [1998] ECR I-621 and also C–13/94 *P v S & Cornwall County Council* [1996] ECR I–2143.

[94] Case C–85/96 *Martínez Sala v Freistaat Bayern* [1998] ECR I–2691.

[95] Ms Sala had in fact worked during intervals between 1976 and 1989 but was, at the time of her application, unemployed.

[96] The Court held that Art 6 was one of the rights and duties which Art 8 (2) (as they were then) EC attaches to EU citizenship. See *Sala*, n 94 above, at para 63.

[97] In which the Court upheld the right of every tourist in the Union to receive services on the basis of a general prohibition of discrimination based on nationality. See Case C–186/86 *Cowan v Trésor Public* [1989] ECR 195.

[98] See Case C–184/99 *Rudy Grzelczyk v Centre public d'aide sociale d'Ottignies-Louvain-la-Neuve* [2001] ECR I–6193.

[99] Within the scope of directive 93/96/EC.

[100] The so-called *minimex* benefit.

student. In order to qualify for the grant, he either had to be a Belgian national or a national of any other EU Member State who was a worker. According to the Court, the social benefit in question was a benefit within the meaning of article 7(2) of Regulation 1612/68[101] which could not be made conditional on having the status of a worker.[102]

These decisions illustrate how the Court has eroded the resistance levels of the legal orders of Member States and that *no state is an island*. Whereas the language of the judgments may be nuanced as to scope, in effect, the Member States' social security systems are not immune to europeanisation. In *Grzelczyk*, for instance, whilst the Court acknowledged that a Member State could revoke the lawful residence of a student if he is no longer able to fulfil the requirements of self-sufficiency needed to qualify for lawful residence, this need not necessarily be the case. The evaluation of whether the student constituted an 'unreasonable' burden on the host State had to include questions of solidarity.[103] This meant that the principle of financial solidarity between citizens of the Member States and the particular situation of students had to be considered.[104] In effect, the Court was providing guidelines for public authorities which is, technically speaking, an exclusive Member State competence. The purpose of this next section is to consider the *dirigism* of the Court in the light of cross border access to health care in the European Union.

THE EUROPEANISATION OF HEALTH CARE

Rights to Health Care in the European Union

Access to health care is not explicitly mentioned in the EC Treaty but has evolved under the aegis of the freedom of movement provisions contained in the EC Treaty and the principle of equal treatment. Whereas there had been some Community activity in this field since the later 1970s, it was not until Maastricht[105] that it evolved into an explicit EU competence,[106]

[101] OJ 1968, L 257/2.

[102] See, however, M Rossi, 'Anmerkung zu C–184/99 Grzelczyk' (2002) 7 *Juristen Zeitung* 249 and also A Iliopoulou and H Toner, 'Case Note on Case C–184/99 Rudy Grzelczyk v Centre public d'aide sociale d'Ottignies-Louvain-la-Neuve [2001] ECR I–6193' (2002) 39 CML Rev 609.

[103] Which appears in the preamble of the directive.

[104] This approach has also been adopted vis-à-vis pensioners. See Case C–326/00 *Idryma Koinonikon Asfalisseon (IKA) v Vasileois Ionnidis* (unreported). See <http://www.curia.eu.int> for the Press Release.

[105] Art 152 (ex 129).

[106] See generally VG Hatzopoulos, 'Killing National Health and Insurance Systems but Healing Patients? The European Market for Health Care Services after the Judgments of the ECJ in Vanbraekel and Peerbooms' (2002) 39 CML Rev 683, TK Hervey, 'Community and National Competence in Health After Tobacco Advertising' (2001) 38 CML Rev 1421;

though it has since then also arisen in other fields of competence.[107] The case law which has evolved in the area of cross-border health care cases has tended to regard health as a mere 'by-product' or 'flanking policy'.[108] In other words, it is not health policy per se that may be regarded as having been comprehensively europeanised. However, europeanisation has occurred on a sectoral basis, despite policy statements which give an impression to the contrary.[109]

Briefly stated, the legal framework for health in the EU is as follows. References in the Treaties are made to a 'high level of social protection, the raising of the standard of living and quality of life'[110] as well as a high level of health protection.[111] A system of coordination of national social security systems developed under the aegis of Regulations 1408/71 and 574/72 facilitates the free movement of workers. In particular, workers have the right to medical treatment,[112] EU citizens have the right to emergency treatment[113] and patients can obtain prior authorisation to be treated in other Member States than that in which they are ordinarily resident.[114] Article 35 of the Charter of Fundamental rights provides a right to health care in the sense that:

> Everyone has the right of access to preventative health care and the right to benefit from medical treatment under the conditions established by national laws and practices.

The principles which have been developed by the European Court of Justice[115] may be summarised as follows: European Community law does not detract from the powers of the Member States to organise their social security systems. Member States must nevertheless comply with Community law when exercising their powers.[116] Prior authorisation for

G Tridimas and T Tridimas, 'The European Court of Justice and the Annulment of the Tobacco Advertisment Directive: Friend of National Sovereignty or Foe of Public Health?' (2002) 14 *European Journal of Law and Economics* 171.

107 See, eg, the Race Directive: Directive 2000/43 [2000] OJ L180/22 which involves harmonisation in the area of health.
108 See Hervey, n 106 above, at 1423.
109 Thus the Laeken Declaration includes better health care as being part of the expectations of EU citizens. It also refers to the need of intensifying cooperation on health matters. See the Laeken Declaration on the Future of the European Union available at <http://european-convention.eu.int/pdf/LKNEN.pdf>.
110 See Art 2 EC Treaty.
111 See Art 3 of the EC Treaty read in conjunction with Art 152.
112 Through use of the E106 form.
113 Through use of the E111 form.
114 Through the use of the E112 form.
115 See below.
116 A further analogy is to be found in the field of education where similar principles have been developed. See Case C–9/74 *Casagrande* [1974] ECR 773 at 12. See also Case C–293/83 *Gravier* [1985] ECR 293 at 19.

treatment in another Member State constitutes a restriction of the freedom to provide services as contained in the Treaty. Restrictions can, however, be objectively justified on the basis of the protection of the financial balance of the system or on grounds of public health, though in practice, this burden of proof has proved difficult to discharge. References to health are scattered across the Draft Constitutional Treaty. Thus, references exist to solidarity,[117] to the 'well-being of its peoples',[118] 'a high level of protection and improvement of quality of the environment'.[119] Article 7 incorporates the rights, freedoms and principles set out in the Charter of Fundamental Rights. Public health matters are included as an area of shared competence alongside inter alia the internal market.[120] The protection and improvement of human health is included as an area of supporting, co-ordinating or complementary action.[121] However, the attempt to codify social rights in the Draft Constitutional Treaty is limited because of the competence clause. Accordingly, the Charter will not give rights in the traditional sense but will provide a framework for policies.[122] This is not, generally speaking an anathema regarding rights to health care.

The language of rights in connection to health care can be misleading. It is more appropriate to speak in terms of interests which may give rise to a duty, all things being equal, and if it is not counteracted by conflicting considerations.[123] However, it is arguably more correct to speak of rights to health care in terms of obligations on behalf of those who are entrusted by the state to provide it, particularly given the underlying tension between the allocation of finite resources for infinite demand. The distinction is an important one as it clarifies that what is *not* meant by a right to health care is an *automatic entitlement* to health care.[124] It does, however, prevent the evolution of any policy which denies reasonable access to readily available resources.[125]

[117] See the Union's values which are outlined in Art 2. Although this reference is not exclusively made to social solidarity but also to solidarity in the face of terrorist attacks and natural disasters. See the solidarity clause contained in Art 42.
[118] Art 3(1).
[119] Art 3(3).
[120] Art 13 (2). See also ch V: Areas where the Union May Take Coordinating Complementary or Supporting Action provided in Art III–179.
[121] Art 16 (2). It is of interest to note that the reference to public health in the list of areas of shared competence was modified. The Praesidium's proposal to divide para 4 of Art 151 EC Treaty into two separate paras was adopted in the final draft. See CONV 724/03 at 75.
[122] See G de Búrca, 'Fundamental Rights and Citizenship' in B de Witte (ed), *Ten Reflections on the Constitutional Treaty for Europe* (San Domenico di Fiesole, Robert Schuman Centre for Advanced Studies, 2003), 11.
[123] See J Raz, *The Morality of Freedom* (Oxford, Clarendon Press, 1986), 166.
[124] See, eg, the decision by the South African Constitutional Court in *Sobramoney v Minister of Health KwaZulu-Natal* (1997) 12 BCLR 1696 (CC), (1997) 50 BMLR 224. Although see *Minister of Health v Treatment Action Campaign* (2002) Constitutional Court – CCT 8/02, 5 July, as a useful illustration of access to health care being framed as a constitutional entitlement.
[125] See JK Mason, RA McCall Smith and GT Laurie, *Law and Medical Ethics* (London, Butterworths, 2002), 377.

The inclusion of rights to health care in constitutions, however, does little to clarify the need to maintain this distinction. Indeed, they go some way towards encouraging the view of rights to health care as being justiciable rights, or what is referred to in German law as subjective rights. In the German case, as in the case of other EU Member States, this is simply not the case. Whereas rights to health care may be articulated as constitutional rights,[126] they are framed as such for the purposes of providing a constitutional basis for a state's health care policy. The distinction between constitutional and legislative social rights is significant. Social rights or entitlements tend to be the latter given that they are too dependent on economic circumstances to be entrenched in the constitution. Indeed constitutions reveal little of a state's health care policy when taken in isolation. Court decisions may go some way towards elucidating some of the principles upon which it is based but there again, regard must be had to the overall institutional and extra-institutional context which is more indicative of the nature of a state's policy as well as the values contained therein. Here again, it is inappropriate to speak of rights to health care in EU Member States without differentiating between respective institutional and indeed extra-institutional arrangements.[127]

The provision of health care varies widely across the Union.[128] Three sources of finance exist, namely, out of pocket payments, voluntary (or private insurance premiums) and compulsory (or public) contributions through insurance or taxation. Three methods of the provision of health care must also be distinguished between reimbursement, benefits in kind and lastly, ownership and management of providers. 'Administrative fragmentation', a phenomenon described as existing at the national level[129] is further accentuated across EU Member States. In Germany, for example,

[126] A right to free health care for all is also included in a number of constitutions of the new Member States. See Art 31 of the Constitution of the Czech Republic; Art 28 of the Estonian Constitution; Art 111 of the Lithuanian Constitution; Art 40 of the Slovak Constitution. Note that in the case of the Bulgarian Constitution, a right to health insurance rather than to actual health care is provided (Art 52) and the Hungarian constitution refers to the right for all those living in its territory to the 'highest possible level of physical and mental health' (Art 70D).

[127] See generally M McCarthy and S Rees, *Health Care Systems and Public Health Medicine in the European Community* (London, Faculty of Public Health Medicine of the Royal Colleges of Physicians of the UK and Royal College of Physicians of London, 1992) which is somewhat dated now but which provides as useful guide to the different arrangements regarding the provision of health care.

[128] The European Observatory on Health Care Systems (EOHCS) is a useful source of information about the health care systems in Europe. See <http://www.observatory.dk>.

[129] In the case, the United Kingdom's National Health Service in relation to Health Authorities, Primary Care Trusts and NHS Trusts. See the National Health Service and Community Care Act 1990 which established District Health Authorities as purchasers of health services on behalf of the local population. See also the Health Act 1999, s 2 which inserted s 16 A into the National Health Service Act 1977. See further the latest proposals by the Department of Health for so-called 'foundation hospitals' which would enable them to be relatively free from central control. See *The Observer*, 2 March 2003 at p 8, 'Split as NHS Trusts Bid for New Freedom'.

health care illustrates the wide distribution of powers and functions between the Federal level, the State level, the courts, the insurance funds and their organisations and the doctors' organisations. The German example is also notable for the absence of centralised control. In the case of Spain, it is the regions which are responsible for the provision of health care but it is the Ministry of Health which determines the overall health budget.[130] Experiences differ markedly as regards implementation of health care policy, particularly between the regions of the north and south,[131] a status quo which in some Member States, such as the United Kingdom, also arises in relation to the street a person lives on.[132] This will be further amplified by EU enlargement which will bring with it a population with a diverse range of health profiles and different systems of health care not to mention levels of resources.[133] The gap is particularly marked by the effects of transition to a market economy which have created considerable fiscal problems. This is problematic since two basic health indicators, namely, infant mortality and life expectancy,[134] reveal that most candidate countries lag well behind the EU Member States.[135]

Added to the internal markers of differentiation, is the impact of Community law which has consequences for the financing of health care systems as a consequence of the application of the free movement provisions, across a variety of levels. Here too, the Court has complemented the EU regulations and the prior authorisation procedure[136] in its decisions concerning cross-border access to health care.[137]

[130] See McCarthy and Rees, n 127 above, at 49.
[131] *Ibid.*
[132] A practice referred to as 'post-coding' whereby the provision of health care is linked to the post-code of where a patient lives. In effect, patients living on opposite sides of the street may fall prey to differential strategies of health care provision.
[133] See B Merkel and K Kärkkäinen, 'Public Health Aspects of Accession' (2002) 8 *Eurohealth* 3.
[134] M Bobak and M Marmont, 'East-West mortality divides and its potential explanations: proposed research agenda' (1996) *British Medical Journal* 312.
[135] Indeed, the level of spending on health in absolute and percentage terms is significantly less than in the EU Health's share of the GDP. The average for the candidate countries has been estimated at 4.5% (although there is considerable variation amongst the candidate countries) whilst the EU average is approximately 8%. What is even more worrying is that the former is in fact decreasing, whilst the latter shows an increase.
[136] Such as E112 which is based on Art 22 of Reg 1408/71 which entitles patients to benefits in kind as well as cash benefits. See also E109 which applies to those working abroad for a short period, E110 which applies to those working in international transport and E111 which provides temporary but emergency medical care for those who are abroad for a short while, such as tourists and business people.
[137] See Case C–238/82 *Duphar* [1984] ECR 523; Case C–158/96 *Kohll* [1998] ECR I-1931; Case C–120/95 *Decker* [1998] ECR I–1831 and more recently cases C–368/98 *Vanbraekel* and C–157/99 *Geraets-Smits and Peerbooms* [2001] ECR I–5363. See also *Attorney General (Society for the Protection of Unborn Children (SPUC) Ltd v Open Door Counselling Ltd and Dublin Wellwoman Centre Ltd* (1988) IRLM 19 (Supreme Court) and Case C–159/90 *Society for the Protection of Unborn Children v Grogan and others* [1990] ECR I–4685.

Cross Border Access to Health Care in the European Union

In *Kohll*[138] and *Decker*,[139] individuals were able to obtain medical treatment in an EU Member State other than where they were resident.[140] *Kohll* was a preliminary reference regarding articles 50 and 60 of the EC Treaty which concerned a Luxembourg national who requested his medical insurers for authorisation for his daughter, a minor, to receive treatment from an orthodontist in Trier, Germany. The Court held that the necessity of obtaining prior authorisation from an institution of the State for treatment in another Member State constituted a restriction on the freedom to provide services within the meaning of articles 59 and 60. It is of interest to note that the court did not accept the objective justification advanced by the defendants, namely, expenditure control and the issue concerning the budget balancing of the social security system and the 'genuine and actual risk' of upsetting the financial balance of that system.

In *Decker*, a Luxembourg national purchased a pair of spectacles with corrective lenses from an optician in Arlon, Belgium on a prescription from an opthalmologist in Luxembourg but was refused reimbursement from his insurers on the grounds that he did not obtain prior authorisation. He argued that this was contrary to articles 30 and 36 EC Treaty, namely, an unjustifiable barrier to the free movement of goods. The Court held that social security and conditions concerning the right or duty to be insured with a social security scheme as well as the conditions for entitlement of benefits was a matter for each Member State but that they must comply with Community law. It rejected an objective justification based on the grounds of public health and ensuring the quality of medical products. The Court referred to the general system concerning the recognition of professional education and training and the fact that the spectacles were purchased on prescription from an opthalmologist, which guarantees the protection of public health. Thus, the quality argument was rejected. Thus, articles 30 and 36 EC Treaty precluded national rules requiring prior authorisation from a social security service for purchase of any medical product abroad, a position which has been upheld in subsequent case law.[141]

[138] Case C–158/96 *Kohll v Union des Caisses de Maladie* [1998] ECR I–1931.
[139] Case C–120/95 *Decker v Caisse de Maladie des Employés Privés* [1998] ECR I–1831. See generally AP van der Mei, 'Cross-Border Access to Medical Care within the European Union: Some Reflections on the Judgments in Decker and Kohll' (1998) 5 *Maastricht Journal of European and Comparative Law* 277.
[140] See Art 22 (1) (c) Reg (EEC) No 1408/71 which allows EU citizens to go to another Member State to receive medical treatment and to obtain reimbursement of the costs at the rates applicable there. Note that this covers public health insurance schemes only. See also Reg (EEC) 574/72.
[141] See Case C–368/98 *Vanbraekel* [2001] ECR I–5382 in which a Belgian social security institution wrongly refused permission to an insured person to seek medical treatment abroad. See also Case C–157/99 *Smits/Peerbooms* [2001] ECR I–5509. See generally M Fuchs, 'Free Movement of Services and Social Security: Quo Vadis?' (2002) 8 *European Law Journal* 536.

A variety of issues arise as a consequence of these cases which include inter alia the idea of 'medical tourism' on behalf of EU citizens for the most favourable services, the protectionism of the medical establishment[142] as regards the labour market and so on.[143] The issue of medical tourism is an example of 'social dumping' whereby individuals seek enhanced social protection across borders. It remains one of the customary objections raised vis-à-vis individuals realising their social citizenship in a state of which they are not a national. However, practice shows that few patients seek treatment in a Member State other than their own. This may, however, increase; it may be too early to tell. Indeed, even taking the cross-border regions into account, it is currently estimated that approximately 2 per cent of the insured population in the EU actually opts for cross-border care,[144] despite the encouragement by some national Member State governments which have adopted policies to send patients abroad in order to reduce waiting lists.[145] The impact of the right to cross-border health care in the EU on the sovereignty and on the resources of Member States is at best minimal, if one takes the frequency of the realisation of these rights as the benchmark. However, this may be because in practice, patients have been faced with considerable administrative hurdles when trying to rely on the right to cross-border access to health care.[146]

See also cases C–385/99 *Müller-Fauré* and C–385/99 *Van Riet* in which standard procedures for obtaining reimbursement for costs of treatment abroad were not followed. Thus, reimbursement was not granted on the basis that the treatment concerned care which was non-urgent (*Müller-Fauré*) or treatment which could have been provided in the country of insurance (*Van Riet*).

142 See an Art in *The Independent*, 13 February 2003 at p 3 entitled, 'GMC [the General Medical Council] "biased" against Foreign Doctors' in which the results of an independent inquiry into Britain's system for disciplining doctors are reported. According to the report, National Health Service (NHS) doctors trained overseas are more than three times as likely to be found guilty of a disciplinary offence than UK trained colleagues despite attracting the same volume of complaints. Doctors from overseas were more likely to be found guilty and get harsher sentences.

143 See generally A Paulus, S Evers, F Fecher, J Van der Made and A Boonen, 'Cross Border Health Care: An Analysis of Recent ECJ Rulings' (2002) 14 *European Journal of Law and Economics* 61.

144 W Palm, J Nickless, H Lewalle and A Coheur, *Implications of Recent Jurisprudence on the Co-ordination of Health Care Protection Systems* (Brussels, AIM, 2000).

145 As in the case of the United Kingdom which has adopted the policy allowing local health authorities to send patients abroad in the event of undue delay in receiving medical treatment. See 'EU backs health care plans', 21 August 2002 reported at <http://www.news.bbc.co.uk/2/hi/health/1511180.stm>.

146 See H Hermans, 'Access to Health Care and Health Service in the European Union: Regulation 1408/71 and the E111 Process' in R Leidl (ed) *Health Care and its Financing in the Single European Market* (Amsterdam, IOS Press, 1998), 324. It remains to be seen to what extent these administrative barriers might be circumvented by the introduction of the so-called European health card.

The extent of the impact is, however, more discernible if one adopts the way in which rational decision-making has been subjected to the forces of europeanisation. It is here where the distinction drawn at the outset of this section must be reiterated. That is to say that it is more appropriate to speak of rights to health in terms of obligations on behalf of those who are entrusted by the state in providing it. Thus, EC law constrains and indeed prevents the evolution of any policy which denies reasonable access to readily available resources to EU citizens. Let us consider a case which is ordinarily not discussed in the context of cross-border access to health care but which illustrates the impact of European rights and in particular, the europeanisation of decision-making of national elites.

The Europeanisation of Rational Decision-making

In *Blood*,[147] an English woman resident in the UK was held not to be precluded from travelling to Belgium for fertility treatment.[148] The facts of the case were rather exceptional. Ms Blood's husband was in a coma after having suffered from an attack of meningitis. Ms Blood wanted access to his sperm so that she could have his child. The Human Fertilisation and Embryology Authority (HFEA) refused access on the grounds that she had not obtained her husband's written consent.[149] The authority subsequently forbade her to travel to Belgium to be treated there, which, the Court of Appeal held, was contrary to EC law and in particular, the freedom to obtain services (Arts 59 [49] and 60 [50] EC).

This case particularly illustrates the authority's reticence to acknowledge the existence of obtaining health care across borders. Indeed, the Authority were unaware of the EC law nexus of the case, electing instead to draw from principles of private international law by maintaining that the plaintiff did not have adequate 'connecting factors' to link her to Belgium.[150] It is arguable that the Authority could be excused for not being aware of the EC law nexus particularly given that as an EU competence, health is both narrowly defined and construed. Moreover, it does not enjoy the same standing as measures which are intended to bring about the internal market, such as free movement.

The Tobacco Advertising case[151] in which the European Court of Justice annulled Directive 98/43 prohibiting the advertising and sponsorship of

[147] *R v Human Fertilisation and Embryology Authority, ex parte Blood* (1996) 35 BMLR 1.
[148] The main provisions on medical treatment are to be found in Title III, Chapter 1 of Reg (EEC) No 1408/71 - OJ L 28 30 January 1997.
[149] As provided by ss 12, sch 3, paras 1, 3, 5 of the Human Fertilisation and Embryology Act 1990.
[150] The Authority was also, however, intent on trying to prevent the creation of a precedent as regards access to gametes where express, written consent has not be given by one of the partners involved.
[151] C–376/98 *Germany v Parliament and Council (Tobacco Advertising)* [2000] ECR I-8419.

tobacco products[152] on the grounds that it did not fall within the scope of the internal market is a case in point. The health and the internal market implications of the directive are inseparable elements of the directive. Indeed, health is seen through the prism of the removal of barriers to trade and the distortion of competition which arise as a consequence of differing national laws regarding the restrictions on the advertising and sponsorship of tobacco products. The Court held that articles 57(2), 66 and 100a of the EC Treaty did not constitute an appropriate legal basis for the adoption of the directive and annulled it.

If anything, the undoing of the Directive was that its public health dimension was too dominant. It was the internal market dimension which ought to have been central, leaving the public health implications with a walk on part, so to speak.[153] The case highlights the limits of the elastic nature of EU competences,[154] it also illustrates the existence of a hierarchy of competences, in which some are more significant than others. It also, however, explains why it is that some have argued in favour of greater clarity regarding the division of competences,[155] an issue which was at the forefront of the European Convention proceedings. In its report on 'Complementary Competencies', Working Group V[156] recommended the use of the term 'supporting measures' instead of 'complementary competencies' to refer to the position where states retain full powers whilst at the same time not precluding the introduction of assisting and co-ordinating 'soft' measures at the European level.[157] Subject matters for 'supporting measures' included sensitive policy areas such as inter alia employment,[158]

[152] Directive 98/43/EC of the European Parliament and of the Council of 6 July 1998 on the approximation of the laws, regulations and administrative provisions of the Member States relating to the advertising and sponsorship of tobacco products (OJ 1992 L213, p 9).

[153] See also Case C–491/01 *British American Tobacco (Investments) Limited and Imperial Tobacco v Secretary of State for Health*, decision of 10 December 2002 (unreported). See <http://www.eu.int/en/cp0299en.htm>.

[154] See generally G de Búrca and B de Witte, 'The Delimitation of Powers between the EU and its Member States' in A Arnull and D Wincott (eds) *Accountability and Legitimacy in the European Union* (Oxford, Oxford University Press, 2002), 201.

[155] See, eg, the proposal of the Prime Minister of Nordrhein-Westfalen, Wolfgang Clement to establish three different categories of competences. W Clement, 'Europa gestalten–nicht verwalten', speech at the Humboldt University, Berlin on 12 February 2001 reproduced at <http://www.whi-berlin.de/clement.htm>. See also the recommendations by the then Council's president under the Belgian presidency, Guy Verhofstadt outlined in the *Frankfurter Allgemeine Zeitung* of 29 June 2001 at p 6.

[156] CONV 375/1/02 REV 1.

[157] That is to say recommendations, resolutions, guidelines, programmes, and other legally non-binding acts as well as legally binding decisions. Union legislation such as regulations and directives may not be adopted as supporting measures unless exceptionally specified in the relevant Treaty article *Ibid* at p 5. The Working Group also proposes that the Open Method of Co-Ordination (OMC) be considered as a 'soft' instrument for these purposes. See Chapter V of Art III-179 of the Final Draft Constitutional Treaty which refers to best practices which are to be used in matters of Public Health.

[158] See Art 125–130 of the EC Treaty.

education and vocational training,[159] culture,[160] industry[161] and public health.[162]

The codification of a division of EU competence and Member State competence,[163] must be qualified by the process of europeanisation of national legal orders of the Member States, a factor which has tended to be notable for its absence as part of the reform process of the EU.[164] The issue of competence is not only the stuff of politicians, however. Put simply, if national elites do not regard a matter as falling within EU competence, then the rights which are contained therein will not be recognised. Given the elastic nature of EU competences, this is arguably easier said than done. This calls into question the loyalties of the Member States' institutions.[165] Access to cross-border health care by EU citizens has qualified decision-making by national public authorities.[166] It has qualified or 'pooled' national sovereignty regarding decision-making. Moreover, this impact has occurred across the various levels across which the responsibility to provide health care is scattered.

In the case of the United Kingdom, for example, financial restraints qualify the Secretary of State's duty to provide health care, such as the provision of hospital accommodation.[167] As in the execution of any statutory duty, the Secretary of State must exercise his discretion reasonably.[168] In the case of the United Kingdom, the rise of judicial review in the United Kingdom in cases relating to medical treatment has been notable for upholding the need to demonstrate reasonableness in decision-making, particularly regarding

[159] Arts 149 and 150 of the EC Treaty.
[160] Art 151 of the EC Treaty.
[161] Art 157 of the EC Treaty.
[162] Art 152 of the EC Treaty. Note that the members of Working Group XI, 'Social Europe' recommended that social matters should remain an area of shared competence, with the Member States having the primary responsibility. See CONV 516/1/03 REV 1.
[163] Whether it be through the adoption of a catalogue or otherwise See the proposal of the German politician Erwin Teufel, CONV 24/02. See also that of Zaplana Hernandez Soro, CONV 26/02 which is framed in less categorical terms.
[164] This does not necessarily mean, however, that this particular fiction, namely, concerning the introduction of a strict list of competences will dominate given the existence of more pragmatic proposals such as those made by the Irish politician John Bruton who has argued in favour of categories of competences. See CONV 27/02 which has received considerable support. See the proposal made by Andrew Duff, Olivier Duhamel and Alain Lamassure *et al*, CONV178/02.
[165] Thus, as John Temple Lang has pointed out that,

> The whole working of the Community system depends on the national authorities fulfilling their role, applying Community law, implementing Community policies, and not adopting national measures, however, well-intentioned, which prevent the Community system from working properly.

See the conclusions of the XIX F.I.D.E. Conference (2000), Helsinki cited in I Pernice and J Dutheil de la Rochère, EU Law and National Constitutions, Questionnaire for F.I.D.E 2002.
[166] And arguably in private authorities in those EU Member States where health care has been privatised.
[167] National Health Service Act 1977, s 3.
[168] See *R v Secretary of State for Social Services, ex p Hincks* (1979) 123 SJ 436.

the issue of the allocation of resources.[169] It has also been used to challenge access to medical treatment as the *Blood* case demonstrates.[170] The case of Diane Blood is also interesting as it illustrates the phenomenon of the impact of europeanisation on the health care systems of the Member States and more importantly the increasing drive towards the internalisation of the European legal order into the domestic legal order. Here again, judicial review provides a useful example of how decision-making by national authorities has had to come to terms with the requirements of European Community law.[171] Thus, in several cases, the justification of domestic legislation has involved EC law, that is to say, that the reasoning employed has drawn from EC law as well as from the domestic legal order. Thus, europeanisation is obligating public bodies to place material before the court which they would otherwise not be required to do, giving rise to greater scrutiny of certain administrative decisions.[172]

Generally speaking, judicial review promotes both transparent and accountable decision-making. In the case at hand, its role is in inculcating public officials with a sense of the desiderata of rational decision-making. This also entails raising awareness of these officials as to the importance of taking EC law and the rights contained therein seriously. This constitutes an impact on state institutions and the legal and administrative culture within which they are located. For national elites, ignorance is no defence. Thus, for example, a national authority (the Human Fertilisation and Embryology Authority in the *Blood* case) entrusted with the decision as to whether a woman could obtain the gametes of her deceased husband to travel to another EU Member State to seek fertility treatment was held by the Court of Appeal not to have been properly advised as to the remit of EC law in declining her application.

To conclude, the *Blood* case is a good illustration of national elites being unaware of the EC law implications for the way in which they reach decisions. Indeed, it sets a precedent for agents of the National Health Service to be aware of the remit of the impact of the EC legal order in a policy area, namely, health, which is customarily referred to as a remaining within the exclusive competence of the Member States albeit through the prism of single issues such as cross-border access to health care. Moreover, it establishes a duty for these elites not only to be aware of the impact but also it establishes a duty to demonstrate this awareness. The former duty is

[169] See, eg, *R v Cambridge Area Health Authority, ex p B (a minor)* (1995) 25 *Butterworths' Medico Legal Reports* 5; revsd (1995) 23 *Butterworths' Medico Legal Reports* 1, CA.

[170] See below.

[171] See C Lewis, 'Judicial Review and the Role of the English Court in European Community Disputes' in M Adenas and F Jacobs (ed), *European Community Law in the English Courts* (Oxford, Clarendon Press, 1998), 101.

[172] See *R v Secretary of State for Employment ex p Equal Opportunities Commission* [1995] 1 AC 1.

dependent on both knowledge and understanding of the Treaty basis regarding matters of Health[173] as well as the jurisprudence of the European Court of Justice which has been pivotal in the development of cross-border access to health care by EU citizens. It has been said that knowledge of the *acquis communautaire* amongst legal elites in the current EU Member States is extremely poor.[174] The case law of the European Court of Justice demonstrates that this also applies to other elites too, such as the health care civil servants, the medical profession and hospital administrators. However, it is difficult to draw assumptions concerning individual Member States as knowledge concerning access to health care services across borders varies. For example, 'Euregios',[175] include health service arrangements as part of their activities.[176] Indeed, some of the regions have even gone as far as to enact measures to ease the administrative burden on patients.[177] It is also difficult to assume that the level of knowledge in the new Member States will be lower than in the old Member States. Indeed, some of the medical professionals in the new Member States, as in Slovenia, have had the experience of cross-border health care for over 50 years.[178] In some of the new Member States, many medical professionals have undergone part of their training in the old EU Member States making them more aware of the possibility of cross border health care.[179]

On the one hand, EU Member States retain a firm hold over matters of health on the basis of the principle of subsidiarity[180] whilst on the other, their competence, like their sovereignty, is not absolute. It has been qualified and/or pooled. In *Vanbraekel* and *Geraets-Smits/Peerbooms*,[181] the assessment of 'undue delay' was held to be one for the medical professionals in the Member State where the EU citizen resided to make. In *Geraets-Smits/Peerbooms*, the

[173] Introduced by the Treaty of Maastricht through Art 129 EC, now amended and renumbered to Art 152 EC.
[174] See Sacha Prechal, National Courts in European Constitution, Paper given at a conference at the European University Institute, The Emerging Constitution of the European Union on 19 and 20 April 2002.
[175] And who benefit from the EU's INTERREG initiative.
[176] As in, eg, the Meuse–Rhine Region (Belgium, Germany and the Netherlands), Rhine–Waal (Germany and the Netherlands), Scheldemond (Belgium and the Netherlands) and Hainaut/Nord-Pas-de-Calais (Belgium and France).
[177] By simplifying the E112 procedure. Thus, in the case of Hainaut/Nord–Pas-de Calais, the E112F form is filled out by the hospital and is sent directly with a request for payment to the relevant institution in the Member State. See A Coheur, 'Integrating Care in Border Regions: An Analysis of the Euregio Projects' (2001) 7 *Eurohealth* 10.
[178] Arising out of the agreements with Italy enabling movement of people and services across the border. (Gorizia, Trieste and Udine Agreements between the Socialist Federal Republic of Yugoslavia and the Republic of Italy, 31 March 1955, Rome, Italy. See T Albrecht, 'Opportunities and Challenges in the Provision of Cross Border Care' (2002) 8 *Eurohealth* 8.
[179] See J Cachia, 'Human Resources in Maltese Healthcare: Solutions for Common Needs' (2002) 8 *Eurohealth* 17 and also S Nicholas, 'Movement of Health Care Professionals: Trends and Enlargement' (2002) 8 *Eurohealth* 11.
[180] See Art 152 (2) EC.
[181] See C–368/98 *Vanbraekel* and C–157/99 *Geraets-Smits and Peerbooms* [2001] ECR I-5363.

two applicants, who were insured under a Dutch social-insurance scheme for persons whose income is below a certain level, received medical treatment outside the Netherlands without obtaining prior authorisation from the fund. The question referred to the ECJ was whether the need to obtain prior authorisation in the circumstances contravened articles 49 and 50 (ex articles 59 and 60). The Court held that the authorisation requirement was a restriction of the freedom to provide and to receive services but that in the case at hand, it was capable of being objectively justified in the interests of maintaining a balanced medical and hospital service available to all and of preventing a social security system becoming seriously undermined. However, it is of interest to note that the Court elected to outline this position by the use of nuance. It held that the decision as to whether the treatment sought should be 'normal'[182] was one for the national (in this case the Dutch doctors) medical professionals to make. So too was the decision as to whether the same or equally effective treatment could be obtained without undue delay from an establishment with which the insured person's sickness insurance fund has contractual arrangements. However, in the case of the former, medical professionals were obligated to take into account the findings of international medical science when deciding whether the treatment sought was 'normal'. Here again, the Court can be seen to be giving guidelines to national authorities in relation to their decision-making, a practice it consolidated in a subsequent decision.

In *Müller-Fauré*,[183] the plaintiff, a Dutch national, had dental treatment while on holiday in Germany over the space of a month without authorisation. On her return to the Netherlands, she applied to her Dutch insurers for reimbursement of the costs of the treatment. The Fund refused on the advice of its advisory dental officer. The plaintiff appealed to the *Ziekenfonsraad*, which is responsible for supervising the management and administration of sickness funds. It upheld the Fund's decision by arguing that insured persons were only entitled to treatment and not reimbursement unless there were exceptional circumstances. The District Court of Rotterdam upheld the decision by stating that no exceptional circumstances had been proven. Moreover, the scale of the treatment was deemed to be unacceptable particularly as it had been obtained over several weeks.

Ms *van Riet*'s doctor requested the Amsterdam Fund's medical advisor to grant authorisation for a procedure (an arthroscopy) to be undertaken in Belgium as the waiting lists were shorter there. The request was rejected on the grounds that the procedure could also be performed in the Netherlands.

[182] This was the first condition laid down by the Dutch social insurance scheme, namely, that the treatment must be regarded as 'normal in the professional circles concerned'. The second condition was that the treatment must be 'necessary' for the person concerned.

[183] Case C–385/99 *V.G Müller-Fauré v Onderlinge Waarborgmaatschappij OZ Zorgverzekeringen UA* and *E.E.M. van Riet v Onderlinge Waarborgmaatschappij ZAO Zorgverzekeringen*, Judgment of 13 May 2003 (unreported).

Ms *van Riet* went ahead with the procedure in Belgium anyway. The results of the arthroscopy indicated the need for an ulnar reduction which was also carried out in Belgium. Ms *van Riet*'s sickness Fund refused to reimburse the cost of care. The *Ziekenfondsraad* confirmed the refusal on the basis that it was not an emergency, there was no medical necessity and appropriate medical treatment was available in the Netherlands within a reasonable period (namely six months). The Referring Court, the *Centrale Raad van Beroep* held that article 22 (1) (a) of Regulation 1408/71 did not apply as the treatment in question was not immediate and because the patient could have been treated in the Netherlands within a reasonable period of time.

At issue was prior authorisation and the nature of the medical cover in the Netherlands, which concerned a system of benefits in kind and not one based on reimbursement. Three questions were referred. First, are national provisions stipulating the need to obtain prior authorisation for treatment outside of the Netherlands with an institution with whom the sickness fund has not concluded an agreement contrary to articles 59 and 60 of the EC Treaty? Secondly, if so, does the nature of the Dutch system justify an exemption? Thirdly, is it relevant that the treatment involved hospital treatment? The Court held that as regards hospital treatment, the prior authorisation requirement does not violate articles 59 and 60. Authorisation may be refused only if treatment which is the same or equally effective for the patient can be obtained without undue delay in an establishment which has an agreement with a fund. As regards non-hospital treatment, however, the prior authorisation requirement does violate articles 59 and 60 even if the system is one of benefits in kind.[184] A variety of issues arise as a consequence of the case, not all of which may be dealt with here. The implications for state sovereignty of the decision necessitate the reconfiguration, or in the words of the Court, 'adjustment' of both the domestic law and culture of the Member States. Thus, the Court reiterated that whereas the sovereignty of the Member States was not undermined, the fundamental freedoms engender the need for the Member States to adjust their systems of social security.[185] Whereas the Court held that the distinction between the

[184] This to some extent mirrors the development of principles of access to education in the context of the application of EC law rules governing freedom to provide services. Here, the European Court of Justice has drawn a distinction between public education, to which the rules on services do not apply because they are not provided 'against remuneration', and private commercial education for which the normal rules on services do apply. In the cases concerning cross-border access to health care and in particular, in the context of hospital services, the Court does not seem to draw such a strict distinction. The Treaty rules on services are applied without special regard to the public nature of hospitals. This raises the issue why education and health are treated differently. Further, and in the alternative, the recent cases on cross-border access to health care may in effect overrule the older education cases. See G Davies, 'Welfare as a Service' (2002) 29 *Legal Issues of European Integration* 27.

[185] *Ibid* at para 102.

types of medical services, namely, benefits in kind and reimbursement was not tenable, it stated that Member States can establish ceilings for reimbursement as long as they are based on objective, non-discriminatory and transparent criteria. It is here that the Court addresses administrative decision-making in the Member States, which according to the Treaty it is bound to respect. Indeed, the Court states that when assessing the issue of undue delay, national authorities are required to consider 'all of the circumstances of each specific case' which include the nature of the medical condition as well as the degree of pain, the nature of the patient's disability in relation to, for example, his professional activity.[186] It is not the first time that the Court has intervened in decision-making by medical professionals and medical insurers regarding patient care. Thus, in *Geraets & Peerbooms* the Court held that when making decisions concerning prior authorisation, regard must be had to what is 'normal in professional circles'. In particular, concerning the issue of undue delay and the necessity of the treatment, practices which have been 'tried and tested by international medical science' and not only national medical opinion.[187] Anyone who has been in the unfortunate position of having to obtain more than one medical opinion regarding a medical complaint will testify to the unlikelihood that the experts will agree as regards diagnosis or methods of treatment. The absence of consensus is a universal as regards medical science. It is contested, subject to vogues and is anything but unitary. Indeed, the treatment in question in *Geraets* concerned a 'multi-disciplinary' approach to Parkinson's disease which involved types of therapy which addressed the socio-psychological effects of the disease for which there was no clinical and scientific evidence according to the plaintiffs. The subjective implications of disease, however, are difficult to measure and receive little attention in medical journals, save for being dismissed as irrelevant. The diagnosis and the treatment of myelo encephalopathy (ME) or what is more commonly referred to as the 'yuppie flu' is a useful case in point, with a considerable proportion of medical science denying its existence. Indeed, what about experimentation, as in the case of *Peerbooms*? The treatment in question concerned experimental treatment, namely neurostimulation, for coma therapy. A useful analogy is provided by the first English cases on human experimentation which still provide the legal standard for experimentation.[188]

In *Slater v Baker and Stapleton*,[189] an English surgeon treated the plaintiff's broken leg by breaking it and disuniting the callous from the leg after

[186] *Ibid* at para 90.
[187] See *Geraets & Peerbooms*, n 137 above, at para 90.
[188] I am indebted to Professor JK Mason for enabling me to develop the following section.
[189] (1797) 95 ER 860.

it had been set by another surgeon. In so doing, Dr Baker decided to try a device which he had recently developed and which he believed would extend the leg. The plaintiff's leg failed to heal and he sued for breach of contract. The court upheld the plaintiff's claim.[190] The court's reasoning, however, is flawed; it is based on paralogic and it is invalid. The conclusion does not follow to the extent that it relies on the consequences. The court's reasoning can be summarised thus:

— If you do something rashly, you may get a bad result.
— If you do something for the first time, you may get a bad result.
— Therefore if you do something for the first time, you are acting rashly.

The error lies in the assumption that because the consequences are the same, the antecedents are the same. However, you could do something for the first time and still get a bad result even though you had considered it very fully and were in no sense 'rash'. The accepted method at the time, as a host of surgeons testified at the trial, involved applying compression until the broken bone knitted together.[191] However, Dr Baker's method was the first recorded instance of the use of modern treatment. It is now common accepted practice in modern medicine to treat a broken leg by putting it in traction, *not* compression. In essence, Dr Slater was treated unfairly. The standard set out in the judgment, 'ignorantly, and unskilfully, contrary to the known rule and usage of surgeons' is false. Dr Baker, is referred to earlier on in the judgment in the most reverential of terms.[192] However, the attitudes of the time come through a few lines down.[193] *Slater v Baker and Stapleton* was a cornerstone for medical malpractice claims; the principles laid down in it should, however, never have been applied to experimentation. Innovation demands an outlook which is inherently prospective, something which the judges and the surgeons in the case regarded with both distaste and caution.

[190] 'For anything that appears to the Court, this was the first experiment made possible with this new instrument; and if it was, it was a rash action, and he who acts rashly acts ignorantly: and although the defendants in general may be as skilful in their respective professions as any two gentlemen in England, yet the Court cannot help saying, that in this particular case they acted ignorantly and unskilfully, contrary to the known rule and usage of surgeons.' (*Slater*, n 189 above, at 863).
[191] *Ibid* at 861.
[192] 'Baker has been above 20 years the first surgeon in St Bartholomew's Hospital, reads lectures in surgery and anatomy, and is celebrated for his knowledge in his profession as well as his humanity; and to charge such a man with ignorance and unskilfulness upon the records of this Court is most dreadful.' (*Ibid* at 862).
[193] 'When we consider the good character of Baker, we cannot well conceive why he acted in the manner he did but many men very skilful in their profession have frequently acted out of the common way for the sake of trying experimentation.' (*Ibid* at 862).

To summarise: the evolution of any policy which denies reasonable access to readily available resources is constrained by the requirements of European integration, an obligation which has arisen as a consequence of decisions by the European Court of Justice which has obvious implications for elites in the Member States. However, as was stated above, whereas some examples, such the *Blood* case, are indicative of the impact of europeanisation on decision-making, it is impossible to draw conclusions concerning the extent of the effects. The reason for this is mainly twofold. First, the way in which discretion is exercised in decision-making is generally very difficult to track, particularly given that the application of judicial review is severely limited in this context. Secondly, there is, as yet, no suitable 'monitoring' device, other than litigation which can signal the extent to which the *acquis communautaire* and European rights in particular are being taken seriously. Litigation, however, occurs on an ad hoc, case by case basis, the access to which is dependent on inter alia sufficient resources. It can, as in the *Blood* case offer clues but cannot provide a peg upon which to hang an evaluation. In other words, you cannot judge the implementation of the *acquis communautaire* by litigation alone.[194]

What is evident from this case study of access to health care across the EU is that undertakings to protect Member States' national identity[195] that is, as the Draft Constitutional Treaty states, 'inherent in their fundamental structures, political and constitutional, inclusive of regional and local self-government'[196] are increasingly hollow claims.

CONCLUSION

Social rights in the EU arose as a by-product of policies designed to overcome barriers to trade and the prevention of the distortion of competition. Whereas many have elected to refer to them in terms of constitutional entitlements, there is clearly a limited basis for this, if one regards rights as being more than rhetorical devices. The study of cross border access to health care in the EU reveals that European social rights are evolving as a reaction to Member State policies which deny reasonable access to EU citizens

[194] Even litigation does not provide a comprehensive overview of the implementation of the *acquis communautaire*. Despite documentation services at the level of the EU such as CELEX and the Commission and the Court of Justice Annual Reports on the monitoring of the application of EC law, and those which exist in the Member States such as JURIS (for Germany), JURIFRANCE (for France), LEXIS (for the United Kingdom), gaps in the coverage arise given that many of the cases of the lower courts are unreported.
[195] See Art 6 (3) of the TEU.
[196] CONV 850/03 at Art 5(1).

to readily available resources. Why then speak of social rights at all? Why seek to adopt the language of constitutionalism, particularly as experience shows that constitutions can achieve very little regarding matters of social welfare? However, in the age of constitutional mainstreaming in the EU ushered in by the Charter of Fundamental Rights and consolidated by the European Convention, it would be illogical, and indeed, ill advised, to isolate social rights from the process of the EU's process of ongoing constitutionalisation.[197] The reasoning is as follows: social rights are an important component of the symbols and rhetoric that serve to consolidate the sense of common identity among EU citizens. Including social justice as one of the constitutive principles upon which the Union is founded sends out an important message to the citizen as well as to those elites upon whom citizens are dependent for the realisation of their rights. For whereas one can safely say that never before has the reform process been closer to the citizen as a consequence of the European Convention,[198] it is doubtful whether it goes far enough in rendering the Union as close to the citizen as possible, despite the proactivity of the *Forum*.[199] This may change with the adoption of a European constitution. However, it remains to be seen whether a constitution would fulfill such high expectations, particularly as regards those who act as the gatekeeper of the *acquis communautaire*, namely the elites of Member States. If they do not pay attention to a European constitution, if they do not take the rights enshrined therein seriously in other words, there can be little gained by such a document. There is little incentive given that the loyalty of public authority officials is directed to the states which they serve. Europeanisation challenges this loyalty, to a certain extent. This extent may not lend itself to being measured in quantitative terms, particularly given the elastic nature of EU competence. Attempting to measure it may be like attempting to establish a strict catalogue of competences. It may of very little practical help but its significance may be linked to the process, namely, the process of coming to terms with the extent of europeanisation which the Member States have undergone. In order to so this, however, loyalty to the state by its officials needs to be, dare one say it, overcome,

[197] See remarks made by Frank Vandenbroucke, Minister for Social Affairs and Pensions, Belgian Federal Government; 'The EU and Social Protection: What Should the European Convention Propose?', Paper presented at the Max Planck Institute for the Study of Societies, Köln, 17 June 2002.

[198] See the Convention's Futurum website: <http://europa.eu.int/futurum/index_en.htm>. Note for instance that in one of the sessions of the European Convention organised with representatives from civil society, there was a separate contact group for social matters. See CONV 126/02. See also the involvement of the European Youth Convention which was convened on 9–12 July 2002. See CONV 205/02.

[199] The Forum is divided into four categories, namely, political or public authorities, socio-economic interests, academic interests and think tanks and other representatives of civil society such as NGOs, etc.

that is, loyalty to a state's tradition, its heritage, its culture and not least the values which are embedded therein. In other words, what is at stake is a state's very identity which the Treaty of European Union protects, but not, as the next chapter will show, at all costs.

5

Implementation of Rights and the Role of Elites

INTRODUCTION

WHEREAS THE EUROPEAN Union's fundamental rights policy is underlined by market rights in the context of negative integration, engineered through the 'creative jurisprudence'[1] of the European Court of Justice,[2] this is no longer exclusively the case. They have also been developed in other policy areas, such as inter alia anti-discrimination,[3] the context of the Charter of Fundamental Rights[4] and latterly, the Draft Constitutional Treaty,[5] which incorporates the Charter. In sum, European rights are a product of the symbiosis which arises between the rights enumerated in the Treaties, the decisions of the European Court of Justice and the constitutional traditions of the Member States,[6] both within and outwith the context of the internal market. Be that as it may, stringent emphasis on market freedoms may undermine both social and political rights as provided by the Member States. Secondly, the ability to take advantage of these rights may vary between states, particularly given that they often require positive measures that the EU is unable to furnish. Thirdly, the interpretation and implementation of European rights may require the EU to adopt some features of the state provoking

[1] See T Tridimas, *The General Principles of EC Law* (Oxford, Oxford University Press, 1999), 205.

[2] See generally J Coppel and A O'Neill, 'The European Court of Justice: Taking Rights Seriously?' (1992) 29 CML Rev 669; JHH Weiler and N Lockhart, '"Taking Rights Seriously": The European Court of Justice and its Fundamental Rights Jurisprudence' (1995) 32 CML Rev 73. P Alston and JHH Weiler, 'An "Ever Closer Union" in Need of a Human Rights Policy: The European Union and Human Rights' in P Alston, M Bustelo and J Heenan (eds) *The EU and Human Rights* (Oxford, Oxford University Press, 1999), 3.

[3] See generally M Bell, *Anti-discrimination Law and the EU* (Oxford, Oxford University Press, 2002).

[4] [2000] OJ C 364/1. See generally P Eeckhout, 'The EU Charter of Fundamental Rights and the Federal Question' (2002) 39 CML Rev 945; R Alonso Garcia, 'The General Provisions of the Charter of Fundamental Rights' (2002) 8 *European Law Journal* 492.

[5] CONV 820/03. This text was revised twice. (CONV 820/1/03 REV 1, CONV 820/1/03 REV 2). See also CONV 847/03, CONV 848/03.

[6] See Art 6 (2) TEU. See also Art 7 (3) of the Draft Constitutional Treaty.

a challenge to the legal cultures of the Member States which may be questionable in terms of sovereignty.

I will not attempt to develop all of the issues mentioned above. This chapter will focus on the third issue, namely, regarding the interpretation and implementation of European rights and the impact thereof on national legal cultures. The implications are twofold. First, I shall address the extent to which the European Convention has shaped the conditions for implementation of the EU's rights regime thereby generating resistance on behalf of many Member States in terms of sovereignty and identity. I shall discuss the citizenship provisions contained in the Draft Constitutional Treaty in conjunction with the principle of loyal co-operation and the protection of national identity, and in particular, the constitutional and administrative structures of the Member States. Secondly, I shall turn my attention to the issue of language rights, arguing that they are important for similar reasons as citizenship and loyal co-operation, namely, they are part of the context of adjunctive or implementation rights which render effective or ineffective the various objectives bound up with the development of a rights regime. Language rights in the EU tend to be viewed in terms of the respect of national identity on the one hand and the clear and harmonised application of the internal market on the other. It will be argued that an efficient language policy in the EU is one which reconciles respect for diversity with the need for effective communication. The contribution of general protocols of good communication to the making of a just, engaged and active polity requires statements concerning rights (political, social, fundamental freedoms and so on) but also a context of implementation which is itself partly legally grounded and supplied, an issue which the discussion concerning access to justice in the EU has tended to overlook.[7]

CITIZENSHIP, SOVEREIGNTY AND IDENTITY

European Rights

Constitutions have traditionally extended rights to the citizens of states, a legacy of the process of state formation in which constitutionalism played a pivotal role.[8] Indeed, the contours of constitutionalisation are the contours of the state which, in the case of rights, has led to the extension of rights by

[7] Tending to concentrate on the relationship between Arts 230 and 234 EC Treaty. E Szyszczak, 'Making Europe More Relevant to its Citizens: Effective Judicial Process' (1996) 21 ELR 351; A Biondi, 'Effectiveness versus Efficiency: Recent Developments on Judicial Protection in EC Law' (2000) 6 *European Public Law* 311. See, however, D Chalmers, 'Judicial Preferences and the Community Legal Order' (1997) 60 MLR 164 at 167ff.

[8] See, eg, UK Preuß, 'Problems of a Concept of European Citizenship' (1995) 1 *European Law Journal* 267; see also generally C Möllers, *Staat als Argument* (München, CH Beck, 2000);

reason of personhood, as provided by classical human rights doctrine, under the slogan of peoplehood or citizenship.

Conceptually speaking, European rights encompass a variety of rights, namely, political, social, cultural and economic rights, distinctions which have not always been easy to maintain, neither in theory nor in practice. There are two dimensions to this uncertainty, namely internal and external. As regards the internal dimension, the ambiguity concerning strict classifications of rights is somewhat exacerbated by the particular nature of EU law. Thus, for example, economic rights may also be social rights.[9] This ambiguity is further amplified by the elastic nature of EU competences. As regards the external dimension, uncertainty arises as a consequence of the impact of supranational rights on a variety of legal cultures which are diverse. As in the case of social rights discussed in the previous chapter, a number of levels of diversity must be distinguished. Diversity exists as between Member States regarding rights and the values upon which they are predicated and according to which they are articulated. Diversity also exists, however, amongst legal and administrative elites within these Member States as to the concept of rights. Indeed, it is difficult to assume the existence of a homogeneous approach to rights amongst those vested with the responsibility of rights recognition and implementation. In the EU, rights debates do not operate on the basis of shared understandings, neither in terms of analysis nor in terms of practice.

Sovereignty and Identity

Rights are part and parcel of a state's constitutional heritage which, together with values, tradition and the culture within which they are embedded, characterise its identity. They are the product of history, testimony to conflicts and revolutions and are the result of both coming to terms with the past (which is referred to in the German case as *Vergangenheitsbewältigung*)[10] and of the process of overcoming it. 'We shall overcome', a song of the 1960s Civil Rights movement in the United States, is a *memento mori* of the process of confronting and indeed overcoming injustices caused be segregation and the institutionalised racism enshrined therein. The Oxford Dictionary distinguishes between three meanings of the word 'overcome'. It refers to dealing with a problem (1), to

M Troper, *La théorie du droit, l'état* (Paris, Presses Universitaires de France, 2001); K-H Ladeur, *Postmoderne Rechtstheorie* (Berlin, Duncker & Humblot, 1992), 207ff.

[9] As in the case of cross-border access to health care which arise in connection with the free movement provisions. See ch 4.

[10] See generally UK Preuß, *Revolution, Fortschritt, Verfassung* (Frankfurt, Suhrkamp, 1992).

dealing with a defeat (2) and to being overwhelmed (3).[11] As we shall see, all three meanings are relevant to the discussion at hand. The first definition, namely dealing with a problem, might usefully describe the respective constitutional traditions in the Member States and the experiences which have generated the acts of constitution-making. The second definition (2) is derivative from the first and conjures up the process whereby a state reconciles itself with a defeat and draws up a constitution in order to consolidate both learning from the past but also, where appropriate, its 'break' with it.[12] Definition (3) may be attributed to the impact of EU constitutionalism on the respective legal orders of the Member States through rights. Taken together with the process of europeanisation of their legal systems and cultures, it is arguable that this impact has to some extent overwhelmed the Member States and their elites, and no more so than in the case of rights which are embedded in a variety of multi-jurisdictional contexts provided by the United Declaration of Human Rights (UDHR),[13] the International Covenant on Civil and Political Rights (ICCPR), the European Convention on Human Rights (ECHR) and the European Union's Charter of Fundamental Rights, taken in conjunction with the jurisprudence of the European Court of Justice and the European Convention of Human Rights.[14]

Generally speaking, rights framed by international organisations pose little threat to state sovereignty to the extent that the 'threat' is contained by the limited remit and applicability of international law. The case of 'supranational' rights, however, is different. It is no coincidence that the UK Government heralded the adoption of the Human Rights Act 1998,[15] which incorporated the European Convention on Human Rights, in terms of 'bringing rights home'.[16] In other words, the Act was a way in which the

[11] See J Pearsall (ed), *The Concise Oxford Dictionary* (Oxford, Oxford University Press, 2001), 1015.
[12] The constitution of the Federal Republic of Germany is a notable example. See E Spevack, *Allied Control and German Freedom: American Political and Ideological Influences on the Framing of the West German Basic Law* (Münster, Hamburg, 2001). Constitution-making as a process of breaking with the past was also a phenomenon which arose in connection with many of the new Member States. See R Elgie and J Zielonka, 'Constitutions and Constitution-Building' in J Zielonka (ed) *Democratic Consolidation in Easten Europe, Vol I: Institutional Engineering* (Oxford, Oxford University Press, 2001), 33; See also the contribution by W Sadurski, 'Conclusions: On the Relevance of Institutions and the Centrality of Constitutions in Post-communist Transitions' in the same volume at p 455.
[13] See generally H Steiner and P Alston, *International Human Rights in Context* (Oxford, Oxford University Press, 2000).
[14] See generally G de Búrca, 'Convergence and Divergence in European Public Law: The Case of Human Rights' in P Beaumont, C Lyons and N Walker (eds) *Convergence and Divergence in European Public Law* (Oxford, Hart Publishing, 2002), 131.
[15] Which entered into force on 2 October 2000. SI 1998 No 2883.
[16] See the pre-legislative White Paper, *Rights Brought Home: The Human Rights Bill* (Cm 3782, 1997).

impact of a supranational legal instrument could be contained. Member States have less room to manoeuvre vis-à-vis EC law given that it creates rights which are directly enforceable by individuals,[17] it has primacy of national law[18] and damages can be sought by EU citizens from their respective Member State governments in the case of failure to implement EC law measures.[19] Notwithstanding, Member States have to some extent retained the competence over fundamental rights, despite several inroads created by the jurisprudence of the European Court of Justice[20] and the promulgation of the EU Charter of Fundamental Rights.[21] Given that the former has been developed on a piecemeal basis in certain policy areas, and the lack of a binding nature of the latter, state sovereignty appears to be intact, relatively speaking. Indeed, it is perhaps of little surprise that the consensus on incorporating the Charter in the European Constitution as part of the Convention was, more or less, unanimous.[22]

The increasing drive towards constitutionalisation of the Union, however, has, however, had a 'spill over effect' on to the constitutional orders of the Member States. This has led to a process of europeanisation over an area which had traditionally been regarded as a Member State competence as regard rights per se as well as their implementation.

Challenging the National Heritage(s)

The link between national identity and the constitutional traditions of the Member States is addressed in article 6 (3) TEU.[23] Furthermore, in respecting fundamental rights, the Union is bound to seek inspiration by the European Convention for the Protection of Human Rights and Fundamental Freedoms as well as the 'constitutional traditions common to the Member States' as general principles of Community law.[24] Rights are integral to a state's constitutional order and the values it seeks to promote both therein and thereby. As a supranational order, European Community law has provoked national constitutional jurists into registering their unease — and indeed, at times even dissent — both in judicial and extra-judicial fora. As was addressed in detail in Chapter Two, the German case serves as a particularly useful indicator of how rights have provided the

[17] Case C–26/62 *Van Gend en Loos (NV) Algemene Transporten Expeditie Onderneming v Nederlandse Administratie der Belastingen* [1963] ECR 1.
[18] Case C–6/64 *Costa (Flaminio) v ENEL* [1964] ECR 585, [1964] CMLR 425.
[19] See Case C–6 & 9/90 *Francovich & Bonifaci v Italy* [1991] ECR I–5357.
[20] See Case C–29/69 *Stauder v Stadt Ulm* [1969] ECR 419.
[21] [2000] OJ C 364/1.
[22] See the final report of the Working Group (II), CONV 354/02.
[23] 'The Union shall respect the national identities of its Member States.'
[24] Art 6 (2) TEU.

basis of such resistance.[25] Notwithstanding, similar trends are discernible in some of the other EU Member States[26] which have provoked some commentators to plead in favour of the adherence to the principle of constitutional tolerance.[27] In other words, the protection of national identity and constitutional traditions is not absolute but is qualified by commitments of the Member States to the European integration project, as the case law of the European Court of Justice regarding the protection of fundamental rights illustrates.[28] This has been further amplified by the introduction of the EU Charter of Fundamental Rights which, though not binding, has been increasingly drawn from by the Court[29] although in the sense of confirming rather than establishing particular fundamental rights.[30] In effect, the Charter applies to Member States only when they are implementing Union law.[31] The case of *Wachauf* has shown the extent to which this is easier said than done, given the varying interpretations of the concept of implementation.[32] The debates concerning the adoption of article 51 (1) have been well documented and are indicative of the wider discords provoked by the issue of the binding nature of the Charter as a whole.[33]

Notwithstanding, the fears of the impact on state sovereignty by EU fundamental rights underpinned much of the deliberations of the European Convention. The reactions to the skeleton draft of 28 October 2002 are a case in point.[34] So too was the publication of the first 16 articles of the Draft Constitutional Treaty[35] to which 1,040 amendments were tabled by delegates to the Praesidium alone. The concern over the chal-lenge to state sovereignty is also noticeable in the other draft constitutions which emerged, as in the case of the Dashwood draft which refers to the 'constitutional order

[25] See the discussion of the decisions by the German Federal Constitutional Court in *Solange I* (BVerfGE 37, 271 and *Solange II* decision (BVerfGE 73, 339) at s 3.2.

[26] See, eg, *Frontini v Ministero delle Finanze* [1974] CMLR 372. See generally the second section of M Cartabia and JHH Weiler, *L'Italia in Europa* (Bologna, Il Mulino, 2000). See also the decision by the Spanish Constitutional Court concerning the ratification of the Treaty on European Union: see *Re Treaty on European Union* [1994] 3 CMLR 101.

[27] See JHH Weiler, 'Federalism without Constitutionalism' in K Nicolaïdis and R Howse (eds) *The Federal Vision* (Oxford, Oxford University Press, 2001), 27.

[28] See generally Alston and Weiler, n 2 above.

[29] See Eeckhout, n 4 above.

[30] *Ibid* at p 947.

[31] As provided by Art 51 (1) of the Charter.

[32] See Case C–55/88 *Wachauf v Germany* [1989] ECR 2609.

[33] In particular see G de Búrca, 'The Drafting of the EU Charter of Fundamental Rights' (2001) 26 ELR 26. J Schönlau, 'Drafting Europe's Value Foundation: Deliberation and Arm-twisting in Formulating the Preamble to the EU Charter of Fundamental Rights' in E Eriksen, JE Fossum and A Menéndez (eds) *The Chartering of Europe* (Oslo, ARENA, 2001), 127. See F Deloche-Gaudez, 'La Convention pour l'Élaboration de la Charte des Droits Fondamentaux: Une Méthode d'Avenir?' (2001) 15 *Études et Recherches* 1, also available at <http://www.notre-europe.assoc.fr>.

[34] See the *Preliminary Draft Constitutional Treaty* prepared by the Secretariat at the request of the Convention President Giscard d'Estaing (CONV 369). For an indication of the reaction to the draft see *The Guardian* (29 October 2002).

[35] See the Draft of Arts 1 to 16 of the Constitutional Treaty (CONV 528/03).

of sovereign states', who have chosen to pool aspects of their respective sovereignties but that this pooling does not impair their respective national identities.[36] However, perceptions of impairment vary. Whilst the Convention spoke the language of respect for national identity, it may, as this next section will show, have been merely a rhetorical device. To some extent, the Convention contributed to the issue of implementation of rights, in the context of the citizenship provisions contained in article 8 of the Draft Treaty establishing a Constitution for Europe of 18 July 2003 and the loyal co-operation clauses contained in article 5.[37]

THE IMPLEMENTATION OF RIGHTS AND THE CONVENTION ON THE FUTURE OF EUROPE

Briefly stated, article 8 of the Draft acts as a sort of 'restatement' of the provisions contained in the existing EC Treaty.[38] The parasitic quality of EU citizenship is retained to the extent that only nationals of EU Member States enjoy the rights and duties associated with it which include the right of free movement, the right to vote and stand as a candidate in the European Parliament and municipal elections, diplomatic and consular protection, the right to petition the European Parliament, the right to apply to the Ombudsman and to write to the institutions and advisory bodies of the Union in any of the Union's languages and obtain a response in the same language. As has been said in another context, however, 'no restatement is simply a restatement'.[39] Certain amendments have been made, such as article 8 (3) which provides that:

> These rights shall be exercised in accordance with the conditions and limits defined by the Constitution and by the measures adopted to give it effect.[40]

[36] 'The Union shall be established as a constitutional order of sovereign States. The Member States have chosen in some measure to exercise their sovereignties in common, through the institutions of the Union, under the conditions laid down by this Treaty. In so combining their sovereignties, for defined purposes and within defined limits, the Member States maintain their national identities. The institutions of the Union, when acting pursuant to powers conferred by this Treaty, shall respect the national identities of the Member States, their cultural and linguistic diversity and their traditions.'

[37] See CONV 820/03. This text was revised twice. (CONV 820/1/03 REV 1, CONV 820/1/03 REV 2). See also CONV 847/03, CONV 848/03.

[38] This section has appeared in an earlier form on the website of the Federal Trust (UK). I am indebted to Jo Shaw for allowing me to publish it in its embryonic form. See <http://www.fedtrust.co.uk/Media/Aziz.pdf>.

[39] N Walker, 'Protection of Fundamental Rights in the European Union: The Charter of Fundamental Rights' in P Cullen and PA Zervakis (eds) *The Post-Nice Process: Towards a European Constitution* (Baden-Baden, Nomos Verlag, 2001), 119.

[40] Interestingly enough the reference to the principle of equality between men and women which was included in the previous draft (CONV 528/03) was dropped.

Notwithstanding, the status quo has been reaffirmed but for a few minor alterations. It is then of little surprise that the response to what was originally article 7 of the Draft Treaty of 28 October 2002 by the Convention's delegates[41] was somewhat constrained leading to somewhat unimaginative proposals such as, for example, of extending EU citizenship to a wider category of individuals, including those who have resided in a EU Member State for more than five years, refugees and stateless person. All in all, however, article 7 offered little by way of innovation.[42]

However, article 8 of the July draft is best understood in the light of the other provisions contained in the constitutional blueprint proposed by the Praesidium and in the light of the existing body of EC law. Indeed, it is suggested that this is how the concept of EU citizenship is best understood, namely as a derivative of the existing Treaty provisions. In particular, I wish to focus my attention on the interplay between the citizenship provisions contained in article 8 of the Draft and the principles of loyal co-operation between the Member States vis-à-vis the Union contained in article 5 (2) and respect of the national identities of the Member States

> inherent in their fundamental structures, political and constitutional, inclusive of regional and local self-government. It shall respect their essential State functions, including those for ensuring the territorial integrity of the State, and for maintaining law and order and safeguarding internal security.[43]

This provision is central to the recognition, interpretation and implementation of European rights in which much depends on the sphere of public administration, public policy and law at the axis of both the national and the supranational legal systems and cultures.

The Principle of Loyal Co-operation

In its Draft (CONV 528/03), it was immediately noticeable that the Praesidium introduced a novel concept, namely, that of loyal co-operation, which is referred to in other sections of the Draft Constitutional Treaty.[44]

[41] See CONV 574/1/03.
[42] See, however, the proposals made by Gráinne de Búrca: G de Búrca, 'Fundamental Rights and Citizenship' in B de Witte (ed) *Ten Reflections on the Constitutional Treaty for Europe* (San Domenico di Fiesole, Robert Schuman Centre for Advanced Studies, 2003), 11.
[43] See Art 5 (1) of the Draft.
[44] And indeed other drafts. See, eg, Art 8 (5). Note that the principle also appears in the draft proposed by Peter Hain and Andrew Dashwood, CONV 345/1/02, CONTRIB 122 at p 25. Note that in the proposal submitted by the European Commission, *Feasibility Study, Contribution to a Preliminary Draft Constitution of the European Union, Working Document*, published on 4 December 2002 at the request of President Prodi in agreement with

The principle appeared in the Skeleton which referred to it in rather opaque terms:

> It sets out the obligation of loyal co-operation of Member States vis-à-vis the Union, and the principle that the acts of the Institutions are implemented by the Member States.[45]

No further guidance was provided in the commentary to the Draft as to where this principle originates from and how it is supposed to function.

What is particularly interesting is the conflation between the principle of loyal co-operation and the protection of national identity, and in particular, the constitutional and administrative structure of the Member States. I use the word 'conflate' with care given that it is not meant to refer to a sense of fusion but rather understanding principles when taken together. The background of these provisions is somewhat explained by the existing Treaty provisions. Thus, to some extent, the Praesidium drew from, article 10 EC,[46] for which article 5 (1) of the July Draft is in effect a summary. However, no mention is made as regards the principle of loyal co-operation in the existing Treaties although, conceptually speaking, it is to be found in a number of the constitutional orders of the Member States, and in particular, in terms of a duty for civil servants towards the state.[47]

Mr Barnier and Mr Vitorino references are made to the principle of 'good faith', see Art 4 (1) which provides that:

> The Member States shall act in good faith in relation to the Union and shall support its initiatives. They shall take all appropriate measures to ensure fulfilment of the obligations arising out of the Constitution. They shall facilitate the achievement of the Union's tasks. They shall abstain from any measure which could jeapardise the attainment of the objectives of the Constitution.

And further at Art 4 (2) which states that:

> In compliance with the subsidiarity principle, the Union shall act in good faith in relation to the Member States and shall preserve their identity and their national and regional diversity. It shall respect the constitutional organisation of the Member States, including in its relations with their territorial units.

Reference is made to the 'spirit of loyalty and mutual solidarity' at Art 5 (Relations between Member States).

[45] See CONV 369/02.

[46] Which provides that:

> Member States shall take all appropriate measures whether general or particular, to ensure fullfillment of the obligations arising out of this Treaty or resulting from action taken by the institutions of the Community. They shall facilitate the achievement of the Community's tasks. They shall abstain from any measure which could jeapardise the attainment of the objectives of this Treaty.

[47] See ch 3, on Access to Public Service Employment p 00–000. See also N Beenen, *Citizenship, Nationality and Access to Public Service Employment: The Impact of European Community Law* (Groningen, Europa Law Publishing, 2001).

Loyalty, Elites and the State

The German concept of loyalty to the constitution or *Verfassungstreue* provides that all civil servants must swear on the constitution. Loyalty is not only presumed but it is a mandatory requirement for employment.[48] Article 33 of the German Basic Law not only upholds a nationality requirement for certain posts in the public service but it also includes a stipulation as to loyalty between members of the public service and the state. The assumption which exists is that non-nationals cannot be trusted to display such loyalty, which further explains why Member States have been so willing to frame those public service positions which qualify as an exception to the freedom of movement as widely as possible. A degree of 'spill over' can also be seen in the academic debate. The concept of constitutional patriotism or *Verfassungspatriotismus*[49] is a case in point, as is the way in which it found favour amongst policy makers both within and outwith Germany. Further examples exist in other EU Member States. Thus, in the case of the United Kingdom, para 4.1.1. of the Civil Service Management Code upholds 'a duty of loyal service to Crown as their employer.' Loyalty to a constitution need not necessary by limited to a state. Much depends on whether one adopts the view that the state is a pre-requisite to a constitution.[50] I do not propose to deal with this here save to say the following: special allegiance or loyalty is very much part of the legacy of the process of state formation and the role of elites in both generating and mediating a sense of national unity.[51]

In particular, it was particularly during its initial phases, such as, for example, during the *Risorgimento* period in Italy, where the role of elites was pivotal in the process of state engineering. Compliance was mostly achieved by recourse to powerful imagery which was employed to conjure up the notion of the state's constitutive elements. The emergence, for example, in the 19th century during the process of state building of a 'canon' in literature published between 1801 and 1849, such as in the case of Italy provides a useful example. Thus, inspiration was sought from 'national-patriotic texts'[52] which defended the idea of the state in order to instil pride, to engender a sense of community and also to mobilise its inhabitants for military conflict if need be or for furthering the economic national cause. The idea of a nation which was perpetuated was one which

[48] 'Die Ausübung hoheitsrechtlicher Befugnisse ist als ständiger Aufgabe in der Regel Angehörigen des öffentlichen Dienstes zuübertragen, die in einem öffentlichrechtlichen Dienst- und Treueverhältnis stehen.' (Art 33 para 4).

[49] See J Habermas, *Die Einbeziehung des Anderen* (Frankfurt am Main, Suhrkamp, 1996).

[50] See the discussion in ch 2 One Legal Order or Two p 00–00.

[51] See generally R Bendix, *Nation-building & Citizenship* (New Brunswick, Transaction Publishers, 1996) at ch 4, 'Administrative Authority in the Nation-State' 127–72.

[52] Such as inter alia de Giusti, Berchet, Foscolo, Niccolini and Manzoni, Botta and even comprising Verdi. See A Banti, M, *La nazione del Risorgimento: Parentela, sanità e onore alle origine dell'Italia unita* (Torino, Einaudi, 2000), 27ff.

was pre-existing, which possessed ontological, natural qualities such as race, territory and language and a sense of common history. In other words, elites were crucial in 'bringing the nation home to the people'. They were central as intermediaries between the state and its subjects whose loyalty was as indivisible as the sovereignty of the state which they served. Indeed, the principle of loyalty is an integral element of the statist legacy.

One wonders to what extent the principle of loyalty is in fact appropriate in the context of a European constitution given its ideological and value based underpinnings.[53] Indeed, it is somewhat curious that the Praesidium elected in favour of the principle of loyalty as opposed to the principle of sincere co-operation developed by the European Court of Justice,[54] and the duty to co-operate in good faith[55] which is arguably more objective and less ideological and, generally speaking, free of the statist legacy.

Two qualifications must be made at this juncture. First, the principle of good faith as outlined in the decision of 22 October 2002 in *Roquette Frères* was raised in the context of competition proceedings. Extrapolating the principle to apply to respecting the *acquis communautaire* as a whole and European rights in particular is slightly tenuous given the 'special relationship' which has been forged between the Commission and the respective national competition authorities whereby the latter in effect act as the former's agent.[56] Secondly, even though the principle of loyalty has been addressed in judicial decisions,[57] the legal basis has been developed in a series of staff cases and in particular in relation to freedom of expression and the duty of loyalty of civil servants who are employed by the EU institutions.[58] Cases such as *Connolly*[59] and *Capitaine*[60] for instance

[53] For a general discussion on the principle of loyalty see K Mortelmans, 'The Principle of Loyalty to the Community (Art 5 EC) and the Obligations of the Community Institutions' (1998) 8 *Maastricht Journal of European and Comparative Law* 67.

[54] See generally B de Witte, 'Institutional Principles: A Special Category of General Principles of EC Law' in U Bernitz and J Nergelius (eds) *General Principles of European Community Law* (The Hague, Kluwer Law International, 2000), 143 at 148. See also Case C–33/76 *Rewe-Zentralfinanz eG and Rewe Zentral AG v Landwirtschaftskammer für das Saarland* [1976] ECR 1989 were the Court at 1997 refers to the principle of co-operation as laid down by Art 5 in relation to the national courts' application of the direct effect of the provisions of Community law.

[55] See Case C–94/00 *Roquette Frères SA v Directeur général de la concurrence, de la consommation et de la répression des fraudes* of 22 October 2002 (unreported) at paras 30–32 which also cites Case 14/83 *Von Colson and Kamann* [1984] ECR 1891, para 26 and Case C–80/86 *Kolpinghaus Nijmegen* [1987] ECR 3969 at para 12.

[56] See, eg, the Preliminary Draft Notice on Co-operation between National Competition Authorities and the Commission in Handling Cases Falling within the Scope of Arts 85 or 86 of the EC Treaty [1996] OJ C262/5.

[57] The word 'arguably' is used here to draw attention to the fact that the principle of loyalty is addressed in this decisions by implication only.

[58] See generally R Hernu, 'Le Devoir de loyauté du fonctionnaire des Communautés européenes' (2002) 38 *Revue Trimestielle de Droit Européenne* 686.

[59] Case C–274/99P *Connolly v Commission* [2001] ECR I–1611.

[60] Case 69/63 *Capitaine v Commission* [1964] ECR I–00239.

are of limited applicability not only because of the *sui generis* nature of the European Union institutional civil service but also because the principle of loyalty has been referred to by the Court of Justice in an interpretative vein. That is to say that the principle of loyalty does not feature in the staff code but has been inferred by the Court. Thus, for example, the Court of Justice in *Connolly* refers to the obligation of loyalty on behalf of EU civil servants vis-à-vis the Treaties as well as the institutions which they serve[61] on the legal basis of staff regulations. Indeed, this principle is not referred to in articles 11 and 12. For its part, article 11 provides that:

> An official shall carry out his duties and conduct himself solely with the interests of the Communities in mind; he shall neither seek nor take instructions from any government, authority, organisation or person outside his institution.

Article 12 provides that:

> An official shall abstain from any action and, in particular, any public expression of opinion which may reflect on his position.[62]

Sections of the judgment in *Connolly* are worth quoting in full if only to illustrate how adept a tribunal can be in referring to a principle in such a persuasive manner that it comes as some surprise when one realises that it is not mentioned once in the staff regulation. Thus, the Court states that:

> Il y a lieu, ensuite, de souligner que l'article 12, premier alinéa, du statut constitue, au même titre que les articles 11 et 21, l'une des expressions spécifiques de l'obligation de loyauté qui s'impose à tout fonctionnaire (voir l'arrêt N/Commission, point 129, confirmé sur pourvoi par l'ordonnance de la Cour du 16 juillet 1998, N/Commission, C-252/97 P, Rec. p I-4874).[63]

And further:

> Il en va de même de l'obligation de loyauté, laquelle, selon la jurisprudence, ne s'impose pas seulement dans la réalisation de tâches spécifiques, mais s'étend aussi à toute la sphère des relations existant entre le fonctionnaire et l'institution.[64]

[61] See *Connolly*, above, at para 117.
[62] The Staff Regulations are reproduced at: <http://europa.eu.int/comm/dgs/personnel_administration/statut/tocen100.pdf>.
[63] See *Connolly* above, at para 127.
[64] *Connolly* above, at para 130, citing its decision in *Williams v Court of Auditors* at para 68. See further at para 168 where the Court states that:

> Étant donné que de telles déclarations sont contraires aux liens de loyauté et de confiance qui doivent régir les relations entre administration et fonctionnaires, et inconciliables avec l'intégrité exigée de tout fonctionnaire (voir, en ce sens, arrêt M./Conseil, précité, point 21),

For its part, article 5(1) of the Draft is notable for keeping up appearances to the extent that the constitutional and administrative structures of the Member States are proclaimed to be an exclusive Member States competence. The provisions must, however, be read in conjunction with the de facto impact of the *acquis communautaire* on the national legal orders of the Member States as well as the concomitant process of europeanisation. Article 5 may well do much by way of symbolism and convince the Member States that their sovereignty has been left largely intact. However, whereas they may contain this impact, they are incapable of immunising the state's constitutional and administrative order from the forces of europeanisation, as the previous chapters have shown. In other words, the borders of the state are permeable, porous and thereby penetrable by virtue of a legal order which created rights which are directly enforceable by individuals.[65] Given the ongoing process of constitutionalisation in which the EU has been entwined, of which the European Convention is but one 'constitutional moment',[66] a 'spill over effect'[67] on the constitutional orders and the public authorities of the Member States is inevitable. Whilst constitutional judges who have found themselves in the role of 'border patrols'[68] are aware of the impact,[69] it is doubtful whether they realise the full implications.

The case of access to public service employment is interesting as it illustrates what the Treaty has given with one hand, namely the protection of exclusion of non-nationals to public service employment on the one hand, it has, in effect, taken away with another. Thus, the European Court of Justice has been adept at construing 'the State' as narrowly as possible[70] as part of its jurisprudence which is in direct contrast to the definition as part of its jurisprudence on direct effect where it has construed it as widely as possible.[71] However, it does not reveal the extent of the impact of

l'AIPN pouvait, dès lors, considérer à juste titre que l'argument du requérant, concernant sa prétendue bonne foi, n'était pas fondé.

[65] Case C–26/62 *Van Gend en Loos (NV) Algemene Transporten Expeditie Onderneming v Nederlandse Administratie der Belastingen* [1963] ECR 1.
[66] See B Ackerman, *We the People* (Cambridge MA, Harvard University Press, 1998). See also B de Witte, 'The Closest Thing to a Constitutional Conversation in Europe: The Semi-Permanent Treaty Revision Process' in P Beaumont, C Lyons and N Walker (eds) *Convergence and Divergence in European Public Law* (Oxford, Hart Publishing, 2002), 39.
[67] First identified by Haas although he did not have the law and the courts in mind. See EB Haas, *The Uniting of Europe: Political, Economic and Social Forces, 1950-1957* (Stanford, Stanford University Press, 1968).
[68] JHH Weiler, 'Epilogue: "Comitology" as Revolution' in C Joerges and E Vos (eds) *EU Committees: Social Regulation, Law and Politics* (Oxford, Hart Publishing, 1999), 339 at 343.
[69] See generally A-M Slaughter, A Stone Sweet and JHH Weiler (eds), *The European Court and National Courts-Doctrine and Jurisprudence. Legal Change in its Social Context* (Oxford, Hart Publishing, 1998).
[70] See generally Beenen, n 47 above, at 71ff.
[71] See eg C–188/89 *Foster (A.) & Others v British Gas plc* [1990] ECR I–3313.

europeanisation on elite decision-making. Several indicators exist such as, for example, judicial review in England and Wales. Indeed, judicial review provides a useful example of how decision-making by national authorities has had to come to terms with the requirements of European Community law.[72] Thus, in several cases, part of the justification of legislation has involved EC law, that is to say, that the reasoning employed has drawn from EC law as well as from the domestic legal order, at times, obligating public bodies in the United Kingdom to place material before the court which they would otherwise would not be required to do, giving rise to greater scrutiny of certain administrative decisions.[73] Generally speaking, judicial review promotes both transparent and accountable decision-making. It is designed to inculcate public officials with a sense of the desiderata of rational decision-making. This also entails raising awareness of these officials as to the importance of taking EU law and the rights contained therein seriously. This gives rise to an impact on the public authorities and the legal and administrative culture within which they are located. In other words, for national elites, ignorance of the *acquis communautaire* and European rights arising therefrom is no defence.[74] The sharing or 'pooling' of sovereignty of the Member States as a consequence of their EU membership also 'pools' sovereignty as regards decision-making by public authorities.[75] Moreover, it also 'pools' the loyalty of elites who work for these authorities leading to a sort of bifurcation,[76] although not necessarily in hierarchical terms. This is to say nothing of the effects of elites who, though vested with the responsibility of implementing European rights, are not public authority officials. Given the increasing drive towards the privatisation of public services in many EU Member States and the concomitant to the public/private divide,[77] public

[72] See C Lewis, 'Judicial Review and the Role of the English Court in European Community Disputes' in M Adenas and F Jacobs (eds) *European Community Law in the English Courts* (Oxford, Clarendon Press, 1998), 101.
[73] See *R v Secretary of State for Employment ex p Equal Opportunities Commission* [1995] 1 AC 1.
[74] See, eg, the case of Diane Blood where a national authority (the Human Fertilisation and Embryology Authority) entrusted with the decision (in accordance with ss 12, sch 3 paras 1, 3, 5 of the Human Fertilisation and Embryology Act 1990) as to whether a woman could obtain the gametes of her deceased husband to travel to another EU Member State to seek fertility treatment was held by the Court of Appeal not to have been properly advised as to the remit of EC law in declining her application. See *R v Human Fertilisation and Embryology Authority, exp Blood* (1996) 35 Butterworths' Medico Legal Reports 1. See Ch 4.
[75] See generally K-H Ladeur (ed), *The Europeanisation of Administrative Law: Transforming National Decision-making Procedures* (Aldershot, Ashgate, 2002).
[76] Or as was suggested to me by a European Commission official, to an 'enrichment' of their duty of loyalty. See, however, the discussion of the European Court of Justice's decision in *Kziber* in ch 2, The Judiciary as Sovereignity's Care (under) taker? at proff in relation to the decision of French public authorities to ignore its impact.
[77] See generally D Oliver, *Common Values and the Public–Private Divide* (London, Butterworths, 1999); S Millns and N Whitty (eds), *Feminist Perspectives on Public Law* (London, Cavendish, 1999).

authority officials no longer have the monopoly over rights implementation. Political participation in the EU, as was discussed in Chapter Three, occurs across national, transnational and supranational lines across a number of levels and by a variety of actors, not all of whom are public authority officials. Indeed, in the case of political lobbying, the points of access to political participation are informal networks which cut across state institutions. As regards judicial activism, access to participatory rights such as in the case of environmental law, is mediated by jurists, not all of whom are civil servants. The implementation of social rights in the EU and in particular, cross-border access to health care illustrate how national decision-making regarding patient care have been europeanised.

Be that as it may, the Draft Treaty has in effect provided a legal framework in which the europeanisation of elite decision-making can be consolidated, though arguably more by default than by design. This poses a dilemma for national elites, who have traditionally been expected to display loyalty to the states they serve which is unquestionable and indivisible. Not only are national elites vested with the task of implementing legal norms which are generated by the state but they are also responsible for the implementation of those which emanate from the EU legal order. Access to European rights by rights holders is mediated through national judges, who retain a filter of considerable importance by virtue of the preliminary reference procedure[78] and through administrative elites who are also responsible regarding rights implementation. As was discussed in Chapter Two, much depends on how these elites perceive the impact of EU law on their legal and administrative orders.[79] In particular, if they regard the recognition of EU law as being mediated through the authority of their own national legal order as opposed to being vested with its own authority, then the substance of the rights of individuals may be lost as a consequence of national judicial translation. This not only means that they may, as some have pointed out, be unlikely to recognise that Community law might prevail over their own national legal orders[80] but also, even where they do recognise this, the substance of this recognition may leave much to be desired. This is particularly apposite in relation to European rights because it is national elites who are responsible for their recognition, interpretation and implementation. What is clearly needed is an adequate reconciliation between national and supranational interests through a two-way loyalty clause. However, it is also essential that the addressees of European rights are able to engage with those norms upon which they can rely. It is here that the Draft Treaty articles concerning citizenship fall short, mainly

[78] Art 234 EC.
[79] See ch 2, the section One Legal Order or Two?
[80] B de Witte, 'Community Law and National Constitutional Values' (1991) 2 *Legal Issues of European Integration* 1 at 4.

in terms of clarity, coherence, consistency and constitutional stability.[81] By clarity, I mean the importance and indeed necessity for the citizen to be able to understand the Treaty. As it stands, articles 8 and 5 (1) and (2) do little to put the citizen in a position of being capable of understanding the rights and duties contained therein, not least those to which he is a party. By coherence, I mean to refer to the debate concerning the Union's competences, that is to say, when it speaks, and when it is obligated to do so but also when it must remain silent. The debates concerning competences did little to foster the hope that we shall at long last be rid of the muddles and complexities which has come to be an indelible part of its legacy. As regards consistency, that is to say, internal and with the existing *acquis communautaire*, it is submitted that the Draft provisions tend towards inconsistency. Finally, the status quo does very little to create a sense of stability as part of the Union's ongoing process of constitutionalisation, which is regrettable to say the least.

The issue of transparency and democratic legitimacy and making the EU more understandable for the EU citizen is emphasised to such an extent at the level of the EU that it is strange that it is not addressed throughout the *acquis communautaire*. The issue of simplification, for example, referred to in the Nice Declaration was framed very much in terms of understanding and greater visibility, an issue which was again taken up in by the European Convention. Thus, the Nice Declaration refers to, 'a simplification of the Treaties with a view to making them clearer and better understood without changing their meaning'. It is of interest to note that the Laeken Declaration is framed in less clear terms. Vague references are made to access to Council documents in a, 'clear, open, effective, democratically controlled Community approach'.[82] Clarity is referred to in conjunction with simplification:

> Thus, the important thing is to clarify, simplify and adjust the division of competence between the Union and the Member States in the light of the new challenges facing the Union.[83]

This also, however, gives rise to a duty to ensure that that the citizen is able to engage with the Community approach, at the stage of both design and implementation. Further attention must be paid to the main tool of active engagement, namely, language. An effective language policy for the EU is needed which is able to reconcile respect for diversity with the need for effective communication.

[81] However, they have been addressed by implication. See the Henry Kissinger Lecture given by Giscard d'Estaing at the Library of Congress in Washington DC on 1 February, 2003.
[82] See the Laeken Declaration on the Future of the European Union available at <http://european-convention.eu.int/pdf/LKNEN.pdf>.
[83] See s II. Challenges and Reforms in a Renewed Union.

LANGUAGE RIGHTS AND THE LANGUAGE OF THE RIGHTS REGIME

The burgeoning debate in European law over its capacity to deal with language rights has traditionally focused on culture.[84] As well as being an expression of culture, however, language is also an instrument of communication. However, the current language rights regime in the European Union emphasises the cultural dimension of language rights through the regulation of the official EU languages (hereinafter referred to as the regulation of 'status') so much so that the regulation of the use of codes or specialist jargon in the official communications of the EU institutions with its citizens has been overlooked (hereinafter referred to as the regulation of 'codes'). There are legal and normative claims to transparent and accessible 'official' language. Transparency and accessibility of 'official' language is of paramount importance for sustaining democratic legitimacy, respect for the rule of law and good governance in the EU. It is argued that that there is a duty of clear and transparent language use both internally and externally in EU official communications which should be mainstreamed[85] into EC law based on the principle of 'good administration' contained in article 41 of the EU Charter of Fundamental Rights, which also has implications regarding freedom to information more generally.[86] Constitutionalism has a vital role to play in promoting recognition and respect for clear and transparent language use in decision-making. A European constitution must proactively promote and structure this process at a number of different levels of governance (international, national, regional, local). Europe's 'constitutional moment' as evidenced by the European Convention, which was established by the Laeken Declaration, is a necessary but insufficient starting point for this process.

Generally speaking, constitutional provisions are generally vaguely stated and often are of a symbolic and rhetorical nature. Embedding language rights in a constitutional framework is an ongoing process that must be progressed by detailed enabling legislation. The recognition of language rights is dependent, in the first instance, on the motivation and willingness of elites, both at the national and the supranational level, to co-operate and

[84] This section draws from an article, M Aziz, 'Mainstreaming the Duty of Clarity and Transparency as Part of Good Administrative Practice in the EU,' (2004) *European Law Journal* (forthcoming). See, eg, N Nic Shuibhne, *EC Law and Minority Language Policy* (The Hague, Kluwer Law International, 2002); J Usher, 'Languages and the European Union' in M Anderson and E Bort (eds) *The Frontiers of Europe* (London, Pinter, 1998), 222; B de Witte, 'Surviving in Babel? Language Rights and European Integration' in Y Dinstein (ed) *The Protection of Minorities and Human Rights* (Dordrecht, Nijhoff, 1992), 277.

[85] As in the case of gender mainstreaming, for instance. See the 1996 Communication on mainstreaming, COM (96) 67 and also COM (1998) 122. M Pollack and E Hafner-Burton, 'Mainstreaming Gender in the EU' (2000) 7 *Journal of European Public Policy* 432.

[86] See eg DM Curtin, 'Citizens' Fundamental Right of Access to EU Information: An Evolving Digital Passepartout?' (2000) 37 CML Rev 7.

comply. It may also require social mobilisation and social learning to support the duty of clear and transparent language use. Some dimensions of Community law, such as food labelling, provide an appropriate model for the duty of clear and transparent language which, it is argued, ought to be mainstreamed as a guiding principle for communication between the EU institutions and the EU citizen.

This section is divided into two parts. The first part deals with the regulation of status, namely, language as an expression of culture and will be used to juxtapose the position in the EU regarding the regulation of codes. I propose to begin by outlining the rationale of the EU's language rights regime. In particular, I shall show how the statist legacy has influenced the EU debate concerning linguistic diversity and the debates concerning the number of official EU languages. In disussing Language Rights Policies, I shall show that cultural heritage continues to be the dominant *Leitmotiv* for the EU's language regime despite attempts of some institutional actors, such as the European Court of Justice, to if not sever, at least recalibrate, the link. Finally under the heading Language and Democratic Legitimacy, I shall deal with the EU language regime in order to show how the law has dealt with the status issue whilst ignoring the separate issue of the use of codes in language. It will be argued that according linguistic rights provide only part of the solution. Rights regimes are heavily dependent on elite compliance. A distinction will be drawn between how the law communicates rights (thus, elite compliance as regards the implementation of rights) and how communication can happen about the law. The latter is dealt with in relation to the language of elites which can be rendered inaccessible through the use of specialised terminology which leaves the citizen at a considerable disadvantage thereby alienating him further from the Union's political processes. This both detracts and undermines democratic legitimacy. It will be argued that in order to counter this, a duty of clarity ought to be extrapolated from existing EC law regarding food labelling and more generally the doctrine of informed consent concerning medical treatment, both of which have been pivotal in securing standards of clarity regarding the communication of information for the benefit of consumers and patients. It will be argued that a duty of clarity should be mainstreamed into EU decision-making based on the principle of good administration which, like the freedom of information, has both quantitative and qualitative implications.

The European Unions's Language Regime: Status

The European Union is composed overwhelmingly of homogenised states in terms of language which is a legacy of the 19th century process of state formation. The linguistic unification of nation-states was an extensive operation and required the mobilisation of considerable resources.[87] To give just one illustration of its scale: at the time of the unification of Italy between 1859 and 1861, the dialects used in the peninsula were so distinct that outside of Tuscany and Rome, where Italian was spoken, only 160,000 in over 20 million individuals could be defined as italophones.[88] The driving force behind an enterprise of such a massive scale drew on powerful motives and transformative ideologies, in addition to resources. The Italian example illustrates how a state and political unity can be manufactured through the invention of a 'national' cultural tradition and the imposition of linguistic homogeneity. Thus, the elites came to regard themselves as having a mission to make 'Italians' through education, mainly through national secular schools and universities.[89] However, whereas education is pivotal in state building it is by no means sufficient.[90] Unity as seen through the prism of nation and a common language enables states to assert not only particularity but also, as Weber's reference to turning peasants into Frenchmen illustrates, superiority.[91] Thus, anyone who speaks Irish or Catalan *is* Irish or *is* Catalan,[92] an issue which has more often than not been linked to the ideology of state building during the 19th century, although the potential of language as an imperial tool was recognised long before this. As Antonio de Nebrija stated in 1492, 'siempre la lengua fue compañera del imperio'.[93]

[87] See A-M Thiesse, *La Création des identités nationales. Europe XVIII–XX siècle* (Paris, Seuil, 2001), 67ff.
[88] See GF Mancini, Democracy and Constitutionalism in the European Union: Collected Essays (Oxford, Hart Publishing, 2000), 59 and also generally T de Mauro, *Storia dell' Italia unita* (Roma, Laterza, 1995).
[89] See R Bellamy, *Modern Italian Social Theory* (Cambridge, Polity Press, 1987), 7ff.
[90] See E Gellner, *Nations and Nationalism* (Oxford, Blackwell, 1983) and also FO Ramirez and J Boli, 'The Political Construction of Mass Schooling: European Origins and Worldwide Institutionalization' (1987) *Sociology of Education* 2 on the nation-building role of compulsory education and R Brubaker, *Citizenship and Nationhood in France and Germany* (Cambridge, MA, Harvard University Press, 1992) on the role of conscription.
[91] E Weber, *Peasants into Frenchmen: The Modernization of Rural France 1870–1914* (London, Chatto & Windus, 1979).
[92] Although the 1998 Linguistic Policy Law passed on 7 January 1998 breaks with language nationalism espoused in the 1983 Linguistic Normalisation Law by insisting that Catalan culture is not synonymous with the Catalan language and by referring to those whose mother tongue is Castilian as 'Catalans', in other words, a territorial rather than a linguistic definition of national identity. For a translation of the key passages of the 1998 Law see S Gore and J MacInnes, 'The Politics of Language in Cataluny', Edinburgh Working Papers in Sociology No 13 (Department of Sociology, University of Edinburgh, 1998). See also Art 3 of the Catalan Statute of Autonomy which provides that the language proper to Catalonia is Catalan (1) but also provides that Catalan is the official language of Catalonia, as is Castilian, the official language of the whole of the Spanish State (2). See <http://www.catalunya-lliure.com/estatut.html>.
[93] A de Nebrija, *Gramática de la lengua Castellana* (Madrid, 1492).

Many EU Member States, such as Spain,[94] have included provisions concerning a 'state language' in their constitutions.[95] Those Member States which have elected against including such provisions in their constitutions have tended to make implicit references by adopting criteria for the naturalisation of immigrants through citizenship provisions, as in the case of Germany.[96]

It has been argued that one of state constitutionalism's heavy biases is the drive of homogeneity and what James Tully has called the 'Empire of Uniformity'.[97] Seen through this lens, constitutionalism is predicated on equal citizenship. In other words, we are all equal in the eyes of the constitution. Recognising difference, however, challenges this assumption, which not only challenges constitutionalism but has also been taken to threaten the very idea of the nation based on a covenant existing between equals. However, one of the most traditional and essential functions of constitutions is that they have gone some way towards protecting diversity, and cultural diversity in particular.[98] Seen in this way, constitutionalism creates a higher law which restrains the actions of actors.

The EU language rights regime has been used to respect the identity of the Member States. The battles fought regarding language rights have been those which concern the number of the official EU languages as well as the dominance of one or two languages in the EU's legislative process.[99] Little, if any, attention has been paid to the need to ensure that the addressees of EU legislation are capable of understanding the immediate impact of the *acquis communautaire* on their daily lives and, in particular, European rights which arise therefrom.

[94] See Art 3 of the Spanish Constitution which provides that:

> (1) Castilian is the official Spanish language of the state. All Spaniards have the duty to know it and the right to use it. (2) The other languages of Spain will also be official in the respective autonomous communities, in accordance with their Statutes. (3) The richness of the linguistic modalities of Spain is a cultural patrimony which will be the object of special respect and protection.' (Translation provided by the International Constitutional Law website at: <http://www.oefre.unibe.ch/law/icl/index.html>.)

[95] As in the case of France, where the reference to the French language in the Constitution was included in 1992. Art 2 now states that, 'The language of the Republic shall be French.' An amendment of Art 12 of the Italian Constitution is currently being debated in order to include a provision stating that Italian shall be the official language of the Republic. See XIV Legislatura — Scheda lavori preparatori. Atto parlamentare: C. 750 (progetto di legge costituzionale) — significa atti della camera n. 750. (Fase iter Camera: 1 ^ lettura. Proponente Angela Napoli. See <http://www.camera.it>.

[96] *Zuwanderung Gestalten, Integration Fördern*, Bericht der Unabhängigen Kommission 'Zuwanderung' (Berlin 4 July 2001), reproduced at <http://www.spiegel.de/politik/deutschland/0,1518,143295,00.html>.

[97] See J Tully, *Strange Multiplicity: Constitutionalism in an Age of Diversity* (Cambridge, Cambridge University Press, 1995) at ch 3.

[98] See F de Varennes, *Language, Minorities and Human Rights* (The Hague, Martinus Nijhoff, 1996).

[99] See V Heutger, 'Law and Language in the European Union' (2003) 3 *Global Jurist* 1.

Language Rights Policies in the European Union Regarding Official Language Use

At present, there are eleven official languages which operate at the level of the EU, a position which will be revised in the period of post-accession when the number of official languages will increase to 21. The EU's language rights policy is both highly symbolic and politically sensitive,[100] mainly because it is one facet of the Member States' identity over which they have traditionally asserted exclusive competence. The legal response of the EU's legal order has been framed accordingly, namely, to avoid head on collisions with Member States which fear that their national identity is under threat.

For example, the European Court of Justice judgment in *Groener* in which it was particularly wary of interfering with the language policy in Ireland is a useful case in point. The *Groener* case[101] concerned a Dutch national working in Ireland as a part-time teacher, whose application for a full-time post was rejected in view of insufficient knowledge of the Irish language. The ECJ held that the implementation of a policy for the protection and promotion of a language of a Member State is not prohibited by the EC Treaty, as long as it does not encroach on a fundamental freedom such as the freedom of movement of workers. The court applied the proportionality test in order to accommodate the sensitive issues concerning national identity and culture.[102]

One of the main aims of language regulation is to preserve a group's national and cultural identity albeit according to different rationales.[103] Thus, for example, modern language legislation in France has been targeted at protecting the purity of the language (which is referred to by linguists as 'corpus planning') and, by extension, the culture from the insidious influence of foreign languages, primarily English. The *loi Toubon* proclaims that the French language is 'a fundamental element of France's personality and heritage'.[104] The *loi* also contains a second dimension, namely, that which

[100] See B de Witte, 'Enlargement and the EU Constitution' in M Cremona (ed) *The Enlargement of the European Union* (Oxford, Oxford University Press, 2003), 209 at 227.
[101] See C–379/87 *Groener v Minister for Education* [1989] ECR 3967, [1990] 1 CMLR 401 at para 19.
[102] *Ibid* at para 18.
[103] In other words, different nations will have different reasons embedded in historical, socioeconomic and cultural contexts which give rise to different rationales.
[104] See Art 1 of the *loi Toubon*. See generally SA Feld, 'Language and the Globalization of the Economic Market: The Regulation of Language as a Barrier to Free Trade' (1998) 31 *Vanderbilt Journal of Transnational Law* 153. See also the decision by the French Constitutional Court: no 99–412 DC, June 1999 in which the Court held that French ratification of the European Charter on Regional or Minority Languages would be unconstitutional on the basis that it was incompatible with the principles of indivisibility of the Republic, equality before the law and unity of the French people.

concerns the regulation of language use (which linguists refer to in terms of 'status planning'). The perennial tradition of linking linguistic diversity and cultural heritage has been reproduced at the level of the EU,[105] mainly in connection with specific policies.[106] The tenor of the provisions have tended to be non-committal, mainly because of the potential challenge to state sovereignty posed by policies affecting a state's identity. Thus, for example, the Charter of Fundamental Rights refers to linguistic diversity in article 22 in the same breath as the protection of cultural and religious diversity although this is slightly ambiguous given that it could relate to EU action and Member States action.[107] The Draft Constitutional Treaty also refers to the need for the Union to respect its 'rich cultural and linguistic diversity, and shall ensure that Europe's cultural heritage is safeguarded and enhanced.'[108]

In practice, the internal use of working languages has been shown to be anything but equal, with English and French accounting for 98 per cent of all internal use, both written and oral.[109] Some official services are not offered in all eleven languages.[110] The policy debate on language use emphasises 'the more languages the better'. In other words, an increase in the number of languages used in the communication between institutions and the citizen brings the Union, to paraphrase the EU Treaty, closer.[111] The European Convention has reiterated the status quo. According to article 8 of the Draft Constitutional Treaty, the citizen has the right to address the institutions and advisory bodies of the Union in any of the Union's languages and obtain a response in the same language,[112] a right which has consistently been upheld by the consecutive restatements of EU citizenship ever since its introduction in the Maastricht Treaty. The Draft Treaty further provides a list of the languages in which the

[105] See, eg, Art 151 EC.

[106] Such as education. See Art 149 (1) of the TEU which provides that:

> The Community shall contribute to the development of quality education by encouraging cooperation between Member States and, if necessary, by supporting and supplementing their action, while fully respecting the responsibility of the Member States for their content of teaching and the organisation of education systems and their cultural and linguistic diversity.

[107] Which states that, 'The Union respects cultural, religious and linguistic diversity'.

[108] CONV 850/03.

[109] See M Strubell, 'Towards a European language policy- una polìtica linguìstica europea', contribution to *The Public Discourse of Law and Politics in Multilingual Societies* held at the International Institute for the Sociology of Law in Oñati, Spain on 6–8 June 2002.

[110] Thus, the portals of the Regional Funds <http://www.inforegio.org> and the Research and Development Website <http://www.cordis.lu> are only in five languages, namely, French, German, English, Italian and Spanish.

[111] Art 1 of the Treaty on European Union (TEU). Although note that the European Convention has proposed that the wording 'ever closer union' be dropped in the new constitutional Treaty. See *The Times* (7 February 2003).

[112] See CONV 850/03.

Constitutional Treaty shall be made available.[113] The current legal provisions governing European Union citizenship provide inter alia that

> every citizen may write to any of the institutions or bodies referred to in this article or in article 7 in one of the languages mentioned in article 314 and have an answer in the same language.[114]

In order to facilitate direct applicability, the whole corpus of European law must also be available in all the eleven official EU languages.[115] All European Court of Justice (ECJ) and Court of First Instance (CFI) decisions must be available in any of the official EU languages.[116] In order to avoid discrimination between economic actors from different countries, the European Commission directorate (DG IV) in charge of competition, for example, must be able to communicate in any of the EU official languages.[117] In the case of the Office for Harmonisation in the Internal Market (OHIM), which deals with trademarks and designs, five official languages are used, namely English, French, German, Italian and Spanish.[118] Even this modest restriction, however, has given rise to vigorous protest on the part of some of those whose mother tongue had been excluded.[119] The cost — in resources, inaccuracies and delays — of operating multilingually at all these levels is huge — it is currently estimated at 800 million euros for all the EU institutions together —[120] and may

[113] See CONV 850/03 Art IV–10 of pt 4 (General and Final Provisions) provides that:

> The Treaty establishing the Constitution, drawn up in a single original in the Danish, Dutch, English, Finnish, French, German, Greek, Irish, Italian, Portuguese, Spanish, Swedish, Czech, Estonian, Latvian, Lithuanian, Hungarian, Maltese, Polish, Slovak and Slovenian languages, the texts in each of these languages being equally authentic, shall be deposited in the archives of the Government of the Italian Republic, which will transmit a certified copy to each of the governments of the other signatory States.

[114] See para 3 of Art 21 of the EC Treaty. Note, however, that this right is confined to EU citizens only and does not include third-country nationals. The EU Charter of Fundamental Rights, however, extends the scope of the right beyond citizenship in the sense that Art 41 (4) refers to 'any person'.

[115] See Art 314 EC in conjunction with Regulation 1/58, [1952–1958] OJ Special Edition 59.

[116] See Arts 29–31 of the Rules of Procedure. This rule has led some commentators to criticise the court's decisions for being inelegant and obscure. See T Koopmans, 'The Future of the Court of Justice of the European Communities' (1991) 11 *Yearbook of European Law* 15 and also GF Mancini and D Keeling, 'Legal Culture and Politics in the Life of the European Court of Justice' (1995) 1 *Columbia Journal of European Law* 397.

[117] See Reg 1/58, [1952–1958] OJ Special Edition 59.

[118] Note that an application may be filed in any of the eleven official EC languages but applicants must specify a second language, which must be an OHIM working language, in which the Office may send written communications.

[119] The European Parliament voted on 10 April 2002 with 256 votes to 187 (with 95 abstentions) to approve the resolution concerning use of five official languages in the adoption of a Community patent. See a report in *El Mundo* (11 April 2002).

[120] See Press Release, 'Commission Prepares its Language Services for Enlargement' on 20 December 2001 (IP/01/1869).

accordingly affect the perceived legitimacy of the European administration, when compared, say, to the US administration and that of each Member State.[121] Using all EU languages means that the quality of the texts will suffer. If the quality of the texts suffer, so too will democratic legitimacy. This problem is, however, intractable given that it would be impossible to adopt only one official language in the EU.

Whilst appearing to be inclusive, however, little can be done to prevent the likelihood that the provisions may in effect entrench the distance between the Union and the citizen particularly given the existence of the use of specialist terminology or 'jargon' by elites. Language operates in a variety of spheres and contexts in order to satisfy a number of aims and functions, some of which cut across class, profession and nationality not to mention sectors or spheres of society. The latter point is particularly apposite as regards the EU given that language policy is scattered across a variety of specialised and highly technical fields of competence which involve linguistic diversity.[122] The ensuing tension between the Commission and the European Parliament on the one hand, which have concentrated largely on the cultural nexus of language policy[123] and the Court of Justice on the other, which has focused on the extent to which minority linguistic claims interfere with trade and the internal market is a case in point.[124] Not all language issues, as the Court has been at pains to point out, are linked to cultural heritage. Thus in *Parliament v Council*[125] the Parliament sought to have a Council decision on the multi-annual programme to promote the linguistic diversity of the Community in the information society[126] annulled on the grounds that it should have specified article 151 as part of its legal basis. In its decision, the Court drew a distinction between the 'essential and indisociable' and the 'incidental' components of the measure. If, as the Court argued, the industrial component was the main or predominant component, then the appropriate legal basis was article 157 of the EC Treaty. In essence, the Court held that the cultural aspects of the contested measure were incidental and that the marginalisation which the legislature sought to

[121] The planned EU enlargement will potentially account for up to ten new languages as of 2004, leading to a further explosion of translation and interpretation costs.

[122] See N Nic Shuibhne, 'Culture, Language, Law and Rights: Tracing an EC Framework', Background Paper as part of the workshop on The Public Discourse of Law and Politics in Multilingual Societies held at the International Institute for the Sociology of Law in Oñati, Spain on 6–8 June 2002.

[123] See, eg, *Community Action in the Cultural Sector*, EC Bulletin Supp. 6/77; *Stronger Community Action in the Cultural Sector*, Bulletin of the European Communities, Supplement 6/82; *New Prospects for Community Cultural Action*, COM (92) [1992].

[124] See, eg, Case C–281/98 *Angonese v Cassa di Risparmio di Bolzano* [2000] ECR I–4139, Case C–274/96 *Bickel and Franz* [1998] ECR I–7637 and Case C–33/97 *Colim v Bigg's* [1999] ECR I–3975.

[125] Case C–42/97 *European Parliament v Council of the European Union* [1999] ECR I–869.

[126] This is aimed particularly at the needs of small and medium-sized companies facing different language markets within the EC. See [1996] OJ L306/40.

ward off was in the commercial sphere of the information society and not the sphere of cultural heritage. What the Court omitted to address, however, was that there are many cases in which the spheres overlap.

Language and Democratic Legitimacy

If one subscribes to the view held by some scholars to equate political legitimacy with political support, it follows that one must also consider the distinction between two types of support, namely, specific and diffuse support.[127] Briefly stated, the former refers to a set of attitudes towards institutions based on the fulfilment of expectations of politics or actions. The latter is more contentious given that every citizen will disagree with, dislike or distrust the policies of political institutions. However, whilst they may disagree with the actions of these institutions, they may nonetheless concede their authority as political decision makers.[128] The importance of maintaining the allegiance of the people to the source of political power emphasises the relational aspect of sovereignty to the extent that it represents the quality of the political relationship that is formed between the state and the people and is thereby tied up with the notion of political power and public law. Trust of the citizens is essential in order to maintain state sovereignty. The very notion of sovereignty as operating at the state level to sustain the affiliation of the citizen is clearly an argument in favour of the nation-state which sees the transfer of sovereignty to supranational instances as weakening the affiliation of the citizen, an issue which is repeatedly discussed in the multiple citizenship discourse, and also the debates, such as those leading up to the reforms of the Citizenship laws in Germany concerning the concept of dual citizenship.[129] My contention is that if one regards sovereignty of the nation-state as being pooled by virtue of European and International obligations that this also gives rise to the following corollary, which goes to the heart of the issue of democratic legitimacy and consent, namely, trust is also 'pooled', or 'qualified' or 'lost' — depending on whichever way one regards the effect of European integration on the sovereignty of the Member States. Whether sovereignty resides at the level of the nation-state or elsewhere is largely irrelevant. What is important is that sovereignty exists. It will, by nature, command affiliation and trust. The level at which sovereignty resides is irrelevant to the affiliation of the trust of the citizen because sovereignty is intrinsic to whether

[127] See G Caldeira and JL Gibson, 'The Legitimacy of the Court of Justice in the European Union: Models of Institutional Support' (1995) 89 *The American Political Science Review* 356 at 357.
[128] *Ibid.*
[129] WW Barbieri, *Ethics of Citizenship: Immigration and Group Rights in Germany* (Durham NC, Duke University Press, 1998).

citizens feel confident that states perform certain duties and the citizens feel comfortable with the obligations. If the EU performs, it will attract both support and affiliation.[130]

Greater access to institutions and their decision-making structures means very little if this access is not accompanied by enabling measures which are able to come to terms with the number of levels at which language operates. It is not enough to provide websites for translation issues[131] and greater access through the internet, for example,[132] and leave its operational aspect to a sort of 'survival of the fittest' contest amongst those are at ease with information technology and those who are less so. This is a phenomenon which is not typical of the EU but is inherent to all official language use as a whole. It might be argued why ought the EU take the lead in a matter which might be construed as being the sole responsibility for the Member States, particularly as it is they who are responsible for implementing the *acquis communautaire*. Notwithstanding, however, the issue of democratic legitimacy of the Union is one over which it is responsible, in conjunction with the Member States. Much is made in the Laeken Declaration, for example, between the link between democracy, transparency and efficiency in the Union as part of its mandate to the European Convention to 'bring the European institutions closer to the citizens.' The citizen must also, however, be brought closer to the institution. Whereas the Convention is to be commended in providing greater visibility of its debates and for ensuring a greater degree of participation of civil society through its Futurum website,[133] it is argued that this falls short of safeguarding democratic legitimacy for a wider section of society given the working assumption that all those affected are (a) computer literate, (b) able to locate documents in the maze of hyperlinks and (c) persevere where most others have failed, which can be particularly arduous when the advice which one receives from EU officials is, 'It's all on the web.'[134]

In the case of the EU, the use of specialist jargon and elite concepts includes *technical* language, EU bureaucratese, some of which not even national public authorities are at ease with. Furthermore, the use of specialist jargon in effect consolidates networks and power of which there are two separate but related dimensions. The first is the external dimension of language, namely the lingua franca of deliberation, be it English, French, German and so on. The second dimension refers to the use of elite codes, that is, language for 'insiders' which operates in spheres of politics, the

[130] See R Rogowski, *Rational Legitimacy: A Theory of Political Support* (Princeton, Princeton University Press, 1974).
[131] See <http://europa.eu.int/comm/translation/index_en.htm>.
[132] See, eg, Curtin, n 86 above.
[133] See the Convention's Futurum website: <http://europa.eu.int/futurum/index_en.htm>.
[134] This is also discussed by Jo Shaw. See J Shaw, 'What's in a Convention? Process and Substance in the Project of European Constitution-building' (2003) *Political Science Series* 89.

law, economics, culture, medicine and so on. It is the latter which the EU language rights regime has neglected given that the absence of enabling provisions governing a duty of clear language renders democratic legitimacy intended by the former relatively meaningless.

Membership of the elite implies the attainment of a position of superiority within society by virtue of qualities and qualifications of distinction which gives them a tendency to be inward looking. If left unchecked elites can in effect monopolise debates. The challenge for the law has been formulated in terms of enabling all those affected to participate in resolving issues whilst, at the same time, leaving some issues for specialised and expert treatment.[135] This is all very well until one starts to realise that dominance can be achieved in more subtle ways. The 'same' language can be used in many different ways so as to inter alia entrench a position of power and authority[136] which may be excessive both in terms of legitimacy and in terms of necessity. Law is a useful case in point given its reliance on 'legalese' in both written and oral proceedings.[137] However, lawyers are not alone in their reliance on codes. This is not to say that codes should be forbidden. Expert terminology and taxonomy are necessary requisites of reasoning. Rather, it is the *over*reliance on codes which is at issue here. The problem with elites is that they sometimes forget that they are speaking a language that only they are capable of understanding.[138] In other words, certain people use codes in speech as a sort of language for 'insiders'. This means that they use words which only they know and moreover which only they are capably of understanding. This is an important point because it is understanding and not the jargon per se which is exclusive. For example, providing access to terminology databases such as TIS (the Council's database), EURODICAUTOM (the Commission's Database)[139] and EUTERPE (*Exploitation unifiée de la terminologie au Parlement européen*) means very little if it is not accompanied by measures which provide for the words and concepts therein to be explained in such a way so that the citizen is capable of understanding them. As has been accepted in some of the Member States,[140] in the absence of such enabling provisions, access to such information gives the appearance of transparency, that is, transparency is seen to being done. In effect, however, the use of specialist concepts and categories

[135] cf J Habermas, *Between Facts and Norms* (Cambridge, Polity Press, 1997), 359–60.

[136] See C Kramarae, C Schulz and WM O'Barr (eds), *Language and Power* (London, Sage, 1984).

[137] See D Curtotti Nappi, *Il Problema delle Lingue nel Processo Penale* (Milan, A. Giuffrè Editore, 2002).

[138] B Bernstein, *Class, Codes and Control* (London, Routledge & Kegan Paul, 1971).

[139] Note that EURODICAUTOM is soon to be included as part of a new interinstitutional database for terminology as part of IATE (Inter-Agency Terminology Exchange) in order to meet the challenge of enlargement which will include some twenty languages.

[140] See, eg, the UK's 'plain English' campaign. This and similar initiatives in other EU Member States is discussed by Heutger, n 99 above.

devised by the 'euro-elites' restricts or at least contains access. Rendering expert knowledge accessible to a wider audience is, however, dependent on the motivation and co-operation of experts. Moreover, even if the elites can be encouraged to comply, care must be taken in ensuring that their explanations do not present the case too selectively. Any act of translation involves interpretation which gives considerable scope for manipulation. In other words, the party who commands language commands the situation. The purpose of this next section is to assess to what extent, if at all, EC law is able to offer an appropriate response to the (ab)use of language by elites.

The Duty of Clarity under EC Law

Language rights in terms of the duty of clarity has not been addressed extensively by the European Union's constitutional framework.[141] However, the duty to use language in a clear and comprehensible manner has arisen in relation to producers in the EC law context of consumer rights.[142] Thus, a duty has been created for all product labels to be in a language which is 'easily understood' by the consumer.[143] Thus, for example the Commission White Paper on Food Safety provides that:

> Consumers have the right to expect information on food quality and constituents that is helpful and clearly presented, so that informed choices can be made.[144]

It is of interest to note that the 'easily understood' requirement has been interpreted as not necessarily being linked to a state's national, official and/or regional languages.[145] The ultimate arbiters of whether language is easily understandable or not are the national courts, guided by the 'invisible hand' of the European Court of Justice,[146] which has drawn on a concept of the 'reasonably circumspect consumer'[147] of its own devising. The consumer which the court has in mind is a 'circumspect consumer', that is to say, 'the presumed expectations of an average consumer who is reasonably

[141] See, however, Art 16(2) of Directive 2000/13 OJ 2000 L109/29.
[142] In ECJ decisions such as, for example, those involving the labelling of Durum Wheat Pasta (Case 407/85 *Drei Glocken v USL Centro Sud* [1988] ECR 4233) and the case of German Beer purity (Case 178/84 *Commission v Germany* [1987] ECR 1227).
[143] See Art 16(1) of Directive 2000/13 (OJ 2000 L109/29) — formerly Art 14 of Directive 79/112 (OJ 1979 L33/1).
[144] COM (1999) 719 final.
[145] See generally Case C–51/93 *Meyhui v Schott Zwiesel Glaswerke* [1994] ECR I–3879; Case C–85/94 *Piageme and others v BVBA Peeters* [1995] ECR I–2955; Case C–33/97 *Colim v Bigg's* [1999] ECR I–3975; Case C–385/96 *Goerres* [1998] ECR I–4431.
[146] See *Piageme and others v BVBA Peeters* [1995] ECR I–2955 at para 30.
[147] See Case C–315/92 *Verband Sozialer Wettbewerb v Clinique Laboratoires and Estée Lauder* [1994] ECR I–397.

well informed and reasonably observant and circumspect.'[148] The circumspect consumer must, however, so the court has conceded, be viewed in terms of social, cultural and linguistic factors.[149] It is submitted that this reasoning ought to be extrapolated to create a duty of EU officials to use language in a clear and comprehensible manner in their dealings with EU citizens. This is particularly apposite when taken in conjunction with arguments concerning democratic legitimacy and gaining the consent of the governed. Endorsing a legal analytical framework which is able to respond to this is not an easy task and may indeed be part of the explanation why the EU has been less active in formulating legal provisions concerning clear and transparent language use than it has regarding status. The law has to be more nuanced, more subtle and indeed more complex than it has to be in relation to the issue of the use of official languages. It has to rely on both hard and soft law and governance, examples of which as regards the use of clear and transparent language do, however, exist.

One is reminded of the doctrine of informed consent to medical treatment which in the United Kingdom has upheld a duty for doctors to explain the risks involved in a medical procedure which is suited to the patient's capacity for understanding.[150] The greatest modern change in medical practice has been founded on the doctrine of informed consent which many physicians like to think is a myth.[151] This is probably because the concept was not introduced by the medical profession. The school of law was responsible for its implantation and it was the lawyer, both practitioner and academic, who nurtured its gestation. It is arguable that the concept has been hijacked by the lawyers as a means of retaliation for what is seen as decades of hegemony by the medical profession.[152] To this extent, informed consent is a battleground

[148] Case C–210/96 *Gut Springenheide and Tusky* [1998] ECR I–4657, para 31. See also Case C–303/97 *Sektkellerei Kessler* [1999] ECR I–513, paras 33 and 36.

[149] Thus, national courts have been held to be permitted to commission an expert opinion in order to assess whether or not a particular promotional statement being challenged is misleading for consumers of a particular Member State. See *Estée Lauder*, n 147 above, at paras 29 and 31.

[150] See M Aziz, *The Regulation of Medical Research Involving Human Subjects. A Comparative Study* (Unpublished Doctoral thesis, Faculty of Law, University of Edinburgh, 1997).

[151] See H Beecher, 'Consent in Clinical Experimentation: Myth and Reality' (1966) 195 *The Journal of the American Medical Association* 34 and also WA Silverman, 'The myth of informed consent: in daily practice and in clinical trials.' (1989) 15 *The Journal of Medical Ethics* 6.

[152] Indeed, the 'law is currently making its presence felt' as the health care delivery system in the United Kingdom is reorganised within a legislative framework over tighter management and greater medical accountability. The use of declarations has increased as has the recourse to litigation which has engendered a climate of distrust. See H Teff, *Reasonable Care: Legal Perspectives on the Doctor / Patient Relationship* (Oxford, Oxford University Press, 1994), 33. Some commentators believe that the law in fact entrenches the medical hegemony. See J Montgomery, 'Medicine, Accountability, and Professionalism' (1989) 16 *Journal of Law and Society* 318.

on which the law and the doctor confront each other.[153] The law has had a pivotal role in establishing rules of good practice. The informed consent doctrine, however, also highlights the pitfalls of endorsing a legal framework which is too rigid. Patients have little to gain from 'defensive medicine' due to a doctor's constant fear of being sued. They do, however, benefit from good practice which is advocated in physicians' codes of conduct complemented by guidelines provided by, for example, a Patient's Charter. Here, the experience in the United States must be distinguished from the United Kingdom. Patients' rights in the United Kingdom are not anchored in the Constitution but evolved from the common law.[154]

In the case of California, for example, rights for medical research subjects are enshrined in statute.[155] The statute provides that research subjects are given the opportunity to sign the 'Experimental Subject's Bill of Rights' before clinical research can take place. The individual must, inter alia, be informed of the nature and purpose of the treatment, of its risks, of any appropriate alternative procedures.[156] The Californian example also highlights the shortfall created by rights which are not articulated in such a way as to come to terms with the context within which they operate. Understanding the risks a medical procedure entails is dependent on expert knowledge, an issue on which the law remains strangely silent. Experts provide a key to understanding the concept of risk in a given context. They play a crucial and indeed, a pervasive role in informing and moulding a consensus. The word pervasive is used given that it is difficult to think of subjects of public policy where expert treatment is not required, be it advice on genetic research, the human genome project and discussions concerning genetically modified crop where the interface between the scientific community and society has been shown to be debilitated by both misinformation and misunderstanding. The challenge is how to ensure that a debate is one based on a collaborative model of well-informed dialogue as opposed to an adversarial contest between the experts and their subjects; this demands a substantial change of attitude on behalf of both the experts and

[153] 'It should not be surprising that on the battlefield of informed consent, law and medicine glare at each other over barricades of suspicion and misunderstanding.' (A Piper, 'Truce on the Battlefield: A Proposal for a Different Approach to Medical Informed Consent' (1994) 22 *Journal of Medical Ethics* 301.)

[154] See SA M McClean, *A Patient's Right to Know* (Dartmouth, Ashgate, 1989) at 22–25.

[155] Calif. Health & Safety Code § 24172 (1978) in D Myers, *The Human Body and the Law* (Edinburgh, Edinburgh University Press, 1990).

[156] The Californian statute further provides what information the consent has to include in order for it to be valid which includes the name, institutional affiliation, if any, and address of the person or persons actually performing and primarily responsible for the conduct of the experiment together with the name of the sponsors or funding source, if any, or manufacturer if the experiment involves a drug or device, and the organisation, if any under whose general aegis the experiment is conducted, to whom the subject may address complaints about the experiment.

the public. The law has its part to play, albeit a modest one. Deriving a duty of clear and transparent use from the right to good administration as contained in the Charter of Fundamental Rights may go some way towards encouraging standards of communication between the institutions of the EU and the EU citizen by including it as part of the desiderata of accountable and transparent decision-making. Until now, the issue of clear and transparent use of language has been neglected.

CONCLUSION

As regards the implementation of European rights, we must be more cognisant of the problems of transforming elite behaviour and ensuring effective compliance in the context of the tensions which arise as a consequence of the impact of EU constitutionalism on the domestic legal cultures of the Member States. As the discussion of language rights has shown, the law can go some way towards protecting, facilitating, safeguarding and encouraging clarity and transparency as part of good administrative practice. The danger is, however, that rights per se may not always be the most appropriate means by which this may be achieved. They may in effect be rhetorical and thereby unable to transform power structures. Indeed, they may in fact provide a distraction from where real power resides and should be distributed by reconfiguring and recalibrating power structures but not necessarily to the benefit of the citizen. Addressing these issues necessarily entails drawing a distinction between the form of law and the rule of law in order to properly evaluate the normative content of capacity and implementation regarding inter alia legal-administrative resources and elite compliance.

The contribution of general protocols of good communication to the making of a just, engaged and active polity requires statements concerning rights (political, social, fundamental freedoms and so on) but also a context of implementation which is itself partly legally grounded and supplied. This involves a supportive generic conception of citizenship, an adequate reconciliation between national and supranational interest through a two-way loyalty clause and an effective language policy which reconciles respect for diversity with the need for effective communication, a facet of European rights implementation which has not been addressed.

6

Conclusion

THE IMPACT OF EUROPEAN RIGHTS

THE IMPACT OF European rights on the national legal cultures of the Member States is multi-faceted, multi-level and also multi-dimensional. It is multi-faceted to the extent that the impact of the law of the European Union with regard to rights is affected by the diverse constitutional systems and cultures of the Member States. It is multi-level in that rights are recognised, interpreted and implemented at the local, regional, national and supranational levels of law and modes of governance in the European Union. It is multi-dimensional in the sense that rights are entrenched in categories and spheres of EU competence which often overlap.[1] The analysis of the case studies of political and social rights presented in this study illustrates the complex inter-relationships and challenges that arise in the practice of European law on rights.

Sovereignty

The impact of European rights on national legal cultures has been linked to the debate on the challenge posed by EU law to the legal systems of the Member States. This challenge is generally viewed in terms of state sovereignty and in particular, the 'ultimate arbiter' or *Kompetenz-Kompetenz* debate. Constitutional courts have tended to adopt hierarchical understandings of the application of EC law in which more often than not, EC law is regarded as aspiring to constituting a separate and higher legal order. Thus far, however, the progress on reconciling different spheres of rights which exist as a consequence of legal pluralism and multi-jurisdictionality has been modest. Furthermore, whilst much is known concerning the juridical

[1] Indeed, health care policy is a useful case in point to the extent that it has also been developed in its own right as well as under the aegis of social protection. See COM (2003) 261 final, *Strengthening the Social Dimension of the Lisbon strategy: Streamlining Open Coordination in the Field of Social Protection* at p 15. See also COM (2003) 57 final, *Scoreboard on Implementing the Social Policy Agenda* at p 20.

debates of respective constitutional courts,[2] little attention has been paid to the impact of European rights across the judicial and bureaucratic spectrum. For the system to work, national judges and other related elites have to be persuaded not only to work within a new system of rules and principles generated by European rights but also be provided with an incentive structure to accelerate their commitment to the process of constitutional adjustment. The case studies employed here have focused on certain categories of rights in order to evaluate the types of benchmarks which ought to inform the process of constitutional adjustment both in theory and in practice.

Political Rights

Political rights in the EU have substantially revised and reconfigured classical notions of representative democracy which have tended to be linked to the citizenship of nation-states. Such citizenship is inappropriate as the basis for political rights in the EU. Whilst policy makers have focused on achieving democratic legitimacy for the Union through citizenship provisions, appealing to the notion of a European demos of citizens in-the-making, concurrently they have underplayed the already existing forms of co-ordination which occur both within and outwith the spheres of law and public administration. In particular, the realisation of political rights is significantly dependent on the commitment of elites who operate in these spheres. Compliance and co-operation with EU law is crucial for the establishment of a European rights regime, which in turn is fundamental for the democratic legitimacy of the Union.

Social Rights

Social rights in the EU arose largely as an unintentional consequence of the policies designed to overcome barriers to trade and the prevention of the distortion of competition. Whereas many have elected to refer to them in terms of constitutional entitlements, there is clearly a limited basis for this. The case study of cross-border access to health care, which arises as a consequence of the free movement provisions, is arguably not the most appropriate test for social rights *stricto sensu*. It does, however, reveal the tension between social rights *stricto sensu* and economic rights with a social dimension. It is this competitive tension which gives rise to an ambiguity at both the policy-making stage and at the level of implementation. Indeed,

[2] See generally A-M Slaughter, A Stone Sweet and JHH Weiler (eds), *The European Court and National Courts: Doctrine and Jurisprudence. Legal Change in its Social Context* (Oxford, Hart Publishing, 1998).

the case study discussed here reveals the extent to which this ambiguity provides an underlying tension to rational decision-making of national elites in the face of europeanisation.

The Emerging Rights Regime in Europe

Three main conclusions may be drawn from this study of the emerging rights regime in Europe. First, there is an increasing trend towards adopting the language of rights and constitutionalism both within and outwith the context of the internal market. Secondly, the policy realms through which rights can be articulated are expanding. Thirdly, policies with a strong rights content are paper tigers in the absence of effective mechanisms of implementation and elites committed to operating such mechanisms. European rights per se do not provide a comprehensive overview of the extent or degree to which the national legal cultures and elites have been europeanised. They do, however, provide important markers of europeanisation. There is a need to distinguish between the formal process of implementation and the legal norms and the legal culture which actually will inform the implementation of European rights on the day-to-day basis. To address the issue of the adaptive capacity of the Member States to the development of a unified legal culture requires an appraisal of the nature of the legal norms, the legal cultures and traditions which inform their diverse constitutional practices. In this respect, it is necessary to view the impact of European rights on the national legal cultures of the Member States in a differentiated manner both with regard to practice and adaptive potential.

While all of the Member States may be regarded as democracies and functioning market economies,[3] they are all different in terms of their constitutional architecture. The markers of differentiation[4] include distinctions between unitary and federal states, states based on plurality elections or proportional representation, a presidential or a parliamentary system, a strongly centralised or decentralised system, judicial review or various hybrids of all of these. Any combination of these features gives rise to different configurations of institutional arrangements. These fundamental distinctions between the Member States will no doubt, on the whole, represent one of the most serious obstacles to a unified EU legal order and to the implementation of European rights.

[3] In the case of the new Member States, the basis of this assumption is provided by the Copenhagen criteria which outlined the political and economic conditions for EU membership established at the Copenhagen European Council of 21–22 June 1993, Bulletin of the European Communities, 6–1993, I.13.
[4] See generally M Tushnet, 'The Possibilities of Comparative Constitutional Law' 108 *Yale Law Journal* 650.

Implementation of Rights and the Role of Elites

The European Convention has created new opportunities and shaped the conditions for the implementation of the EU's rights regime thereby generating resistance from many Member States who are suspicious of any threat to their sovereignty and identity. The citizenship provisions contained in the Draft Constitutional Treaty in conjunction with the principle of loyal co-operation and the protection of national identity, and in particular, the constitutional and administrative structures of the Member States, are one of the key dimensions along which the European constitutional debate is being conducted. Language rights, are important for similar reasons as citizenship and loyal co-operation, namely, they are part of the context of adjunctive or implementation rights which make effective or ineffective the enforceability of rights. Language rights in the EU tend to be viewed as intrinsic to the claims for respect for national identity of the Member States on the one hand, and the clear and harmonised application of the internal market on the other. An efficient language policy in the EU is one which reconciles respect for diversity with the need for effective communication. The contribution of general protocols of good communication to the making of a just, engaged and active polity requires statements concerning rights (political, social, fundamental freedoms and so on) but also a context of implementation which is itself partly legally grounded and delivered. The discussion concerning access to justice in the EU has tended to overlook this fundamental aspect of the deliverability and enforceability of rights.[5]

Indeed, procedural guarantees are needed in order to ensure that the rights holders have rights of access to a court and the right to an effective remedy. It is regrettable that access to justice was not an overriding concern of the Convention,[6] though it has been recognised by other institutional actors, such as the European Court of Justice, as requiring Treaty amendment.[7] The law can go only so far in enabling effective access to justice. Indeed, all too often, the law is overburdened by unrealistic expectations. Constitutionalism per se cannot deliver access to justice, though it could certainly better institutionalise European rights in a meaningful and effective sense. It is argued that the 'constitutional moment' is a necessary but

[5] Tending to concentrate on the relationship between Arts 230 and 234 EC Treaty. E Szyszczak, 'Making Europe More Relevant to its Citizens: Effective Judicial Process' (1996) 21 ELR 351; A Biondi, 'Effectiveness versus Efficiency: Recent Developments on Judicial Protection in EC Law' (2000) 6 *European Public Law* 311. See, however, D Chalmers, 'Judicial Preferences and the Community Legal Order' (1997) 60 MLR 164 at 167ff.

[6] It might have been the subject of a working group in its own right as opposed to being included in the deliberations of the Working Group on the Charter. See the report which can be found at <http://european-convention.eu.int>. See also the contribution to the Working Group by Francis Jacobs, Advocate General of the European Court of Justice: WG II–WD 020.

[7] See Case C–50/00 *P Union de Pequeños Agricultores v Council*, judgment of 25 July 2002.

insufficient starting point for an ongoing process that must be progressed by enabling legislation and enabling devices to secure elite co-operation in the implementation process. EU constitutionalism has a part to play in encouraging societies to recognise and respect European rights and in proactively advancing and structuring processes at a number of levels (international, national, regional and local). We should recognise, however, the modesty of what Europe's constitutional moment can deliver. Endorsing a legal analytical framework which is able to come to terms with diversity necessarily involves multi-level constitutionalism but it must also be sensitive to the reality of diversity in Member State governance as key socio-political contexts.

European rights through law and modes of governance is of particular relevance for the transformation of the societies, legal systems and administrative practices, economies and polities of all the Member States. Moreover, issues of implementation arise in ways from which lessons may be learned by all of the EU Member States which are faced with the double challenge of europeanisation and transition. This is particularly important as regards contemporaneous developments in the EU such as the Convention, the subsequent Intergovernmental Conference in 2004[8] and further Treaty revisions.

How viable and how sustainable are the different modes of implementation of rights in the EU? One way to examine this question is to consider the impact of enlargement on the EU's constitutional development. Each wave of enlargement has provided an opportunity which has enabled the adoption of new policies,[9] including rights. It has also revealed the pivotal role of elites in mediating the impact of the *acquis communautaire* as a whole.[10] Experience gained through the accession process has in effect provided a mirror of the nature of the EU itself. Much can be learned by the old Member States of the from the new Member States which have had to address the issue of rights within a new supranational architecture. The flexibility and speed with which the new Member States have had to both reassess and reconfigure their own traditions of state theory and practice in the face of EU membership, particularly as regards rights, may serve as a useful example to existing members, both in terms of the benefits and the

[8] Indeed, both the Convention and the subsequent IGC must be taken in conjunction, given the former's role in setting the agenda of the latter. See, eg, COM (2003) 548 final, *Une Constitution Pour L'Union. Avis de la Commission au titre de l'Art 48 du traité sur l'Union européenne, sur la réunion d'une Conférence des représentants des gouvernements des États membres en vue de reviser les traités.*

[9] G Avery and F Cameron, *The Enlargement of the European Union* (Sheffield, Sheffield Academic Press, 1999).

[10] J Hughes, G Sasse and C Gordon, 'Saying "Maybe" to the "Return to Europe": Elites and the Political Space for Euroscepticism in Central and Eastern Europe' (2002) 3 *European Union Politics* 3.

burdens of legal adaptation.[11] It would be erroneous to consider the new Member States, however, without also differentiating between their respective experiences. Even if it is accepted that communism provided a sort of 'shared legacy', it is clear that intra-regional experiences of communism differed markedly,[12] particularly as regards sovereignty.[13]

Transforming Elite Behaviour

Generally speaking, we must be more modest in our expectations of what EU constitutionalism can achieve, and be more cognisant of the problems of transforming elite behaviour and ensuring effective compliance with the process of constitutionalism in the European Union and to European rights in particular. Constitutional rights may, as we have seen, in effect be rhetorical and are not always capable of transforming power structures. They may in fact provide a distraction from where real power resides in a political system. Addressing these issues necessarily entails drawing a distinction between the form of law and the rule of law in order to properly evaluate the normative content of capacity and implementation. By normative content I refer to the legal-administrative resources and elite behaviour necessary for the delivery and enforceability of rights.

The issue of elite compliance is, however, subjected to the variable dynamics of europeanisation which arise at the structural *external* level of the state and also at the *internal* level of elite decision-making within the state. As regards the latter, it is doubtful that elites are familiar with the multi-jurisdictionality of European rights arising from European Union law. In particular, it is unlikely that they are aware of the extent to which rational decision-making procedures in the national institutions of the Member States in which they serve have been 'europeanised'. The difficulty here is that national elites are trained to serve their respective Member States. The impact of European rights, as has been demonstrated in the case of political and social rights, challenges and reconfigures their duties not to mention their loyalty towards the state they serve. Ultimately, it may recalibrate their loyalty also. This has important implications for legal education in the European Union as well as the training of those elites who have key roles in

[11] See C Dupré, *Importing the Law in Post-communist Transitions: The Hungarian Constitutional Court and the Right to Human Dignity* (Oxford, Hart Publishing, 2003); F Emmert, 'Administrative and Court Reform in Central and Eastern Europe' (2003) 9 *European Law Journal* 288; W Sadurski, 'Charter and Enlargement' (2002) 8 *European Law Journal* 340.

[12] See eg, the Report of the Reflection Group on the Political Dimension of EU Enlargement: Looking Towards Post-Accession (San Domenico di Fiesole, The Robert Schuman Centre for Advanced Studies, European University Institute with the Group of Policy Advisors, 2001) at p 55.

[13] As was discussed in ch 2, section Sovereignty and the Legacy of Communism in the New Member States.

the implementation of rights. As a whole, lawyers are trained to serve their own domestic legal orders.[14] Lawyers tend to think of law in terms of the nation-state. Indeed, the nation-state lies at the apex of legal reasoning.[15] Few legal disciplines encourage the legal profession to think beyond the limits of their national legal training, a notable exception being the discipline of public international law and comparative law not to mention the recent development of supranational legal bodies such as the arbitration authority established by the World Trade Organisation.[16] To some extent, comparative law fosters the pursuit of ideas within a multi-jurisdictional context. The *ratio* of this discipline, however, remains the domestic legal system which is first and foremost the point of departure of this form of legal analysis which encourages a compartmentalised view of law along the lines of the nation-state. The Issue of European rights goes someway towards illustrating the need to recalibrate the link between law and the nation-state and the concomitant effect on legal reasoning as a whole. It is debatable to what extent law degrees and professional training are designed so as to be sensitive to the impact of europeanisation. The same may be said in relation to administrative elites although the introduction of the Open Method of Co-ordination (OMC), which provides for inter alia the exchange of good practices and bench-marking, arguably goes some way towards highlighting the impact of europeanisation on administrative practice across the Member States, albeit so far focused on certain policy spheres. Empirical research is vital concerning the implementation of European rights across the EU with particular emphasis on administrative law.[17] This includes observing the behaviour of the constitutional courts, the administrative courts and bodies[18] and the lower courts, the reforms of legal education as well as the informal changes to the respective legal cultures of the Member States, the aim of which, however, would be more than an exercise in mere legal pathology. The aim of such research ought to be targeted to the reception of European rights into the national legal cultures whilst acknowledging the particular characteristics of the legal systems and cultures of the Member States.

[14] P Legrand, 'European Legal Systems Are Not Converging' (1993) 45 *International and Comparative Law Quarterly* 52.

[15] See ch 2, section Endogenous Judicial Reasoning at p 38 and also generally M Douglas, *How Institutions Think* (London, Routledge, 1987), 12ff.

[16] The role of the state is, however, not obsolete as the rules regarding standing provide: States and not individuals have standing as parties to the proceedings. Individuals are still dependent on institutions of the state for the recognition and implementation of their rights.

[17] This argument has, as yet, only been made in relation to the old Member States although it must be made in relation to the new Member States also. See C Harlow, 'European Administrative Law and the Global Challenge' in P Craig and G de Búrca (eds) *The Evolution of EU Law* (Oxford, Oxford University Press, 1999), 261.

[18] See, eg, K-H Ladeur, 'Conflict and Co-operation between European Law and the General Administrative Law of the Member States' in K-H Ladeur (ed) *The europeanisation of Administrative Law: Transforming National Decision-making Procedures* (Dartmouth, Ashgate, 2003), 1.

EU CONSTITUTIONALISM IN THEORY AND IN PRACTICE

An analytical framework which is able to address EU constitutionalism, the constitutionalisation process of the EU and the European Constitution, both in terms of theory and practice is vital. In particular, care must be taken in establishing and evaluating indicators of the impact of European rights on the respective constitutional legal orders and cultures of the Member States, both actual and potential. One way forward would be for a greater level of multi-disciplinarity by drawing on, synthesising and further developing a range of theoretical approaches within the law which are sensitive to those contained in other disciplines, namely, political science, sociology, history and economics. A comprehensive multi-disciplinary approach would allow jurists to map, classify and monitor the respective constitutional orders and cultures, modes of governance, the relevant elites, and any transformative dimensions in response to European rights.

Numerous levels of diversity must, however, be distinguished. Diversity exists as between Member States regarding rights and the values upon which they are predicated and according to which they are articulated. Diversity also exists amongst the elites within these Member States as to the concept of rights. Indeed, it is difficult to assume the existence of a homogeneous approach to European rights amongst jurists and other institutional actors. The reasons may be partly explained by political tradition. They may also be regionally structured. Moreover, there is diversity across the academic disciplines as to definitions of European rights. It is also unlikely that one could assume the existence of a unified understanding of European rights amongst the political actors involved. Variation further exists at the level of the EU citizen who tends to view European rights in terms of domestic constitutional and legal provisions and the values and practices enshrined therein. Here again, different markers are evident as a consequence of political tradition and regional location and history. Debates concerning European rights today do not operate on the basis of shared understandings, neither analytically speaking nor practically speaking.

Thus, as regards analysis, there is a need to qualify the use of the term rights. Generally speaking, careful distinctions must be drawn between rights which give rise to a duty of another party, rights which permit a right holder to perform an action or a right which may be used in such as way that it upholds the invalidity of behaviour of someone other than the right holder.[19] European rights do not lend themselves to a strict demarcation or disaggregation of the general concept of a 'right' particularly given the various spheres of law and the different types of claims

[19] NE Simmonds, 'Rights at the Cutting Edge' in MH Kramer, NE Simmonds and H Steiner (eds) *A Debate Over Rights. Philosophical Enquiries* (Oxford, Oxford University Press, 1998), 112 at p 149ff.

which exist. For example, it is virtually impossible to speak of social rights in the same breath as one speaks of civil rights. In the case of the former, a right to social security, for instance, does not necessarily bind another party by way of a duty, particularly given that the recognition of such a right has implications for public resources. It is arguable that European rights ought to be viewed as interests which may give rise to a duty, all things being equal, and if it is not counteracted by conflicting considerations.[20] In other words, rights provide reasons for imposing duties but do not impose duties in a strict sense.[21] Whereas this might accord with a view of the EU predicated on the doctrine of subsidiarity, leaving each Member State a certain degree of discretion whether or not and to what extent rights are recognised, as in the case of directives, it is unclear whether this is really the case. European rights are made up of a mixture of European Union law as well as of the laws and legal traditions and cultures of the respective Member States.[22]

This 'fusion' has obvious implications for the rich tapestry which makes up EU law. Just as constitutionalism is subject to the systemic failure of being unable to live up to expectations which are unrealistic, so too is EU law unable to deliver regarding the institutionalisation of European rights in a significant and effective sense, when considered as a system *propre* that is. EU law is *sui generis* in nature, a characteristic which may, however, be conceived of as an inherent strength and not, as is often the case, as a weakness. The flexibility with which it is endowed given the variety of legal mechanisms at its disposition, each with their own terms of reference of applicability and effect, potentially offers a multiplicity of routes to the effective articulation, delivery and enforceability of rights. An interest theory of rights would arguably enable the thin sense of rights (the EU) to come to terms with the thick sense existent in some of the Member States, allowing for and indeed facilitating symbiosis between the two. Accordingly, the challenge for legal science is mainly two-fold. First, it must be able to formulate a legal response to the articulation and recognition of rights across the EU, whilst coming to terms with the different conceptions of rights which arise as a consequence of diversity of the respective legal traditions and cultures of the Member States.[23] Secondly, this response needs to be able to better empirically demonstrate the means for the articulation and recognition of rights.

[20] J Raz, *The Morality of Freedom* (Oxford, Clarendon Press, 1986), 166. See also C Hilson and T Downes, 'Making Sense of Rights: Community Rights in EC Law' (1999) 24 ELR 121.
[21] N MacCormick, 'Rights in Legislation' in PMS Hacker and J Raz (eds) *Law, Morality and Society* (Oxford, Clarendon Press, 1977), 203.
[22] The latter is particularly important as it qualifies the applicability of the Interest Theory of rights in relation to the EU.
[23] Bearing in mind that there is no uniform model of a Bill of Rights in the existing Members States nor in the new Member States.

As regards rights in practice, there is a need for an appropriate framework within which the process of constitutional development and adjustment in the European Union can be monitored. This involves assessing the impact of EU constitutionalism according to commonly defined criteria and indicators. Methods should be developed in law and in the social sciences generally to analyse and evaluate modes of incorporating and implementing European rights across several dimensions, both quantitative and qualitative[24] so that it may be used by researchers across the European Research Area (ERA) as well as by users in the EU Member States in a variety of contexts and sectors of law, governance, policy-making and industry for evaluating adherence to the constitutional rule of law in the European Union not only in Europe, but also as a general international reference tool.

The Modest Proposal of EU Constitutionalism

The current EU constitutionalisation process, as the European Convention has shown, is underwritten not only by grand aspirations but also by expectations, some of which are legitimate whilst others are unreasonable.[25] This is partly explained by the fact that there is little consensus amongst elites as to what constitutionalism can effectively address or deliver. This is further amplified by the use of the language of constitutionalism for the purposes of persuasion and in particular the quest for democratic legitimacy. There is too fine a line in EU constitutionalism between gaining consent and manufacturing consent. There are certain issues which constitutionalism is able to address. There are others, however, which it ought, in turn, to pass over in silence. Moreover, however, there is the need to recognise that the capacity for constitutionalism to meet the demands posed by rights claims is dependent on structures which exist both within and outwith the law. Certain aspects of protection, for example, are matters of 'soft law',[26] of governance and also administrative practice. Nevertheless EU constitutionalism has a part to play in encouraging the Member States to recognise and respect European rights. We must be more modest of our expectations of what constitutionalism can achieve in this respect and be more cognisant of the problems of transforming elite behaviour and ensuring effective compliance. This

[24] Arguably drawing from existing programmes of monitoring such as the EU Accession Monitoring Programme (EUMAP). Although the role of EUMAP has been to focus on governmental compliance with the political criteria for EU membership as defined by the 1993 Copenhagen European Council. See <http://www.eumap.org>.

[25] See generally Y Mény, 'The Achievements of the Convention' (2003) 14 *Journal of Democracy* 57.

[26] See generally L Senden, *Soft Law in European Community Law* (Nijmegen, Wolf Legal Publishers, 2003).

includes endorsing an analytical framework regarding European rights which is capable of being monitored for its effectiveness.

The 'modest proposal of constitutionalism'[27] in the EU is hinged on the fact that access to rights may be mediated through what has been referred to as 'hard' or 'soft' law. Not only does this recognise the importance of speaking of rights in a differentiated manner but also it acknowledges the different media which exist both within and outwith the state's apparatus — and indeed the law — for enabling and facilitating access to justice. The age of state formation in Europe has in effect bedevilled constitutional development and has acted as a restraining order. Constitutions are capable, as some have pointed out, of much more.[28] A central challenge of the process of constitution-making in the EU is how it necessarily entails qualifying the impact of European rights on national legal cultures, both in terms of theory and in practice. How this challenge is resolved will be critical for the establishment of a unified European legal order.

[27] 'Language, Rights and Diversity: the Modesty of the Constitutional Moment', prepared for a Workshop on 'The Public Discourse of Law and Politics in Multilingual Societies' held at the International Institute for the Sociology of Law (IISL) in Oñati, Spain in June 2002 to be published in an edited collection by Hart Publishing edited by Dario Castiglione and Richard Bellamy (forthcoming).

[28] N Walker, 'Beyond the Unitary Conception of the United Kingdom Constitution?' (2000) PL 384.

Select Bibliography

ACKERMAN, B, *We the People* (Cambridge MA, Harvard University Press, 1998).

ADENAS, M (ed), *Article 177 References to the European Court: Policy and Practice* (London, Butterworths, 1994).

ADORNO, T, *The Culture Industry* (London, Routledge, 1991).

AJANI, G, *Diritto del'Europa Orientale* (Torino, UTET, 1996).

ALBI, A, 'Postmodern versus Retrospective Sovereignty: Two Different Discourses in the EU and the Candidate Countries' in Walker, N (ed) *Sovereignty in Transition* (Oxford, Hart Publishing, 2003).

ALBRECHT, T, 'Opportunities and Challenges in the Provision of Cross Border Care' (2002) 8 *Eurohealth* 8.

ALEXY, R, *Theorie der Grundrechte* (Frankfurt am Main, Suhrkamp, 1996).

ALLISON, JWF, 'Transplantation and Cross-Fertilisation' in Beatson, J and Tridimas, T (eds) *New Directions in European Public Law* (Oxford, Hart Publishing, 1998), 169.

ALONSO GARCIA, R, *Derecho comunitario y derechos nacionales: autonomia, integración e interacción* (Buenos Aires, Abeledo-Perrot, 1999).

——, 'The General Provisions of the Charter of Fundamental Rights' (2002) 8 *European Law Journal* 492.

ALSTON, P, BUSTELO, M and HEENAN, J (eds), *The EU and Human Rights* (Oxford, Oxford University Press, 1999).

ALSTON, P and WEILER, JHH, 'An "Ever Closer Union" in Need of a Human Rights Policy: The European Union and Human Rights' in Alston, P, Bustelo, M and Heenan, J (eds), *The EU and Human Rights* (Oxford, Oxford University Press, 1999), 3.

ALTER, KJ, *Establishing the Supremacy of European Law: The Making of an International Rule of Law in Europe* (Oxford, Oxford University Press, 2001).

ANDERSON, B, *Imagined Communities* (London, Verso, 1983).

ANDERSON, M, DEN BOER, M and MILLER, G, 'European Citizenship and Co-operation in the Fields of Justice and Home Affairs' in Duff, A, Pinder, J and Bryce, R (eds) *Maastricht and Beyond* (London, Routledge, 1994), 104.

ARCHIBUGHI, D and HELD, D (eds), *Cosmopolitan Democracy: An Agenda for a New Word Order* (Cambridge, Polity Press, 1995).

ARCHIBUGHI, D, HELD, D and KOHLER, M (eds), *Reimagining Political Communities* (London, Polity Press, 1998).

AREEDA, P, 'Essential Facilities: An Epithet in Need of Limiting Principles' (1990) 58 *Antitrust Law Journal* 841.

ARNULL, A, 'Modernising Community Courts' (2000) 3 *Cambridge Yearbook of European Legal Studies* 37.

ARNULL, A and WINCOTT, D (eds), *Accountability and Legitimacy in the European Union* (Oxford, Oxford University Press, 2002).

ASHFORD, DE, *The Emergence of the Welfare States* (Oxford, Blackwell, 1986).

AVERY, G and CAMERON, F, *The Enlargement of the European Union* (Sheffield, Sheffield Academic Press, 1999).

AZIZ, M, 'The Federal Constitutional Court Decision Concerning the Financial Equalization between the States of the Federal Republic of Germany: The "Länderausgleich" judgment' (2000) 6 *European Public Law* (Survey).

——, 'Constitutional Tolerance and EU Enlargement: The Politics of Dissent?' in Zumbansen, P and Miller, R (eds) *The Annual of German and European Law* (New York, Berghahn, 2002).

——, 'Sovereignty Lost, Sovereignty Regained? The European Integration Project and the Bundesverfassungsgericht' (2002) 9 *Columbia Journal of European Law* 109.

——, 'Sovereignty über Alles: (Re)Configuring the German Legal Order' in Walker, N (ed) *Sovereignty in Transition* (Oxford, Hart Publishing, 2003).

AZOULAY, L, 'The Judge and the Community's Administrative Governance' in Joerges, C and Dehousse, R (eds), *Good Governance in Europe's Integrated Market* (Oxford, Oxford University Press, 2002), 109.

BALDASSARRE, A, *Diritti sociali in Encylopaedia Giuridico* (Rome, Treccani 1989).

BANDRÉS MOLINÉ, E, FERNÁNDEZ, G and GARCÍA-MORENO, FC (eds), *Derecho, economía y sociedad en España* (Madrid, Escuela Libre Editorial - Las Estructuras del Bienestar, 1997).

BANTI, AM, *La nazione del Risorgimento: Parentela, sanità e onore alle origine dell'Italia unita* (Torino, Einaudi, 2000).

BANTING, KG, 'The Welfare State as Statecraft: Territorial Politics and Canadian Social Policy' in Leibfried, S and Pierson, P (eds), *European Social Policy: Between Fragmentation and Integration* (Washington DC, Brookings Institute, 1995), 269.

BAQUERO CRUZ, J, *Between Competition and Free Movement: The Economic Constitutional Law of the European Community* (Oxford, Hart Publishing, 2002).

BARBIERI, WW, *Ethics of Citizenship: Immigration and Group Rights in Germany* (Durham NC, Duke University Press, 1998).

BARNARD, C, 'The Economic Objectives of Article 119' in Hervey, T and O'Keefe, D (eds) *Sex Equality Law in the European Union* (London, Wiley, 1996).

——, 'EC "Social Policy" in Craig, P and de Búrca, G (eds) *The Evolution of EU Law* (Oxford, Oxford University Press, 1999), 479.

——, 'Flexibility and Social Policy' in de Búrca, G and Scott, J (eds) *Flexibility and Models of Governance for the EU* (Oxford, Hart Publishing, 2000), 197.

——, 'Social Dumping and the Race to the Bottom' (2000) 25 ELR 57.

BARNARD, C and DEAKIN, S, 'Corporate Governance, European Governance and Social Rights' in Hepple, B (ed) *Social and Labour Rights in a Global Context: International and Comparative Perspectives* (Cambridge, Cambridge University Press, 2002), 122.

BARRON, C and SCOTT, J, 'The Charter Programme' (1992) 55 MLR 526.

BEAUMONT, P, 'Human Rights: Some Recent Developments and Their Impact on Convergence and Divergence of Law in Europe' in Beaumont, P, Lyons, C and Walker, N (eds) *Convergence and Divergence in European Public Law* (Oxford, Hart Publishing, 2002), 151.

BEECHER, H, 'Consent in Clinical Experimentation-Myth and Reality' (1966) 195 *The Journal of the American Medical Association* 34.

BEENEN, N, *Citizenship, Nationality and Access to Public Service Employment: The Impact of European Community Law* (Groningen, Europa Law Publishing, 2001).

BELL, M, *Anti-discrimination Law and the EU* (Oxford, Oxford University Press, 2002).

BELLAMY, R, *Modern Italian Social Theory* (Cambridge, Polity Press, 1987).

——, 'Citizenship and Rights' in Bellamy, R (ed) *Theories and Concepts of Politics* (Manchester, Manchester University Press, 1993), 43.

——, 'The "Right to have Rights": Citizenship Practice and the Political Constitution of the European Union' in Bellamy, R and Warleigh, A (eds) *Citizenship and Governance in the European Union* (London, Pinter/Continuum, 2001), 41.

BELLAMY, R and WARLEIGH, A (eds), *Citizenship and Governance in the European Union* (London and New York, Continuum, 2001).

BENDIX, R, *Nation-building & Citizenship* (New Brunswick, Transaction Publishers, 1996).

BENGOA, E, ARANTZAZU, R and TAPIA, F, 'The Principle of Subsidiarity and the European Union: A New Political Sphere for the Basque Government' (1995) International Institute for Sociology of Law, Oñati (unpublished paper)

BENHABIB, S (ed), *Democracy and Difference* (Princeton, Princeton University Press, 1996).

BERCUSSON, B, 'Fundamental Social and Economic Rights in the European Community' in Cassesse, A, Clapham, A and Weiler, JHH (eds) *Human Rights and the European Community: Methods of Protection* (Baden-Baden, Nomos Verlag, 1991), 207.

BERNSTEIN, B, *Class, Codes and Control* (London, Routledge & Kegan Paul, 1971).

BIEBER, R and SALOMÉ, I, 'Hierarchy of Norms in European Law' (1996) 33 CML Rev 907.

BIONDI, A, 'Effectiveness versus Efficiency: Recent Developments on Judicial Protection in EC Law' (2000) 6 *European Public Law* 311.

BIRNBAUM, P, *La France imaginée: déclin des rêves unitaires* (Paris, Fayard, 1998).

BLANCHARD, D, *La Constitutionalisation de l'Union européenne* (Rennes, Apogée, 2001).

BOBAK, M and MARMONT, M, 'East-West Mortality Divides and its Potential Explanations: Proposed Research Agenda' (1996) *British Medical Journal* 312.

BÖCKENFÖRDE, EW, 'Die sozialen Grundrechten im Verfassungsgefüge' in Böckenförde, EW, Jekemitz, J and Ramm, T (eds), *Soziale Grundrechte: Von der bürgerlichen zur sozialen Rechtsordnung* (Heidelberg, CF Müller, 1981), 7.

BOGDAN SZTYBER, W, 'Market and State in Times of Globalisation' (2001) 12 *European Journal of Law and Economics* 145.

BONNER, D and GRAHAM, C, 'The Human Rights Act 1998: The Story So Far' (2002) 8 *European Public Law* 177.

BONNIE, A, 'The Constitutionality of Transfers of Sovereignty: The French Approach' (1999) 4 *European Public Law* 517.

BORN, G and PROSSER, T, 'Culture and Consumerism: Citizenship, Public Service Broadcasting and the BBC's Fair Trading Obligations' (2001) 64 MLR 657.

BRAUN, E, *EC Competition Rules in National Courts (III): Germany* (Baden-Baden, Nomos Verlag, 1996).

BRIGHAM, J, *Constitutional Language* (Westport, Greenwood Press, 1978).

BROWNLIE, I, *Principles of Public International Law* (Oxford, Clarendon Press, 1990).
BRUBAKER, R, *Citizenship and Nationhood in France and Germany* (Cambridge MA, Harvard University Press, 1992).
BRUNNER, G (ed), *Before Reforms: Human Rights in the Warsaw Pact States 1971–1988* (London, Hurst & Co, 1990).
BULTERMAN, M, *Human Rights in the Treaty Relations of the European Community* (Antwerp, Groningen and Oxford, Intersentia-Hart, 2001).
BURLEY, A-M and MATTLI, W, 'Europe before the Court: A Political Theory of Legal Integration' (1993) 47 *International Organization* 41.
BURROWS, R and LOADER, B (eds), *Towards a Post-Fordist Welfare State?* (London, Routledge, 1994).
CACHIA, J, 'Human Resources in Maltese Healthcare. Solutions for Common Needs' (2002) 8 *Eurohealth* 17.
CALDEIRA, G and GIBSON, JL, 'The Legitimacy of the Court of Justice in the European Union: Models of Institutional Support' (1995) 89 *The American Political Science Review* 356.
CALHOUN, C, *Critical Social Theory* (Oxford, Blackwell, 1995).
CALLIES, C and RUFFERT, M (eds), *Kommentar zu EUV and EGV* (Neuwied, Luchterhand, 2002).
CAPOTORTI, F (ed), *Il primato del diritto comunitario e i guidici italiani* (Milan, Franco Angeli Editore, 1978).
CARRINO, A, *Ideologia e coscienza: Critical Legal Studies* (Napoli, ESI, 1992).
CARTABIA, M, *Principe inviolabili e integrazione Europea* (Milano, Giuffrè, 1995).
CARTABIA, M and WEILER, JHH, *L'Italia in Europa* (Bologna, Il Mulino, 2000).
CASTRO JOVER, A (ed), *Educación como transmisión de valores* (Oñati, The Oñati International Institute for the Sociology of Law, 1995).
CASTRO OLIVIERA, Á, 'Workers and Other Persons: Step-by-Step from Movement to Citizenship. Case Law 1995–2001' (2002) 39 CML Rev 77.
CHALMERS, D, 'Judicial Preferences and the Community Legal Order' (1997) 60 MLR 164.
——, 'Inhabitants in EC Environmental Law' in Craig, P and de Búrca, G (eds) *The Evolution of EU Law* (Oxford, Oxford University Press, 1999), 653.
CHITI, MP, *Diritto amminstrativo europeo* (Milano, A. Giuffrè, 1999).
——, 'The Emergence of a Community Administration: The Case of European Agencies' (2000) 37 CML Rev 309.
CLAPHAM, A, 'A Human Rights Policy for the European Community' (1990) 10 *Yearbook of European Law* 309.
CLAUWERT, S, *Fundamental Social Rights in the European Union: Comparative Tables and Documents* (Brussels, European Trade Union Institute, 1998).
CLOOS, J, *Le Traité de Maastricht: genèse, analyse, commentaires* (Paris, Bruylant, 1993).
CLOSA, C, 'The Concept of Citizenship in the Treaty on European Union' (1992) 29 CML Rev 1137.
——, 'Improving EU Constitutional Politics? A Preliminary Assessment of the Convention' (2003) Constitutionalism Web-Papers, ConWEB: <http://www.les1.man.ac.uk/conweb 1>.
COHEUR, A, 'Integrating Care in Border Regions: An Analysis of the Euregio Projects' (2001) 7 *Eurohealth* 10.

COLLINS, D, *The European Communities: The Social Policy of the First Phase* (London, Martin Robertson, 1975).
CONANT, L, *Justice Contained: Law and Politics in the EU* (Ithaca, Cornell University Press, 2002).
CONSORTIUM, YHE, *Evaluation of Treating Patient's Overseas* (York, The University of York, 2002).
CONSTANTINESCO, V and JACQUÉ, JP, 'L'Application du droit international et communautaire au regard de la Constitution' in Koernig, P and Rüfner, W (eds) *Le Contrôle de la constitutionalité en France et en République féderale d'Allemagne* (Paris, Heymann, 1985), 174.
COPPEL, J and O'NEILL, A, 'The European Court of Justice: Taking Rights Seriously?' (1992) 29 CML Rev 669.
COSTA, P, *Civitas. Storia della cittadinanza in Europa. 1. Dalla civilità comunale al Settecento* (Roma and Bari, Laterza, 1999).
COSTA, P and ZOLO, D (eds), *Lo stato di diritto: Storia, teoria, critica* (Milano, Feltrinelli, 2002).
COULMAS, F (ed), *A Language Policy for the European Community* (Berlin and New York, Mouton de Gruyter, 1991).
CRAIG, P, 'What Constitution does Europe Need? The House that Giscard Built: Constitutional Rooms with a View' (2003) <http://www.fedtrust.co.uk>.
CRAIG, P and DE BÚRCA, G (eds), *The Evolution of EU Law* (Oxford, Oxford University Press, 1999).
——, *EU Law: Text, Cases and Materials* (Oxford, Oxford University Press, 2002).
CRAUFURD SMITH, R, 'Remedies for Breaches of EU Law in National Courts: Legal Variation and Selection' in Craig, P and de Búrca, G (eds) *The Evolution of EU Law* (Oxford, Oxford University Press, 1999), 287.
CULPITT, I, *Welfare and Citizenship: Beyond the Crisis of the Welfare State* (London, Sage, 1992).
CURTIN, D, *Postnational Democracy: The European Union in Search of a Political Philosophy* (The Hague, Kluwer, 1997).
CURTIN, DM, 'The Constitutional Structure of the European Union: A Europe of Bits and Pieces' (1993) 30 CML Rev 83.
——, '"Civil Society" and the European Union: Opening Spaces for Deliberative Democracy?' in Alston, P, de Búrca, G and de Wilte, B (eds) *Collected Courses of the Academy of European Law* (Florence, European University Institute, 1999), 185.
——, 'Citizens' Fundamental Right of Access to EU Information: An Evolving Digital Passepartout?' (2000) 37 CML Rev 7.
CURTIN, DM and DEKKER, IF, 'The European Union as a "Layered" International Organization: Institutional Unity in Disguise' in Craig, P and de Búrca, G (eds) *The Evolution of EU Law* (Oxford, Oxford University Press, 1998).
CURTOTTI NAPPI, D, *Il problema delle lingue nel processo penale* (Milano, A. Giuffrè Editore, 2002).
DAHRENDORF, R, 'The Challenge for Democracy' (2003) 14 *Journal of Democracy* 102.
DASHWOOD, A and HILLION, C (eds), *The General Law of EC External Relations* (London, Sweet & Maxwell, 2000).
DAVID, R, *Les Grands systèmes de droit contemporains* (Paris, Dalloz, 1988).
DAVIES, G, 'Welfare as a Service' (2002) 29 *Legal Issues of European Integration* 27.

De Búrca, G, 'The Quest for Legitimacy in the European Union' (1996) 59 MLR 349.
——, 'The drafting of the EU Charter of Fundamental Rights' (2001) 26 ELR 126.
——, 'Convergence and Divergence in European Public Law: The Case of Human Rights' in Beaumont, P, Lyons, C and Walker, N (eds) *Convergence and Divergence in European Public Law* (Oxford, Hart Publishing, 2002), 131.
——, 'Fundamental Rights and Citizenship' in de Witte, B (ed) *Ten Reflections on the Constitutional Treaty for Europe* (San Domenico di Fiesole, Robert Schuman Centre for Advanced Studies, 2003), 11.
De Búrca, G and De Witte, B, 'The Delimitation of Powers between the EU and its Member States' in Arnull, A and Wincott, D (eds) *Accountability and Legitimacy in the European Union* (Oxford, Oxford University Press, 2002), 201.
De Búrca, G and Scott, J (eds) *Flexibility and Models of Governance for the EU* (Oxford, Hart Publishing, 2000).
De Búrca, G and Walker, N, 'Law and Transnational Civil Society: Upsetting the Agenda?' (2003) 9 *European Law Journal* 387.
De Castro, JL, *La emergente participación política de las regiones en el proceso de construcción europea* ([Oñati], Instituto Vasco de Administración Pública-Herri-Arduralaritzaren Euskal Erakundea, 1994).
De Mauro, T, *Storia dell' Italia unita* (Roma, Laterza, 1995).
De Nebrija, A, *Gramática de la lengua Castellana* (Madrid, 1492).
De Schutter, O, 'Europe in Search of its Civil Society' (2002) 8 *European Law Journal* 198.
De Varennes, F, *Language, Minorities and Human Rights* (The Hague, Martinus Nijhoff, 1996).
De Witte, B, 'Community Law and National Constitutional Values' (1991) 2 *Legal Issues of European Integration* 1.
——, 'Surviving in Babel? Language Rights and European Integration' in Dinstein, Y (ed) *The Protection of Minorities and Human Rights* (Dordrecht, Nijhoff, 1992), 277.
——, 'Cultural Legitimation: Back to the Language Question' in Garcia, S (ed) *European Identity and the Search for Legitimacy* (London, Pinter, 1993), 154.
——, 'The Past and Future Role of the European Court of Justice in the Protection of Human Rights' in Alston, P, Bustelo, M and Heenan, J (eds) *The EU and Human Rights* (Oxford, Oxford University Press, 1999), 859.
——, 'Institutional Principles: A Special Category of General Principles of EC Law' in Bernitz, U and Nergelius, J (eds) *General Principles of European Community Law* (The Hague, Kluwer Law International, 2000), 143.
——, 'The Closest Thing to a Constitutional Conversation in Europe: The Semi-Permanent Treaty Revision Process' in Beaumont, P, Lyons, C and Walker, N (eds) *Convergence and Divergence in European Public Law* (Oxford, Hart Publishing, 2002), 39.
——, 'Politics versus Law in the EU's Approach to Ethnic Minorities' in Zielonka, J (ed), *Europe Unbound: Enlarging and Reshaping the Boundaries of the European Union* (London, Routledge, 2002), 137.
——, 'Enlargement and the EU Constitution' in Cremona, M (ed) *The Enlargement of the European Union* (Oxford, Oxford University Press, 2003), 209.

DEBRAY, R, *L'État séducteur, les révolutions médiologiques du pouvoir* (Paris, Gallimard, 1993).
DEHOUSSE, R, 'Comparing national law and EC law: The Problem of the Level of Analysis' (1994) 42 *American Journal of Comparative Law* 201.
——, 'Towards a Regulation of Transitional Governance? Citizens' Rights and the Reform of Comitology Procedures' in Joerges, C and Vos, E (eds) *EU Committees: Social Regulation, Law and Politics* (Oxford, Hart Publishing, 1999), 109.
——, 'The Juridification of the Political Process' in Snyder, F (ed) *The Europeanisation of Law: The Legal Effects of European Integration* (Oxford, Hart Publishing, 2000), 15.
DELANTY, G, *Inventing Europe: Idea, Identity, Reality* (London, Macmillan Press, 1995).
DELOCHE-GAUDEZ, F, 'La Convention pour l'Élaboration de la Charte des Droits Fondamentaux: Une Méthode d'Avenir?' (2001) 15 *Études et Recherches* 1.
DEMMKE, C and LINKE, U, 'Who's a National and Who's a European? Exercising Public Power and the Legitimacy of Art. 39 4 EC in the 21st Century' (2003) 2 *EIPAscope* 2.
DOBSON, L, 'Citizenship, Political Authority and Constitutionalism in the European Union: A Normative Theoretical Approach' (2002) 23 *Journal of European Integration* 335.
D'OLIVEIRA, H, 'European Citizenship: Its Meaning, its Potential' in Monar, J, Ungerer, W and Wessels, W (eds) *The Maastricht Treaty on European Union: Legal Complexity and Political Dynamic* (Brussels, Interuniversity Press, 1994).
DONATI, P, *Riposte alle crisi dello stato sociale: Le nuove politiche sociali in prospettiva sociologica* (Milano, Franco Angeli, 1984).
DORAU, C and JACOBI, P, 'The Debate over a "European Constitution": Is it Solely a German Concern?' (2000) 6 *European Public Law* 413.
DOUGAN, M, 'The Convention's Draft Constitutional Treaty: A "Tidying-Up Exercise" That Needs Some Tidying-up of its Own' (2003) <http://www.fedtrust.co.uk>.
DOUGLAS, M, *How Institutions Think* (London, Routledge, 1987).
DOWNES, T, 'Market Citizenship: Functionalism and Fig-leaves' in Bellamy, R and Warleigh, A (eds) *Citizenship and Governance in the European Union* (London, Continuum, 2001), 93.
DOWNS, A, *An Economic Theory of Democracy* (London, Harper & Row, 1957).
DUPRÉ, C, *Importing the Law in Post-communist Transitions: The Hungarian Constitutional Court and the Right to Human Dignity* (Oxford, Hart Publishing, 2003).
DUTHEIL, J, 'Droits de l'homme: La Charte des droits fondamentaux et au delà' (2002) 10/01 Jean Monnet Working Papers <http://www.jeanmonnetprogram.org>.
DWORKIN, R, *Taking Rights Seriously* (Cambridge, Cambridge University Press, 1978).
——, *Freedom's Law: The Moral Reading of the American Constitution* (Cambridge MA, Harvard University Press, 1996).
DYZENHAUS, D (ed), *Recrafting the Rule of Law* (Oxford, Hart Publishing, 1999).
EECKHOUT, P, 'The EU Charter of Fundamental Rights and the Federal Question' (2002) 39 CML Rev 945.

EGEBERG, M, 'Transcending Intergovernmentalism. Identity and Role Perceptions of National Officials in EU Decision-making' (1999) 6 *European Journal of Public Policy* 456.

EHLERMANN, C-D, 'The European Administration and the Public Administration of Member States with regard to Competition Law' (1995) 16 ECLR 454.

EHLERMANN, C-D and DJRIBER, B, 'Procedural Protection of Enterprises: Administrative Procedure, In Particular Access to Files and Confidentiality' (1996) 7 ECLR 375.

EHRLICH, E, *Grundlegung des Soziologie des Rechts* (Berlin, Duncker & Humblot, 1989).

EIDE, A, KRAUSE, C and ROSAS, C (eds), *Economic, Social and Cultural Rights: A Textbook* (Dordrecht, Kluwer, 1995).

ELEFTHERIADIS, P, 'Cosmopolitan Law' (2003) 9 *European Law Journal* 241.

ELGIE, R and ZIELONKA, J, 'Constitutions and Constitution-building' in Zielonka, J (ed) *Democratic Consolidation in Easten Europe, Vol I: Institutional Engineering* (Oxford, Oxford University Press, 2001), 33.

ELLIS, E, 'Recent Developments in EC Sex Equality Law' (1998) 35 CML Rev 379.

ELSTER, J (ed), *The Roundtable Talks and the Breakdown of Communism* (Chicago, Chicago University Press, 1996).

ELSTER, J, OFFE, C and PREUß, UK (eds), *Institutional Design in Post-communist Societies: Rebuilding the Ship at Sea* (Cambridge, Cambridge University Press, 1997).

ELY, JH, *Democracy and Distrust: A Theory of Judicial Review* Cambridge MA, Harvard University Press, 1980).

EMMERICH, V, *Kartellrecht* (München, CH Beck, 1994).

EMMERT, F, 'Administrative and Court Reform in Central and Eastern Europe' (2003) 9 *European Law Journal* 288.

ENNEN, E, *The Medieval Town* (Amsterdam, North-Holland, 1979).

ESPING-ANDERSON, G, *The Three Worlds of Welfare Capitalism* (Princeton, Princeton University Press, 1990).

ESTELLA, A, *The EU Principle of Subsidiarity and its Critique* (Oxford, Oxford University Press, 2002).

EVANS, PB, Rueschemeyer, D and Skopcpol, T, 'On the Road toward a More Adequate Understanding of the State' in Evans, PB, Rueschemeyer, D and Skopcpol, T (eds) *Bringing the State Back In* (Cambridge, Cambridge University Press, 1985), 347.

EVERSON, M, 'The Legacy of the Market Citizen' in Shaw, J and Moore, G (eds) *New Legal Dynamics of the European Union* (Oxford, Clarendon Press, 1995), 73.

——, 'Administering Europe' (1998) 36 *Journal of Common Market Studies* 195.

FACCHI, A, *I diritti nell'Europa multiculturale* (Milano, Laterza, 2001).

FAIST, T, 'A Medieval City: Transnationalizing Labor Markets and Social Rights in Europe' (1994) 9/94 *ZeS—Arbeitspapier*.

FAIT, B, 'In einer Atmosphäre von Freiheit: Die Rolle der Amerikaner bei der Verfassunggebung in den Ländern der US Zone 1946' (1985) 33 *Vierteljahrshefte für Zeitgeschichte* 420.

FALCON, G, 'La tutela giurisdizionale' in Chiti, MP and Greco, G (eds) *Trattato di diritto amminstrativo* (Milano, Giuffrè, 1997), 337.

FELD, SA, 'Language and the Globalization of the Economic Market: The Regulation of Language as a Barrier to Free Trade' (1998) 31 *Vanderbilt Journal of Transnational Law* 153.

FINK, J, 'Silence, Absence and Elision in Analyses of "the family" in European Social Policy' in Fink, J, Lewis, G and Clarke, J (eds) *Rethinking European Welfare* (London, Sage, 2001), 163.

FINK, J, LEWIS, G and CLARKE, J (eds), *Rethinking European Welfare* (London, Sage, 2001).

FLEISCHER, H, 'Gezielte Kampfpreisunterbindungen im Recht der Vereinigten Staaten: der Supreme Court zwischen Chicago School and Post-Chicago Economics' (1995) 45 *Wirtschaft und Wettbewerb* 798.

FOSTER, N, *German Law and Legal System* (London, Blackstone, 1993).

FRANCK, C and PYSZNA-NIGGE, D, *Positions of 10 Central and Eastern European Countries of EU Institutional Reforms: Analytical Survey in the Framework of the CEEC-DEBATE project* (Louvain-la-Neuve, Université catholique de Louvain, 2003).

FUCHS, M, 'Free Movement of Services and Social Security-Quo Vadis?' (2002) 8 *European Law Journal* 536.

FULLER, L, 'The Forms and Limits of Adjudication' (1978) 92 *Harvard Law Review* 353.

FURSE, M, 'The "Essential Facilities" Doctrine in Community Law' (1995) 8 ECLR 469.

FÜßER, K, 'Grundrecht auf wirtschaftliche Freizügigkeit und Art. 8 a EGV als Auffangbeschränkungsverbot des Gemeinschaftsrechts' (1999) *Die öffentliche Verwaltung* 96.

GALANTER, M, 'Why the "Haves" Come Out Ahead: Speculations on the Limits of Legal Change' (1974) 10 *Law and Society* 95.

GARCÍA DE ENTERRÍA, E and ORTEGA, L, 'Spanish Report' in Schwarze, J (ed), *Le Droit administratif sous l'influence de l'Europe* (Baden-Baden, Nomos Verlag, 1996), 722.

GARDE, JA (ed), *Políticas sociales y estado de bienestar en España* (Madrid, Trotta, 1999).

GATI, C, *The Bloc that Failed Soviet-East European Relations in Transition* (Oxford, Oxford University Press, 1990).

GEDDES, A, *Protection of Individual Rights under EC Law* (London, Butterworths, 1995).

GELLNER, E, *Nations and Nationalism* (Oxford, Blackwell, 1983).

——, *Nationalism* (London, Phoenix, 1997).

GERSTENBERG, O, 'Proceduralisation of Law and the Transformation of Adjucative Functions in the EC and the WTO' (2002) *European Law Journal*.

GERSTENBERG, O and SABEL, C, 'Directly-Deliberative Polyarchy: An Institutional Ideal for Europe?' in Joerges, C and Dehousse, R (eds) *Good Governance in Europe's Integrated Market* (Oxford, Oxford University Press, 2002), 289.

GLENN, PH, *Legal Traditions of the World: Sustainable Diversity in Law* (New York, Oxford University Press, 2000).

——, 'La tradition juridique nationale' (2003) 2 *Revue International de Droit Comparé* 263.

GREAVES, R, 'Magill est arrivé ... RTE and ITP v Commission of the European Communities' (1995) 4 ECLR 244.

GRECO, G, 'Rapporti tra ordinamento comunitario e nazionale' in Chiti, MP and Greco, G (eds) *Trattato di diritto amministrativo europeo* (Milano, Giuffrè, 1997), 566.

GREENWOOD, J, *Representing Interests in the European Union* (London, MacMillan Press, 1997).

GRILLER, S, 'Judicial Enforceability of WTO Law in the European Union' (2000) 3 *Journal of International Economic Law* 441.

GRIMM, D, 'Die Zukunft der Verfassung' in Preuß, UK (ed), *Zum Begriff der Verfassung* (Frankfurt am Main, Fischer, 1994), 283.

——, 'Does Europe Need a Constitution?' (1995) 1 *European Law Journal* 282.

GUIBENTIF, P and BOUGET, D, *Minimum Income Policies in the European Union* (Lisbon, União das Mutualidades Portuguesas, 1997).

GUILD, E, *The Developing Immigration and Asylum Law of the EU* (The Hague, Kluwer Law International, 1995).

——, *European Community Law from a Migrant's Perspective* (Nijmegen, Katholieke Universiteit Nijmegen, 1999).

GUIRAUDON, V, 'The Marshallian Triptych Re-Ordered: The Role of Courts and Bureaucracies in Furthering Migrant Social Rights' (1998) European University Institute Working Paper 98/4.

GURVITCH, G, *The Bill of Social Rights* (New York, International Universities Press, 1946).

HAAS, EB, *The Uniting of Europe: Political, Economic and Social Forces, 1950–1957* (Stanford, Stanford University Press, 1968).

HÄBERLE, P, *Europäische Rechtskultur: Versuch einer Annährung in zwölf Schriften* (Baden-Baden, Nomos Verlag, 1994).

HABERMAS, J, *Die Einbeziehung des Anderen* (Frankfurt am Main, Suhrkamp, 1996).

——, *Between Facts and Norms* (Cambridge, Polity Press, 1997).

——, 'Toward a Cosmopolitan Europe' (2003) 14 *Journal of Democracy* 86.

HAILBRONNER, K and THIERY, C, 'Asylrecht und Einwanderung sowie Überführung des Schengen-Besitzstands aud EU-Ebene' (1998) 5 *Europarecht* 583.

HALLSTEIN, W, *Der unvollendete Bundesstaat* (Düsseldorf, Econ Verlag, 1969).

HAMMAR, T, *European Immigration Policy: A Comparative Study* (Cambridge, Cambridge University Press, 1983).

HARDING, A and ÖRÜCÜ, E (eds), *Comparative Law in the 21st Century* (The Hague, Kluwer Law International, 2002).

HARDING, C, 'Who Goes to Court in Europe? An Analysis of Litigation against the European Community' (1992) 17 ELR 105.

HARLOW, C, 'Towards a Theory of Access for the European Court of Justice' (1992) 12 *Yearbook of European Law* 213.

——, 'Codification of EC Administrative Procedures? Fitting the Shoe to the Foot' (1996) 2 *European Law Journal* 3.

——, 'Access to Justice as a Human Right: The European Convention and the European Union' in Alston, P, Bustelo, M and Heenan, J (eds) *The EU and Human Rights* (Oxford, Oxford University Press, 1999), 187.

——, 'European Administrative Law and the Global Challenge' in Craig, P and de Búrca, G (eds) *The Evolution of EU Law* (Oxford, Oxford University Press, 1999), 261.

HARLOW, C and RAWLINGS, R, *Pressure through Law* (London, Routledge, 1992).

HARTLEY, TC, *Constitutional Problems of the European Union* (Oxford, Hart Publishing, 1999).

HATZOPOULOS, VG, 'Killing National Health and Insurance Systems but Healing Patients? The European Market for Health Care Services after the Judgments of the ECJ in Vanbraekel and Peerbooms' (2002) 39 CML Rev 683.

HECHTER, M, *Containing Nationalism* (Oxford, Oxford University Press, 2000).

HEDEMANN-ROBINSON, M, 'An Overview of Recent Legal Developments at Community Level in Relation to Third Country Nationals Resident within the European Union, with Particular Reference to the Case Law of the European Court of Justice' (2001) 38 CML Rev 525.

HEGEL, *Grundlinien der Philosophie des Rechts* (Frankfurt am Main, Suhrkamp, 1970).

HELD, D, 'Between State and Civil Society: Citizenship' in Andrews, G (ed) *Citizenship* (London, Lawrence and Wishart, 1991).

——, *Democracy and the Global Order: From the Modern State to Cosmopolitan Governance* (Cambridge, Polity Press, 1995).

HEPPLE, B, 'The Implementation of the Community Charter of Fundamental Social Rights' (1991) 53 MLR 643.

——, *European Social Dialogue: Alibi or Opportunity* (London, The Institute of Employment Rights, 1993).

HERDEGEN, M, *Europarecht* (München, CH Beck, 1999).

HÉRITIER, A, 'Elements of Democratic Legitimation in Europe: An Alternative Perspective' (1999) 6 *Journal of European Public Policy* 269.

——, 'New Modes of Governance in Europe: Increasing Political Efficiency and Policy Effectiveness?' in Boerzel, T and Chicowski, E (eds) *State of the European Union* (Oxford, Oxford University Press, 2003).

HERMANS, H, 'Access to Health Care and Health Service in the European Union: Regulation 1408/71 and the E111 Process' in Leidl, R (ed) *Health Care and its Financing in the Single European Market* (Amsterdam, IOS Press, 1998), 324.

HERNU, R, 'Le Devoir de loyauté du fonctionnaire des Communautés européennes' (2002) 38 *Revue Trimestrielle de Droit Européenne* 686.

HERVEY, TK, 'Migrant Workers and their Families in the European Union: the Pervasive Market Ideology of Community Law' in Shaw, J and Moore, G (eds) *New Legal Dynamics of the European Union* (Oxford, Clarendon Press, 1995), 110.

——, 'Community and National Competence in Health After Tobacco Advertising' (2001) 38 CML Rev 1421.

HESSE, K, *Grundzuge des Verfassungsrechts der Bundesrepublik Deutschland* (Heidelberg, Müller, 1995).

HEUTGER, V, 'Law and Language in the European Union' (2003) 3 *Global Jurist* 1.

HILSON, C and DOWNES, T, 'Making Sense of Rights: Community Rights in EC Law' (1999) 24 ELR 121.

HIX, S, 'The Study of the European Union II: The New Governance Agenda and Its Rivals' (1998) 5 *Journal of European Public Policy* 38.

HOFFMANN, TRHL, 'A Sense of Proportion' in Adenas, M and Jacobs, F (eds) *European Community Law in the English Courts* (Oxford, Oxford University Press, 1998), 149.

HOHFELD, WN, *Fundamental Legal Conceptions as Applied in Judicial Reasoning* (New Haven, Yale University Press, 1978).

HOLMES, OW, 'The Path of the Law' in his *Collected Legal Papers* (New York, Peter Smith, 1952).

HONDIUS, E, 'Towards a European Civil Code' in Hartkampf, A, Hesslink, M, Hondius, E, Joustra, C and du Perron, E (eds) *Towards a European Civil Code* (The Hague, Kluwer Law International, 1998).

HUGHES, J, SASSE, G and GORDON, C, 'Saying "Maybe" to the "Return to Europe": Elites and the Political Space for Euroscepticism in Central and Eastern Europe' (2002) 3 *European Union Politics* 3.

HUME, D, *A Treatise of Human Nature* (Oxford, Clarendon Press, 1978).

ILIOPOULOU, A and TONER, H, 'Case Note on Case C–184/99 Rudy Grzelczyk v. Centre public d'aide sociale d'Ottignies-Louvain-la-Neuve [2001] ECR I-6193' (2002) 39 CML Rev 609.

INGLEWOOD, R, *Culture Shift* (Princeton, Princeton University Press, 1990).

JACKSON, V and TUSHNET, M (ed), *Comparative Constitutional Law* (New York, Foundation Press, 1999).

JACOBS, D (ed), *The Communist Manifesto and Related Documents* (New York, Harper Torchbooks, 1962).

JACQUÉ, JP, 'Cours générale de droit communautaire' in Clapham, A (ed) *Collected Courses of the Academy of European Law* (Dordrecht, Martinus Nijhoff, 1990), 247.

JARVIS, M, *The Application of EC Law by National Courts: The Free Movement of Goods* (Oxford, Clarendon Press, 1998).

JÉSUS-GIMENO, B, 'International and Community Obligations of the Member States in the Field of Social Security Schemes: Which Impact for Migrant Workers?' in Kronenberger, V (ed) *The EU and the International Legal Order: Discord or Harmony?* (The Hague, TMC Asser Press, 2001), 297.

JOERGES, C, 'European Economic Law, the Nation State and the Maastricht Treaty' in Dehousse, R (ed) *The European Union Treaty* (München, CH Beck, 1994), 29.

JOERGES, C and DEHOUSSE, R (ed), *Good Governance in Europe's Integrated Market* (Oxford, Oxford University Press, 2002).

JOERGES, C, MÉNY, Y and WEILER, JHH (eds), *What Kind of Constitution for What Kind of Polity? Responses to Joschka Fischer* (Florence, Robert Schuman Centre for Advanced Studies at the European University Institute; Cambridge MA, Harvard Law School, 2000).

—— (eds), *Mountain or Molehill?: A Critical Appraisal of the Commission White Paper on Governance* Jean Monnet Working Paper 6/01 (Florence, Robert Schuman Centre for Advanced Studies at the European University Institute; New York, New York University School of Law, 2001).

JOERGES, C and NEYER, J, 'From Intergovernmental Bargaining to Deliberative Political Processes: The Constitutionalization of Comitology' (1997) 3 *European Law Journal* 273.

JOERGES, C and VOS, E (eds), *EU Committees: Social Regulation, Law and Politics* (Oxford, Hart Publishing, 1999).

JOHNSON, E and O'KEEFE, D, 'From Discrimination to Obstacles to Free Movement: Recent Developments Concerning the Free Movement of Workers 1989–1994' (1994) 31 CML Rev 1313.

JOSSELIN, J-M and MARCIANO, A, 'Displacing your Principal: Two Historical Case Studies of Some Interest for the Constitutional Future of Europe' (2000) 10 *European Journal of Law and Economics* 217.

KADELBACH, S, 'European Administrative Law and the Law of a Europeanized Administration' in Joerges, C and Dehousse, R (eds) *Good Governance in Europe's Integrated Market* (Oxford, Oxford University Press, 2002), 167.

KAKOURIS, CN, 'The Case Law of the European Court of Justice on Immigration' in Korella, GD and Twomey, PM (eds) *Towards a European Immigration Policy* (Brussels, European Interuniversity Press, 1994), 155.

KALMAN, L, *The Strange Career of Legal Liberalism* (New Haven, Yale University Press, 1996).

KANT, I, *Zum ewigen Frieden: Ein philosophischer Entwurf* (Königsberg, Nicholovius, 1795).

——, *Die Metaphysik der Sitten, Rechtslehre* (Frankfurt am Main, Suhrkamp, 1977).

——, *Political Writings* (Cambridge, Cambridge University Press, 1991).

KAYE, J, 'No One Such Place: "Home" in Austrian and Swedish "Landscapes"' (Doctoral thesis) (Florence, European University Institute, 2003).

KELSEN, H, *A Pure Theory of Law* (Berkeley and Los Angeles, University of California Press, 1967).

KIRCHHOF, P, 'Deutsches Verfassungsrecht und Europäisches Gemeinschaftsrecht' (1991) *Special Edition of Europarecht* 12.

——, 'Europäische Einigung und der Verfassungsstaat der Bundesrepublik Deutschland' in Isensee, J (ed) *Europa als politische Idee und als rechtliche Form* (Berlin, Duncker & Humblot, 1993), 79.

——, 'The Balance of Powers between National and European Institutions' (1999) 5 *European Law Journal* 225.

——, 'Der Weg Europas ist der Dialog' (1999) 12 *Zeitschrift für Wirtschaftsrecht* 353.

KOHLER-KOCH, B, 'Catching up with the Change: The Transformation of Governance in the European Union' (1998) 3 *European Journal of Public Policy* 359.

KOKOTT, J, 'Report on Germany' in Slaughter, A-M, Stone Sweet, A and Weiler, JHH (eds) *The European Courts and National Courts: Doctrine and Jurisprudence* (Oxford, Hart Publishing, 1998), 79.

KOMMERS, DP, *The Constitutional Jurisprudence of the Federal Republic of Germany* (Durham NC, Duke University Press, 1989).

KOOPMANS, T, 'The Future of the Court of Justice of the European Communities' (1991) 11 *Yearbook of European Law* 15.

KOSKENNIEMI, M, 'The Effect of Rights on Political Culture' in Alston, P, Bustelo, M and Heenan, J (eds), *The EU and Human Rights* (Oxford, Oxford University Press, 1999), 99.

KRAMARAE, C, SCHULZ, C and O'BARR, WM (eds), *Language and Power* (London, Sage, 1984).

KRAMER, MH, SIMMONDS, NE and STEINER, H, *A Debate over Rights: Philosophical Enquiries* (Oxford, Clarendon Press, 1998).

KRASNER, S, *Sovereignty* (Princeton, Princeton University Press, 1999).

KÜCHENMEISTER, D (ed), *Honecker-Gorbatschow: Vieraugengespräche* (Berlin, Dietz, 1993).

KÜHN, K-U, 'Germany' in Graham, EM and Richardson, JD (eds), *Global Competition Policy* (Washington DC, Institute for International Economics, 1997), 117.

KUHN, T, *The Structure of Scientific Revolutions* (Cambridge, Cambridge University Press, 1962).

KYMLICKA, W, *Multicultural Citizenship* (Oxford, Oxford University Press, 1995).
LA TORRE, M (ed), *European Citizenship: An Institutional Challenge* (The Hague, Kluwer Law International, 1998).
——, 'Legitimacy for a Supranational European Political Order — Derivative, Regulatory or Deliberative?' (2002) 15 *Ratio Juris* 63.
LACHMANN, P, 'Some Danish Reflections on the Use of Article 235 of the Rome Treaty' (1981) CML Rev 447.
LADEUR, K-H, *Postmoderne Rechtstheorie* (Berlin, Duncker & Humblot, 1992).
——, 'Towards a Legal Theory of Supranationality: The Viability of the Network Concept' (1997) 3 *European Law Journal* 33.
——, 'Towards a Legal Concept of the Network in European Standard-setting' in Joerges, C and Vos, E (eds) *EU Committees: Social Regulation, Law and Politics* (Oxford, Hart Publishing, 1999), 151.
—— (ed), *The Europeanisation of Administrative Law: Transforming National Decision-making Procedures* (Aldershot, Ashgate, 2002).
——, 'Conflict and Co-operation between European Law and the General Administrative Law of the Member States' in Ladeur, K-H (ed) *The Europeanisation of Administrative Law: Transforming National Decision-making Procedures* (Dartmouth, Ashgate, 2003), 1.
LEGRAND, P, 'European Legal Systems Are Not Converging' (1993) 45 *International and Comparative Law Quarterly* 52.
LEITÃO MARQUES, MM, 'Iniziativa economica e concurrenza nell'ordinamento guiridico portoghese' in Mezzetti, L (ed), *Costituzione economica e libertà di concurrenza* (Torino, G. Giappichelli, 1994), 75.
LENAERTS, K and DE SMIJTER, E, 'A "Bill of Rights" for the European Union' (2001) 38 CML Rev 273.
LEWIS, A, 'Earl Warren' in Sayler, RH, Boyer, BB and Gooding Jr, RE (eds) *The Warren Court: A Critical Analysis* (New York, Chelsea House, 1969), 1.
LEWIS, C, 'Judicial Review and the Role of the English Court in European Community Disputes' in Adenas, M and Jacobs, F (eds) *European Community Law in the English Courts* (Oxford, Clarendon Press, 1998), 101.
LIÑÁN NOGUERAS, DJ and ROLDÁN BARBERO, J, 'The Judicial Application of Community Law in Spain' (1993) 30 CML Rev 1135.
LINKLATER, A, 'Cosmopolitan Citizenship' (1998) 2 *Citizenship Studies* 23.
——, *The Transformation of Political Community: Ethical Foundations of the Post-Westphalian Era* (Cambridge, Polity Press, 1998).
LO FARO, A, *Regulating Social Europe: Reality and Myth of Collective Bargaining in the EC Legal Order* (Oxford, Hart Publishing, 2000).
LODGE, J, 'Social Europe: Fostering a People's Europe?' in Lodge, J (ed) *The European Community and the Challenge of the Future* (London, Pinter, 1989), 303.
LOUIS, B, 'Une Distinction nécessaire dans l'État nation: la Communauté-nation et l'État-citoyenneté. L'identité des sociétés occidentales modernes face à l'immigration musulmane' (1993) 31 *Revue Interdisciplinaires d'Études Juridiques* 25.
LUHMANN, N, *Legitimation durch Verfahren* (Frankfurt am Main, Suhrkamp, 1983).
——, *Das Recht der Gesellschaft* (Frankfurt am Main, Suhrkamp, 1989).
——, *Political Theory in the Welfare State* (Berlin, de Gruyter, 1990).
LUKES, S, 'Political Ritual and Social Integration' (1975) 9 *Sociology* 289.
——, 'Can a Marxist Believe in Human Rights?' (1982) 1 *Praxis International* 334.

LYONS, C, 'Citizenship in the Constitution of the EU: Rhetoric or Reality'? in Bellamy, R (ed) *Constitutionalism, Democracy and Sovereignty: American and European Perspectives* (Aldershot, Avebury, 1996).
MACCORMICK, N, 'Rights in Legislation' in Hacker, PMS and Raz, J (eds) *Law, Morality and Society* (Oxford, Clarendon Press, 1977), 203.
——, 'Beyond the Sovereign State' (1993) 50 MLR 1.
——, 'The Maastricht Urteil: Sovereignty Now' (1995) 1 *European Law Journal* 255.
——, *Questioning Sovereignty: Law, State and Nation in the European Commonwealth* (Oxford, Oxford University Press, 1999).
——, 'A Comment on the White Paper' in Joerges, C, Mény, Y and Weiler, JHH (eds) *Maintain or Molehill?: A Critical Appraisal of the Commission White Paper on Governance* Jean Monnet Working Paper 6/01 (Florence, Robert Schuman Centre for Advanced Studies at the European University Institute; New York, New York University School of Law, 2001), 195.
MACINTYRE, A, *After Virtue:A Study in Moral Theory* (London, Duckworth, 1981).
MACRORY, R and TURNER, S, 'Participatory Rights, Transboundary Environmental Governance and EC Law' (2002) 39 CML Rev 489.
MAJONE, G, *Regulating Europe* (London, Routledge, 1996).
——, 'Europe's "Democratic Deficit": The Question of Standards' (1998) 4 *European Law Journal* 5.
——, 'Delegation of Regulatory Powers in a Mixed Polity' (2002) 8 *European Law Journal* 319.
MAMPEL, S, *Die sozialistiche Verfassung der DDR* (Frankfurt am Main, Metzner, 1982).
MANCINI, GF, 'Europe: the Case for Statehood' (1998) 4 *European Law Journal* 29.
——, *Democracy and Constitutionalism in the European Union: Collected Essays* (Oxford, Hart Publishing, 2000).
MANCINI, GF and KEELING, D, 'Legal Culture and Politics in the Life of the European Court of Justice' (1995) 1 *Columbia Journal of European Law* 397.
MANGAS MARTÍN, A, *Derecho comunitario europeo y derecho español* (Madrid, Tecnos, 1987).
MANNONI, S, 'Stato nazionale di diritto e diritto internazionale' in Costa, P and Zolo, D (eds) *Lo Stato di diritto* (Milan, Feltrinelli, 2002), 485.
MARKESINIS, B, *The Gradual Convergence: Foreign Influences and English Law on the Eve of the 21st Century* (Oxford, Clarendon Press, 1994).
——, *Foreign Law and Comparative Methodology* (Oxford, Hart Publishing, 1998).
MARKS, G, HOOGHE, L and BLANK, K, 'European Integration from the 1980s: State-centric v. Multi-level Governance' (1996) 34 *Journal of Common Market Studies* 341.
MARQUAND, D, 'The Irrestible Tide of Europeanisation' in Hall, S and Jacques, M (eds) *New Times* (London, Lawrence and Wishart, 1991).
MARSCHANG, B, 'Mißtrauen, Abschottung, Eigensinn — Entwicklungslinien der europäischen Asylrechts <harmonisierung> bis zum Amsterdamer Vertrag' (1998) 69 *Kritische Justiz* 69.
MARSHALL, TH, *Citizenship and Social Class and Other Essays* (Cambridge, Cambridge University Press, 1950).
MASON, JK, MCCALL SMITH, RA and LAURIE, GT, *Law and Medical Ethics* (London, Butterworths, 2002).

MAYER, F, *Kompetenzüberschreitung und Letztentscheidung* (München, CH Beck, 2000).
MCCARTHY, M, *Evolution and Implementation of the Italian health service reform of 1978* (London, Chadwick Press, 1992).
MCCARTHY, M and REES, S, *Health Care Systems and Public Health Medicine in the European Community* (London, Faculty of Public Health Medicine of the Royal Colleges of Physicians of the UK and Royal College of Physicians of London, 1992).
MCCLEAN, S, *A Patient's Right to Know* (Dartmouth, Ashgate, 1989).
MCCRUDDEN, C, 'A Common Law of Human Rights?: Transnational Judicial Conversations on Constitutional Rights' (2000) 4 OJLS 499.
MÉNY, Y, 'The Achievements of the Convention' (2003) 14 *Journal of Democracy* 57.
MERKEL, B and KÄRKKÄINEN, K, 'Public Health Aspects of Accession' (2002) 8 *Eurohealth* 3.
MEZZETTI, L (ed), *Costituzione economica e libertà di concurrenza* (Torino, G. Giappichelli, 1994).
MICKLITZ, H-W and REICH, N (eds), *Public Interest Litigation before European Courts* (Baden-Baden, Nomos Verlag, 1996).
MILLER, D, 'Citizenship and Pluralism' (1995) 43 *Political Studies* 432.
MILLNS, S, 'The Treaty of Amsterdam and Constitutional Revision in France' (1999) 5 *European Public Law* 61.
MILLNS, S and WHITTY, N (eds), *Feminist Perspectives on Public Law* (London, Cavendish, 1999).
MILWARD, AS, *The European Rescue of the Nation-State* (London, Routledge, 1992).
MISCHLER, W and ROSE, R, 'Learning and Re-learning Regime Support: The Dynamics of Post-communist Regimes' (2002) 41 *European Journal of Political Research* 5.
MÖLLERS, C, *Staat als Argument* (München, CH Beck, 2000).
MONAR, J, 'Justice and Home Affairs in the Treaty of Amsterdam: Reform at the Price of Fragmentation' (1998) 23 ELR 320.
MONTGOMERY, J, 'Medicine, Accountability, and Professionalism' (1989) 16 *Journal of Law and Society* 318.
MOORE, M, 'Freedom of Movement and Migrant Workers' Social Security: An Overview of the Court's Jurisprudence 1992–1997' (1998) 35 CML Rev 409.
MORAN, M and WOOD, B, *States, Regulation and the Medical Profession* (Buckingham, Open University Press, 1993).
MORAVCSIK, A, 'Review Essay on Larry Siedentop, *Democracy in America*: Despotism in Brussels? Misreading the European Union' (2001) 80 *Foreign Affairs* 114.
MORIN, E, *L'Identité humaine* (Paris, Seuil, 2001).
MORTELMANS, K, 'The Principle of Loyalty to the Community (article 5 EC) and the Obligations of the Community Institutions' (1998) 8 *Maastricht Journal of European and Comparative Law* 67.
MOUFFE, C, 'Democratic Citizenship and the Political Community' in Mouffe, C (ed), *Dimensions of Radical Democracy* (London, Verso, 1992), 226.

MURKENS, J, 'The Integrative Function of a European Constitution: Discussion of Christian Dorau's Book: *Die Verfassungsfrage der Europäischen Union*' (2002) 3 *German Law Journal*.

MYERS, D, *The Human Body and the Law* (Edinburgh, Edinburgh University Press, 1990).

NEHL, HP, *Principles of Administrative Procedure in EC Law* (Oxford, Hart Publishing, 1999).

NELKEN, D, *Comparing Legal Cultures* (Aldershot, Dartmouth, 1997).

NELKEN, D and FEEST, J (ed), *Adapting Legal Cultures* (Oxford, Hart Publishing, 2001).

NELSON-JONES, R and BURTON, F, *Medical Negligence Case Law* (London, Butterworths Law, 1995).

NEUMAN, GL, '"We are the People": Alien Suffrage in German and American Perspective.' (1992) 35 *Michigan Journal of International Law* 237.

NIC SHUIBHNE, N, *EC Law and Minority Language Policy* (The Hague, Kluwer Law International, 2002).

——, 'The European Union and Fundamental Rights: Well in Spirit but Considerably Rumpled in Body?' in Beaumont, P, Lyons, C and Walker, N (eds) *Convergence* and *Divergence in European Public Law* (Oxford, Hart Publishing, 2002), 178.

NICHOLAS, S, 'Movement of Health Care Professionals: Trends and Enlargement' (2002) 8 *Eurohealth* 11.

NICOLAÏDIS, K and VERNON, R, 'Competition Policy and Trade Policy in the European Union' in Graham, EM and Richardson, JD (eds) *Global Competition Policy* (Washington DC, Institute for International Economics, 1997), 273.

NIELSON, R and SYZSZCZAK, E, *The Social Dimension of the European Community* (Copenhagen, Handelshøjskolens, 1991).

OFFE, C, 'Demokratie und Wohlfahrtsstaat' in Streeck, W (ed) *Internationale Wirtschaft und nationale Demokratie: Herausaforderung für die Demokratietheorie* (Frankfurt am Main, Campus, 1998), 99.

O'KEEFE, D, 'Judicial Interpretation of the Public Service Exeption in Article 48, paragraph 4 of the EEC Treaty' in Curtin, D and O'Keefe, D (eds) *Constitutional Adjudication in European Community and National Law* (Dublin, Butterworths, 1992), 89.

ÖLANDER, J, 'European Integration as an Instrument for Breaking State Sovereignty: A Discussion on the Relativity of Sovereignty. The Example of Euzkadi'. (Oñati Master's Tesinas) (Oñati, International Institute for the Sociology of Law, 1996).

O'LEARY, S, 'The Relationship between Community Citizenship and the Protection of Fundamental Rights in Community Law' (1995) 32 CML Rev 519.

——, *The Evolving Concept of Community Citizenship: From the Free Movement of Persons to Union Citizenship* (The Hague, Kluwer Law International, 1996).

OLIVER, D, *Common Values and the Public–Private Divide* (London, Butterworths, 1999).

——, 'The Frontiers of the State: Public Authorities and Public Functions under the Human Rights Act' (2000) 9 PL 476.

ONAINDÍA, M, *La Construción de la nación española* (Barcelona, Bailén, 2002).

ONDOUA, A, *L'Étude des rapports entre le droit communautaire et la Constitution en France: l'ordre juridique constitutionnel comme guide au renforcement de l'intégration européenne* (Paris, L'Harmattan, 2001).

OPPENHEIMER, A, *The Relationship between European Community Law and National Law: The Cases*. Vol 1 (Cambridge, Cambridge University Press, 1994).

——, *The Relationship between European Community Law and National Law: The Cases. Vol 2* (Cambridge, Cambridge University Press, 2003).

OSIATYNSKI, W, 'Rights in New Constitutions of East Central Europe' (1994) 26 *Columbia Human Rights Law Review* 111.

PALM, W, NICKLESS, J, LEWALLE, H and COHEUR, A, *Implications of Recent Jurisprudence on the Co-ordination of Health Care Protection Systems* (Brussels, AIM, 2000).

PAPER, W, 'Rights Brought Home: The Human Rights Bill' (1997) *Cm. 3782*.

PAREKH, B, *Rethinking Multiculturalism: Cultural Diversity and Political Theory* (Cambridge, Cambridge University Press, 2000).

PAULUS, A, EVERS, S, FECHER, F, VAN DER MADE, J and BOONEN, A, 'Cross Border Health Care: An Analysis of Recent ECJ Rulings' (2002) 14 *European Journal of Law and Economics* 61.

PEARCE, D, 'Welfare is not for Women: Why the War on Poverty Cannot Conquer the Feminisation of Poverty' in Gordon, L (ed), *Women, the State and Welfare* (Madison WI, Wisconsin University Press, 1990), 269.

PEARSALL, J (ed), *The Concise Oxford Dictionary* (Oxford, Oxford University Press, 2001).

PECHSTEIN, M and KOENIG, M, *Die Europäische Union: Die Verträge von Maastricht und Amsterdam* (Tübingen, Mohr, 1998).

PEERS, S, 'Equality, Free Movement and Social Security' (1997) 22 ELR 342.

——, 'Towards Equality: Actual and Potential Rights of Third-Country Nationals in the European Union' (1997) ELR 341.

——, 'Aliens, Workers, Citizens or Humans? Modes for Community Immigration Law' in Guild, E and Harlow, C (eds), *Implementing Amsterdam: Immigration and Asylum Rights in EC Law* (Oxford, Hart Publishing, 2000), 291.

PENNINGS, F, *Introduction to European Social Security Law* (The Hague, Kluwer Law International, 1998).

PENNINGTON, K, *The Prince and the Law 1200–1600. Sovereignty and Rights in the Western Legal Tradition* (Berkeley, University of California Press, 1993).

PERNICE, I, 'Multilevel Constitutionalism and the Treaty of Amsterdam: European Constitution-making Revisted?' (1999) 36 CML Rev 703.

PETERSMANN, E-U, 'European and International Constitutional Law: Time for Promoting "Cosmopolitan Democracy" in the WTO' in de Búrca, G and Scott, J (eds) *The EU and the WTO: Legal and Constitutional Issues* (Oxford, Hart Publishing, 2001), 81.

PETTIT, P, *Republicanism: A Theory of Freedom and Government* (Oxford, Clarendon Press, 1999).

PHELAN, DR, 'Right to Life of the Unborn v. Promotion of Trade in Services: The European Court of Justice and the Normative Shaping of the European Union' (1992) 55 MLR 670.

PHILIPPART, E and SIE DHIAN HO, M, 'From Uniformity to Flexibility: The Management of Diversity and its Impact on the EU System of Governance' in

de Búrca, G and Scott, J (eds) *Flexibility and Models of Governance for the EU* (Oxford, Hart Publishing, 2000), 299.
PIPER, A, 'Truce on the Battlefield: A Proposal for a Different Approach to Medical Informed Consent' (1994) 22 *Journal of Medical Ethics* 301.
POIARES MADURO, M, *We, the Court* (Oxford, Hart Publishing, 1998).
——, 'Balancing Economic Freedom and Social Rights' in Alston, P, Bustelo, M and Heenan, J (eds), *The EU and Human Rights* (Oxford, Oxford University Press, 1999), 449.
——, 'Is There Any Such Thing as Free of Fair Trade? A Constitutional Analysis of the Impact of International Trade on the European Social Model' in de Búrca, G and Scott, J (eds), *The EU and the WTO: Legal and Constitutional Issues* (Oxford, Hart Publishing, 2001), 257.
POLANYI, K, *The Great Transformation* (Boston, Beacon Press, 1944).
POLLACK, M, 'Delegation, Agency, and Agenda Setting in the European Community' (1997) 51 *International Organization* 99.
POLLACK, M and HAFNER-BURTON, E, 'Mainstreaming Gender in the EU' (2000) 7 *Journal of European Public Policy* 432.
POSTIGLIOLA, A, 'De Malebranche à Rousseau: Les Apories de la volonté générale et la revanche du "raisonneur violent"' (1980) 39 *Annales de la Société Jean-Jacques Rousseau* 134.
PRAWER, J, 'Crusader Cities' in Miskimin, HA, Herlihy, D and Udovitch, UL (eds) *The Medieval City* (New Haven, Yale University Press, 1977).
PRECHAL, S, *Directives in European Community Law* (Oxford, Clarendon Press, 1995).
PREUß, UK, *Revolution, Fortschritt, Verfassung* (Frankfurt, Suhrkamp, 1992).
——, 'Problems of a Concept of European Citizenship' (1995) 1 *European Law Journal* 267.
——, 'The Roundtable Talks in the German Democratic Republic' in Elster J (ed) *The Roundtable Talks and the Breakdown of Communism* (Chicago, Chicago University Press, 1996), 99.
PRODI, R, *Europe as I See it* (Cambridge, Polity Press, 2000).
PUNTSCHER RIEKMANN, S, 'The Myth of European Unity' in Hosking, G and Schöpflin, G (eds) *Myths & Nationhood* (New York, Routledge, 1997).
RAMIREZ, FO and BOLI, J, 'The Political Construction of Mass Schooling: European Origins and Worldwide Institutionalization' (1987) *Sociology of Education* 2.
RAMOS, F, 'Judicial Cooperation in the European Courts: Testing Three Models of Judicial Behavior' (2002) 2 *Global Jurist Frontiers* 1.
RAWLS, J, *A Theory of Justice* (Cambridge MA, Harvard University Press, 1971).
RAZ, J, *The Morality of Freedom* (Oxford, Clarendon Press, 1986).
REICH, N, 'Judge Made "Europe à la Carte": Some Remarks on Recent Conflicts between European and German Constitutional Law Provoked by the Banana Litigation' (1996) 7 *European Journal of International Law* 103.
——, 'Union Citizenship: Metaphor or Source of Rights?' (2001) 7 *European Law Journal* 4.
RETUERTO BUADES, M, *Demandas ciudadanas sobre proteción social en España* (Madrid, Ilustre Colegio Nacional de Dotores y Licenciados en Ciencias Políticas y Sociología, 1989).

RHODES, M, FERRERA, M and HEMERIJCK, A, 'The Future of the European "Social Model" in the Global Economy' (2001) 3 *Journal of Comparative Policy Analysis* 1.

RIMLINGER, GV, *Welfare Policy and Industrialization in Europe, America and Russia* (New York, Wiley, 1971).

ROBERTS, A, 'Multilateral Institutions and the Rights to Information: Experience in the European Union' (2002) 8 *European Public Law* 255.

RODRÍGUEZ IGLESIAS, GC, LIÑÁN NOGUERAS, D and ABELLÁN HONRUBIA, V (eds), *El derecho comunitario europeo y su aplicación* (Madrid, Civitas, 1993).

ROGOWSKI, R, *Rational Legitimacy: A Theory of Political Support* (Princeton, Princeton University Press, 1974).

ROOM, G, 'Social Quality in Europe. Perspectives on Social Exclusion' in Beck, W, Van der Maesen, L and Walker, A (eds) *The Social Quality of Europe* (The Hague, Kluwer Law International, 1997), 255.

ROSSI, M, 'Anmerkung zu C–184/99 Grzelczyk' (2002) 7 *Juristen Zeitung* 249.

ROUSSEAU, J-J, 'Les Confessions' in Gagnebin, B and Raymond, M (eds) *Oeuvres complètes de Jean-Jacques Rousseau* (Paris, Pléiade, 1959), 237.

RUGGIE, JG, 'International Regimes, Transactions and Change: Embedded Liberalism in the Postwar Economic Order' (1982) 36 *International Organization* 379.

RUIZ, G and RUIZ, R, 'La libertà di impresa nella costituzione economica spagnola: con particolare riguardo al principio di libera concurrenza' in Mezzetti, L (ed), *Costituzione economica e libertà di concurrenza* (Torino, G. Giappichelli, 1994), 37.

SADURSKI, W, 'Conclusions: On the Relevance of Institutions and the Centrality of Constitutions in Post-communist Transitions' in Zielonka, J (ed) *Democratic Consolidation in Eastern Europe, Vol I: Institutional Engineering* (Oxford, Oxford University Press, 2001), 455.

——, 'Charter and Enlargement' (2002) 8 *European Law Journal* 340.

——, 'Postcommunist Charters of Rights in Europe and the U.S. Bill of Rights' (2002) 65 *Law and Contemporary Problems* 223.

SAJO, A, 'How the Rule of Law Killed Hungarian Welfare Reform' (1996) 5 *East Constitutional Review* 31.

SANDHOLZ, W and STONE SWEET, A (eds), *European Integration and Supranational Governance* (Oxford, Oxford University Press, 1998).

SASSEN, S, *Losing Control? Sovereignty in an Age of Globalization* (New York, Columbia University Press, 1996).

SCHARPF, F, *Governing in Europe: Effective and Democratic?* (Oxford, Oxford University Press, 1999).

SCHILLING, T, 'The Autonomy of the Community Legal Order: An Analysis of Possible Foundations' (1996) 17 *Harvard International Law Journal* 389.

——, 'Bestand und allgemeine Lehren der bürgerlichen allgemeinen Rechtsgrundsätze des Gemeinschaftsrechts' (2000) *Europäische Grundrechte-Zeitschrifte* 3.

SCHMIDT, C, 'From Pont d'Avignon to Ponte Vecchio: The Resolution of Constitutional Conflicts between the European Union and the Member States through Principles of Public International Law' (1998) 18 *Yearbook of European Law* 415.

SCHMITT, C, *Verfassungslehre* (Berlin, Duncker & Humblot, 1928).

SCHMITTER, PC, *How to Democratize the European Union. And Why Bother?* (Maryland, Rowman and Littlefield, 2000).

——, 'Democracy in Europe and Europe's Democratization' (2003) 14 *Journal of Democracy* 71.

SCHÖNLAU, J, 'Drafting Europe's Value Foundation: Deliberation and Arm-twisting in Formulating the Preamble to the EU Charter of Fundamental Rights' in Eriksen, E, Fossum, JE and Menéndez, A (eds) *The Chartering of Europe* (Oslo, ARENA, 2001), 127.

SCHUCK, PH, *Citizens, Strangers and In-Betweens: Essays on Immigration and Citizenship* (Boulder, Westview Press, 1998).

SCHUDSON, M, *The Good Citizen: A History of American Civic Life* (New York, The Free Press, 1998).

SCHULZE, H, *Staat und Nation in der Europäischen Geschichte* (München, CH Beck, 1994).

SCHUMPETER, J, *Capitalism, Socialism and Democracy* (London, Allen & Unwin, 1942).

SCHWARZE, J (ed), *Administrative Law under European Influence: On the Convergences of the Administrative Laws of the EU Member States* (London, Sweet & Maxwell; Baden-Baden, Nomos Verlag, 1996).

SCOTT, A, PETERSON, J and MILLAR, D, 'Subsidiarity: A "Europe of the Regions" v. the British Constitution?' (1994) 32 *Journal of Common Market Studies* 1.

SEN, A, *Development as Freedom* (Oxford, Oxford University Press, 1999).

SENDEN, L, *Soft Law in European Community Law* (Nijmegen, Wolf Legal Publishers, 2003).

SHAW, J, 'The Many Pasts and Futures of Citizenship in the European Union' (1997) 22 ELR 554.

——, 'From the Margins to the Centre: Education and Training Law and Policy' in Craig, P and de Búrca, G (eds) *The Evolution of EU Law* (Oxford, Oxford University Press, 1999), 555.

——, 'Constitutional Change in the EU: From Uniformity to Flexibility?' in de Búrca, G and Scott, J (eds) *Constitutional Change in the EU: From Uniformity to Flexibility?* (Oxford, Hart Publishing, 2000), 337.

—— (ed), *Social Law and Policy in an Evolving EU* (Oxford, Hart Publishing, 2000).

——, 'Process, Responsibility and Inclusion in EU Constitutionalism' (2003) 9 *European Law Journal* 45.

——, 'What's in a Convention? Process and Substance in the Project of European Constitution-building' (2003) *Political Science Series* 89.

SHAW, J, MAGNETTE, P, HOFFMANN, L and VERGÉS BAUSILI, A, *The Convention on the Future of the Union: Working Towards an EU Constitution* (London, Federal Trust/Kogan Page, 2003).

SHAW, J and WIENER, A, 'The Paradox of the European Polity' in Green Cowles, M and Smith, M (eds) *State of the European Union 5: Risks, Reform, Resistance and Revival* (Oxford, Oxford University Press, 2000).

SHORE, C, *Building Europe: The Cultural Politics of European Integration* (London and New York, Palgrave, 2000).

SILVERMAN, WA, 'The myth of informed consent: in daily practice and in clinical trials.' (1989) 15 *The Journal of Medical Ethics* 6.

SIMMA, B, 'The Role of German Courts in the Enforcement of International Human Rights' in Conforti, B and Francioni, F (eds) *Enforcing International Human Rights in Domestic Courts* (Oxford, Oxford University Press, 1997), 107.

SIMMONDS, NE, 'Rights at the Cutting Edge' in Kramer, MH, Simmonds, NE and Steiner, H (eds), *A Debate over Rights: Philosophical Enquiries* (Oxford, Oxford University Press, 1998), 112.

SLAUGHTER, A-M, 'A Typology of Transjudicial Communication' (1994) 99 *University of Richmond Law Review* 137.

SLAUGHTER, A-M, STONE SWEET, A and WEILER, JHH (eds), *The European Court and National Courts: Doctrine and Jurisprudence. Legal Change in its Social Context* (Oxford, Hart Publishing, 1998).

SMITH, A, *National Identity* (Oxford, Clarendon Press, 1991).

SNYDER, F, 'The Effectiveness of European Community Law' (1993) 56 MLR 19.

SORRENTINO, F, *Profili costituzionali dell'integrazione comunitaria* (Torino, Giappichelli, 1996).

SOYSAL, Y, *Limits of Citizenship: Migrants and Postnational Membership in Europe* (Chicago, Chicago University Press, 1994).

SPAAK, H, *Comité intergouvernmental crée par la conférence de Messine: Rapport des chefs de délégations aux ministères des affaires étrangères* (Messina, 1956).

SPEVACK, E, *Allied Control and German Freedom: American Political and Ideological Influences on the Framing of the West German Basic Law* (Münster, LIT Verlag, 2001).

STAPLES, E, *The Legal Status of Third Country Nationals Resident in the European Union* (The Hague, Kluwer Law International, 1999).

STARK, D, 'Path Dependence and Privatisation Strategies in East Central Europe' (1992) 6 *East European Politics and Societies* 17.

STEIN, E, 'Lawyers, Judges and the Making of a Transnational Constitution' (1981) 75 *American Journal of International Law* 1.

STEINER, H and ALSTON, P, *International Human Rights in Context* (Oxford, Oxford University Press, 2000).

STOLLEIS, M, *Geschichte des öffentlichen Rechts in Deutschland* (München, CH Beck, 1992).

STONE SWEET, A, *Governing with Judges* (Oxford, Oxford University Press, 2000).

STONE SWEET, A and BRUNELL, TL, 'Constructing a Supranational Constitution: Dispute Resolution and Governance in the European Community' (1998) 92 *American Political Science Review* 63.

STONE SWEET, A, FLIGSTEIN, N and SANDHOLZ, W, 'The European Courts and the National Courts: A Statistical Analysis of Preliminary References, 1961–1995' (1998) 5 *Journal of European Public Policy* 66.

STROZZI, G, 'Alcuni interrogativi a proposito della limitazione di competenza dell'Unione Europea' (1994) 77 *Rivista di Diritto Internazionale* 136.

SUBIOTTO, R, 'The Right to Deal with Whom One Pleases under EEC Competition Law: A Small Contribution to a Necessary Debate' (1992) 6 ECLR 234.

SYKES, R, PALIER, B and PRIOR, PM (eds), *Globalization and European Welfare States* (London, Palgrave, 2001).

SZYSZCZAK, E, 'Making Europe More Relevant to its Citizens: Effective Judicial Process' (1996) 21 ELR 351.

——, 'Social Policy in the Post-Nice Era' in Arnull, A and Wincott, D (eds), Accountability and Legitimacy in the European Union (Oxford, Oxford University Press, 2002), 329.

TEFF, H, *Reasonable Care: Legal Perspectives on the Doctor / Patient Relationship* (Oxford, Oxford University Press, 1994).

TÉLO, M, 'Governance and Government in the European Union: The Open Method of Co-ordination' in Rodrigues, MJ (ed) *The New Knowledge Economy in Europe: A Strategy for International Competitiveness and Social Cohesion* (Cheltenham, Edward Elgar Publishing, 2002), 242.

TEUBNER, G, *Law as an Autopoetic System* (Oxford, Blackwell, 1993).

——, '"Global Bukowina": Legal Pluralism in the World Society' in Teubner, G (ed) *Global Law without a State* (Aldershot, Dartmouth, 1997), 3.

THIESSE, A-M, *La Création des identités nationales. Europe XVIII - XX siècle* (Paris, Seuil, 2001).

THRÄNHARDT, D, 'Europe — A New Immigration Continent. Politics and Policies since 1945 in Comparative Perspective' in Thränhardt, D (ed) *Europe: A New Immigration Continent. Policies and Politics in Comparative Perspective* (Münster, Lit, 1992), 15.

TOMKINS, A, 'Transparency and the Emergence of a European Administrative Law' (1999) 19 *Yearbook of European Law* 219.

TOMUSCHAT, C, 'The Interaction between different systems for the protection of Human Rights' in Bieber, R, de Gucht, K, Lenaerts, K and Weiler, JHH (eds), *Au nom des peuples européens – In the Name of the Peoples of Europe. Un catalogue des droits fondamentaux de l'Union européene – A Catalogue of Fundamental Rights in the European Union* (Baden-Baden, Nomos Verlag, 1996), 29.

TONIATTI, R (ed), *Diritto, diritti, giurisdizione: La carta dei diritti fondamentali dell'Unione Europea* (Padova, CEDAM, 2002).

TRIANDAFYLLIDOU, A, *National Identity Reconsidered: Images of Self and Other in a 'United' Europe* (Lampeter, Edwin Mellen Press, 2002).

TRIDIMAS, G and TRIDIMAS, T, 'The European Court of Justice and the Annulment of the Tobacco Advertisment Directive: Friend of National Sovereignty or Foe of Public Health?' (2002) 14 *European Journal of Law and Economics* 171.

TRIDIMAS, T, *The General Principles of EC Law* (Oxford, Oxford University Press, 1999).

TROPER, M, *La Théorie du droit, l'état* (Paris, Presses Universitaires de France, 2001).

TRUBECK, DM, DEZALAY, R, BUCHANAN, R and DAVIS, JR, 'Global Restructuring and the Law: Studies of the Internationalization of Legal Fields and the Creation of Transnational Arenas' (1994) 44 *Case Western Reserve Law Review* 407.

TRZASKOWSKI, R, 'National Report Poland' in Franck, C and Pyszna, D (eds) *Positions of 10 Central and Eastern European Countries on EU Institutional Reforms: Analytical Survey in the Framework of the CEEC-DEBATE Project* (Louvain-la-Neuve, Université catholique de Louvain, 2003), 70.

TULLY, J, *Strange Multiplicity: Constitutionalism in an Age of Diversity* (Cambridge, Cambridge University Press, 1995).

TULLY, J and GAGNON, AG (eds), *Multinational Democracies* (Cambridge, Cambridge University Press, 2001).

TUSHNET, M, 'The Possibilities of Comparative Constitutional Law' 108 *Yale Law Journal* 650.

——, *Taking the Constitution Away from the Courts* (Princeton NJ, Princeton University Press, 1999).
UNGER, RM 'The Critical Legal Studies Movement' (1983) 3 *Harvard Law Review* 563.
USHER, J, 'Languages and the European Union' in Anderson, M and Bort, E (eds) *The Frontiers of Europe* (London, Pinter, 1998), 222.
VAN DER MEI, AP, 'Cross-border Access to Medical Care within the European Union: Some Reflections on the Judgments in Decker and Kohll' (1998) 5 *Maastricht Journal of European and Comparative Law* 277.
——, *Free Movement of Persons within the European Community: Cross-border Access to Public Benefits* (Oxford, Hart Publishing, 2002).
VAN RAEPENBUSCH, S and HANF, D, 'Flexibility in Social Policy' in De Witte, B, Hanf, D and Vos, E (eds) *The Many Faces of Differentiation in EU Law* (Antwerp, Intersentia, 2001), 65.
VENCE, V, 'Riqueza desde la diversidad: disparidades regionales y cohesión en la Unión Europea' in Vence, V and Outes, JL (eds), *La Unión Europea y la crisis del estado del bienestar* (Madrid, Síntesis, 1998).
VILLIERS, C, *The Spanish Legal Tradition* (Dartmouth, Ashgate, 1999).
VOGEL-POLSKY, E and VOGEL, J, *L'Europe sociale 1993. Illusion, alibi ou réalité* (Brussels, Éditions de l'Université libre de Bruxelles, 1991).
VOLKAI, J, 'The Application of the Europe Agreement and European Law in Hungary: The Judgment of an Activist Constitutional Court on Activist Notions' (1999) <http://www.jeanmonnetprogram.org>.
VON BOGDANDY, A, 'The European Union as a Human Rights Organization?' (2000) 37 CML Rev 1307.
——, 'The Science of European Law' (2000) 6 *European Law Journal* 213.
VON BOGDANDY, A and NETTESHEIM, M, 'Die Europäische Union: Eine einheitlicher Verband mit eigener Rechtsordnung' (1996) *Europarecht* 3.
VOS, E, 'EU Committees: the Evolution of Unforeseen Institutional Actors in European Product Regulation' in Joerges, C and Vos, E (eds) *EU Committees:* Social Regulation, Law and Politics (Oxford, Hart Publishing, 1999), 19.
VOSGERAU, U, 'Der Begriff des Rechts bei Kant' (1999) 30 *Archiv der Rechtstheorie* 277.
VRANES, E, 'The Final Clauses of the Charter of Fundamental Rights: Stumbling Blocks for the First and Second Convention' (2003) European Integration OnLine Papers <http://eiop.or.at.eiop/texte/2003-007a.htm>.
WALKER, N, 'Beyond the Unitary Conception of the United Kingdom Constitution?' (2000) PL 384.
——, 'Flexibility within a Metaconstitutional Frame' in de Búrca, G and Scott, J (eds) *Flexibility and Models of Governance for the EU* (Oxford, Hart Publishing, 2000), 9.
——, 'Human Rights in a Postnational Order: Reconciling Political and Constitutional Pluralism' in Campbell, T, Ewing, KD and Tomkins, A (eds) *Sceptical Essays on Human Rights* (Oxford, Oxford University Press, 2001), 119.
——, 'Protection of Fundamental Rights in the European Union: The Charter of Fundamental Rights' in Cullen, P and Zervakis, PA (eds) *The Post-Nice Process: Towards a European Constitution* (Baden-Baden, Nomos Verlag, 2001).
——, 'The Idea of Constitutional Pluralism' (2002) 65 MLR 317.

——, 'Constitutionalising Enlargement, Enlarging Constitutionalism' (2003) 9 *European Law Journal* 365.

WARD, I, *A Critical Introduction to European Law* (London, Butterworths, 1996).

WARLEIGH, A, 'The Hustle: Citizenship Practice, NGOs and "Policy Coalitions" in the European Union: The Cases of Auto Oil, Drinking Water and Unit Pricing' (2000) 7 *Journal of European Public Policy* 229.

WEATHERILL, S, 'Finding Space for Closer Cooperation in the Field of Culture' in de Búrca, G and Scott, J (eds) *Flexibility and Models of Governance for the EU* (Oxford, Hart Publishing, 2000), 237.

WEBER, E, *Peasants into Frenchmen. The Modernization of Rural France 1870–1914* (London, Chatto & Windus, 1979).

WEILER, JHH, 'The Community System: the Dual Character of Supranationalism' (1981) 1 *Yearbook of European Law* 267.

——, 'The Transformation of Europe' (1990) 100 *Yale Law Review* 2403.

——, 'Does Europe Need a Constitution? Demos, Telos and the German Maastricht Decision' (1995) 1 *European Law Journal* 259.

——, *The Constitution of Europe: 'Do the New Clothes Have an Emperor?'* (Cambridge, Cambridge University Press, 1999).

——, 'Epilogue: "Comitology" as Revolution' in Joerges, C and Vos, E (eds) *EU Committees: Social Regulation, Law and Politics* (Oxford, Hart Publishing, 1999), 339.

——, 'Does the European Union Truly Need a Charter of Rights' (2000) 6 *European Law Journal* 95.

——, 'Forward' in Eric Stein, *Thoughts from a Bridge: A Retrospective of Writings on New Europe and American Federalism'* (Ann Arbor, University of Michigan, 2000), ix.

——, 'Federalism without Constitutionalism' in Nicolaïdis, K and Howse, R (eds) *The Federal Vision* (Oxford, Oxford University Press, 2001), 27.

——, 'A Constitution for Europe? Some Hard Choices' (2003) 40 *Journal of Common Market Studies* 563.

WEILER, JHH and FRIES, SCF, 'A Human Rights Policy for the European Community and Union: The Question of Competences' in Alston, P, Bustelo, M and Heenan, J (eds) *The EU and Human Rights* (Oxford, Oxford University Press, 1999), 147.

WEILER, JHH and LOCKHART, N, '"Taking Rights Seriously": The European Court of Justice and its Fundamental Rights Jurisprudence' (1995) 32 CML Rev 73.

WENDELL HOMES, O, 'Review of C.C. Langdell "Summary of the Law of Contracts"' (1880) 14 *American Law Review* 233.

WESEL, U, *Juristische Weltkunde: eine Einführung in das Recht* (Frankfurt am Main, Suhrkamp, 1984).

——, *Geschichte des Rechts: Von den Frühformen bis zum Vertrag von Maastricht* (München, CH Beck, 1997).

WESSELING, R, *The Modernisation of EC Antitrust Law* (Oxford, Hart Publishing, 2000).

WESSELS, W, 'Staat und (westeuropäische) Integration: Die Fusionsthese' in Kreile, M (ed) *Die Integration Europas* 1992), 36.

WILKINSON, M, 'Civil Society and the Re-imagination of European Constitutionalism' (2003) 9 *European Law Journal* 451.

WILLIAMS, A, 'Enlargement of the Union and Human Rights Conditionality: A Policy of Distinction?' (2000) 25 ELR 601.

WITTGENSTEIN, L, *On Certainty* (Oxford, Blackwell, 1969).

WOUTERS, J, 'National Constitutions and the European Union' (2000) 27 *Legal Issues of European Integration* 25.

ZAJAC, M, 'EU Accession. Implications for Poland's Healthcare Personnel' (2002) 8 *Eurohealth* 13.

ZILLER, J (ed), *The Europeanisation of Constitutional Law in the Light of the Constitutional Treaty for Europe* (Paris, L'Harmattan, 2003).

——, *La Nouvelle constitution européenne* (Paris, La Découverte, 2003).

ZIMMERMANN, R, 'Civil Code and Civil Law: The Europeanisation of Private Law within the European Community and the Re-emergence of a European Legal Science' (1994) 1 *Columbia Journal of European and Transnational Law* 82.

——, 'Savigny's Legacy: Legal History, Comparative Law and the Emergence of a European Legal Science' (1996) 112 LQR 576.

——, 'Roman Law and European Legal Unity' in Hartkampf, A, Hesslink, M, Hondius, E, Joustra, C and du Perron, E (eds) *Towards a European Civil Code* 2nd rev edn (The Hague, Kluwer International Law 1998), 27.

ZOLBERG, A, 'Modes of Incorporation: Towards a Comparative Framework' in Bader, V (ed) *Citizenship and Exclusion* (London, MacMillan, 1997), 140.

ZOLO, D (ed), *La Cittadinanza* (Rome and Bari, Laterza, 1999).

ZULEEG, M, 'The European Constitution under Constitutional Constraints: The German Scenario' (1997) 22 ELR 19.

ZUMBANSEN, P, 'Carl Schmitt und die Suche nach politischer Einheit' (1997) 30 *Kritische Justiz* 63.

——, 'Die vergangene Zukunft des Völkerrechts' (2001) 35 *Kritische Justiz* 46.

——, 'Making Day-to-Day Sense of European Governance' in Zumbansen, P and Miller, R (eds), *The Annual of German and European Law* (Oxford and New York, Berghahn Books, 2002),

ZÜRN, M, *Regieren jenseits des Nationalstaates: Globalisierung und Denationalisierung als Chance* (Frankfurt am Main, Suhrkamp, 1998).

ZÜRN, M and WOLF, D, 'European Law and International Regimes: The Features of Law Beyond the Nation-State' (1999) 5 *European Law Journal* 272.

ZWEIGERT, K and KÖTZ, H, *An Introduction to Comparative Law* (Amsterdam, North-Holland, 1977).

Index